Never Let Go

Never Let Go
A Philosophy of Lifting, Living and Learning

Dan John

Introduction
Pavel Tsatsouline

Foreword
Dave Draper

Preface
Dan John

On Target Publications
Santa Cruz, California

Never Let Go
A Philosophy of Lifting, Living and Learning

Dan John

Introduction: Pavel Tsatsouline

Foreword: Dave Draper

Cover photo: Mark Twight

Articles originally published by Testosterone Muscle

Copyright © 2009, Daniel Arthur John
ISBN-10: 1-931046-38-7 — ISBN-13: 978-1-931046-38-1

On Target Publications
P. O. Box 1335
Aptos, CA 95001 USA
(888) 466-9185
info@ontargetpublications.net
www.ontargetpublications.net

Library of Congress Cataloging-in-Publication Data
    John, Dan.
      Never let go : a philosophy of lifting, living and learning / Dan John ;
    introduction, Pavel Tsatsouline ; foreword, Dave Draper.
          p. cm.
      Includes index.
       ISBN 978-1-931046-38-1 (pbk.)
      1. Weight lifting. 2. Weight training. 3. Bodybuilding. 4. Physical
    education and training. I. Title.
       GV546.3.J64 2009
       613.7'1301--dc22
                                        2009012888

To all my mentors past, present and future

To Tiffini,
who believed in my dreams and became them

Contents

Introduction

Any scientist who can't explain to an eight-year-old what he is doing is a charlatan. Kurt Vonnegut could have said the same about strength coaches and bodybuilding writers.

My publisher, John Du Cane, once told me one chooses Latin words to impress, not to communicate. A great number of strength authors do just that, liberally sprinkling their books — pardon me, opera, the plural of opus, Latin for work — with the likes of transverse plane and transversus abdominis.

Not Dan John. Having reached the deepest understanding of his subject, this coach extraordinaire has no need to impress, only the desire to teach. A Fulbright Scholar with advanced degrees in history and religious education, he could have written his books entirely in Latin, yet he chooses to communicate with strong and simple Anglo-Saxon words of old England.

Like his language, Dan's method is simple. Complexity on one level implies simplicity on another. There is even a scientific term, simplexity, which refers to the emergence of simple rules from underlying disorder and complexity.

John's deceptively simple training plans cover a great many fitness attributes, safely and quickly, and are always a hit with athletes. I am writing this introductino on a plane on my way back from a Russian Kettlebell course (RKC) taught to a SEAL team. Using kettlebells no heavier than fifty-three pounds, in five minutes we safely smoked a group of extremely conditioned and tough men — while simultaneously developing their hip flexibility, spine stability and breathing skills… with one of Dan's "simplex" workouts.

John has made an art form out of collecting the highest "interest" on the strength training his athletes "put in the bank." His sixteen-year-old girls who compete in track can deadlift 300 pounds any time — without touching anything heavier than 150 in training. Boys who train with a measly 35-100 pounds in Dan's patented goblet squat can uncork 400 in the back squat any time they feel like maxing.

The pursuit of the quality Gray Cook calls durability stands out in Dan John's training philosophy. He throws farther in his fifties than he ever has and routinely beats athletes with huge benches and zits. He and his athletes keep getting stronger without getting injured. If this does not personify coaching wisdom, I don't know what does.

The author of this book is open-minded in the best sense of that word. The majority of strength coaches and athletes fall into two categories. The first doggedly stick to the old training methods. The second fall for every new fad. Predictably, the former have limited success and the latter have only soreness to show for their efforts. Dan John has found the happy medium, that sweet spot between continuity and evolution. "The art of progress," wrote Alfred North Whitehead, "is to preserve order amid change and to preserve change amid order." Dan has been doing exactly that, advancing the cutting edge without losing his roots.

When it comes to teaching strength, Dan John has no superiors and only a handful of equals such as Marty Gallagher or Arkady Vorobyev. I have learned a great deal from Dan over the years I've known him, and have become a better athlete and coach for it. I strongly encourage you to read *Never Let Go* to do the same.

Pavel Tsatsouline
Author, *Enter the Kettlebell!*

Foreword

Dan John can toss metal, hoist rocks, drag sleds, launch a discus and clean and jerk loaded Olympic bars with the biggest and best of strongmen. Give him a kettlebell and he'll make it dance; give him a hammer and he'll make it sing. With one hand, he'll send a shot put whistling through the air into the next county. He's a heavy-weight composer; he's a world-wide record-holder who never lets go.

Extraordinary power, marvelous skill and masterful technique have been earned through years of training and practice and scrutiny, failure and success. The road Dan traveled is long, the track circuitous and the field weedy and potholed. No other trek would do. A man doesn't get from here to there, if there is somewhere, by taking a shortcut, the easy way, a limo or a mule.

So what, the guy is super-persistent, disciplined, gutsy and powerful? Take away the aspirin, you've got another headache. Not exactly! I've just begun to list Dan John's attributes.

Get this: He's intelligent, sharp and creative. He teaches, he coaches, he writes and he speaks. He has Masters degrees in history and religious education, and studied in Universities in Cairo and Haifa, as well as in good ole America. His day job is Head Strength and Track and Field Coach at Juan Diego Catholic High School in Utah.

How does one so devoted to education spare the time to lift, tug and press? The same way one who loves to lift and tug finds time to learn. He has blended the two as one. This brings me to the point of my comments: Dan craves knowledge and understanding, and is compelled to pass along what he discovers. Knowing is not enough; applying what he knows helps; instructing makes him complete.

A generous servant, a giver of gifts, his words come alive with experience and fact for the reader, the hungry student, the one bound to learn. Dan doesn't design a paint-by-number and help you pick out the colors. He draws a picture and invites you, encourages you, inspires you to become a part of it.

He's done more research in the physics and mechanics of hefting and heaving, and knows clearly what makes man a more efficient, enduring and forceful machine. He's applied the knowledge to himself, observed it in his colleagues, shared it with competitors and fine-tuned the learning for his subsequent applications. Dan's wrapped, unwrapped and rewrapped knowledge and fact and theory and invention until they're his without doubt or missing parts.

Me? I'd rather listen to the ocean than study a thing. I'm nowhere near lazy, but I want to get down to doing — lifting and living and learning and growing. Dan takes you to those places in a marvelous journey of words and word pictures and unfolding truths and bare facts. Further, comprehensive methodology is barren without philosophy and purpose. These, too, are colorfully, critically woven into the raw materials of power and might.

Lucky you! You're about to become bigger, stronger, faster and robustly entertained.

I haven't yet mentioned he has a wife, Tiffini, and two daughters, Kelly and Lindsay, who absolutely love him. This in itself is spectacular for a mound of muscle throwing imposing objects across a grassy patch of earth for the fun of it.

Let's go. *Never Let Go.*
Dave Draper
Author, *Brother Iron Sister Steel*

Preface

When I was about twelve, it became obvious my athletic career was at a crossroads. Now, I'm sure most preadolescent males probably worry about a lot of things, but I had this odd notion time was running out on my sports career. I didn't know it at the time, but there were dozens of other fun things to worry about like acne, girls, cars, wars and money, but in my little world, I knew I was far too weak.

A year or so earlier, my Aunt Florence died and left us, my brothers and me, a few hundred dollars. We invested in a Sears barbell set with plastic-covered cement plates. Like everyone in the late 1960s, we picked up the bar in a way similar to what we saw on the Olympic coverage, and pressed the weight over our heads. The workouts with brothers and friends consisted of simply doing that movement long enough for everybody to hoist as much as they could lift.

And, I was lagging behind. It never occurred to me I was the youngest and several of the guys were phenomenal high school athletes and collegians. I'm not sure the information would have mattered at the time; the answer for me was clear — I needed to go to the library.

Somewhere in my first years of education, I began this love affair with books, and I still turn to books for much of my inspiration and answers. Towards the back wall of my hometown library, I found very little on exercise and even less on weightlifting. There were books on tumbling and gymnastics that were helpful for doing a Crow's Nest on the pull-up bars, but these texts wouldn't help me crack the fifty-pound barrier in the press.

Sliding down the aisles a bit, I found books on football. I remember leafing through Vince Lombardi's *Run to Daylight*, and enjoying the way plays were diagramed. Would I ever be big enough to play high school football?

Then I found a book that changed my life: Eliot Asinof's *Seven Days to Sunday*. Lucky for me, I popped the book open in the middle and read about a linebacker named Ken Avery. He was undersized, and by working harder than anyone else and looking for answers in other disciplines, he ended up playing in what could easily be the most competitive level of sport in the world, the National Football League. I still own a copy of this book, falling apart at the seams from countless readings, with one small item stuck between the pages: Ken Avery's football card, the kind we bought for a nickel, complete with a piece of gum.

Eventually, I found books on strength training, diet, exercise and Olympic sports, filling the gaps in my weightlifting knowledge. *Strength and Health Magazine* was available at the time and I began buying these at the corner pharmacy. I learned the technical problems that held me back from lifting more, and discovered that my ignorance of basic diet was going to prevent long-term progress. Some of the information was bogus, but much of it stands the decades of research in sports and nutrition done since my first foray to the library.

I began visiting the local library as many of my friends visited young ladies — yes, I was *that* kid. One evening, I was strolling along and found a librarian had displayed T. H. White's *The Sword in the Stone* as a recommended read. I enjoyed the Disney movie when I was six, and eagerly checked the book out to read. As I devoured the pages, I found Wart — the name White gives young King Arthur — was trying to teach me as much as Merlyn was trying to teach him.

In the section on hawks and falcons, I learned the First Law of the Foot: *Never Let Go.* That short phrase stopped me. It would inspire me to hold on during tough times through the death of my parents, and cling to the lessons of my mentors. Literally, I will Never Let Go.

I never stopped reading. I never stopped listening. I never stopped learning.

A few years ago, I was asked to write a few sentences about a young man in our community for a newsletter and was told simply, "You write well." Not long after, the late Jack Schroeder noted I should consider "writing a few things," possibly for a column in a local paper. He gave me some sage advice: People like to hear stories, usually about people.

With the growth of the internet, I found myself answering basic questions in weightlifting forums. Soon, I discovered parts of my answers became passed-around quotes. Not long after, I was asked to give a small workshop on basic lifting. Then Chris Shugart, now an editor and feature writer for *Testosterone Muscle Magazine* and the author of the *Velocity Diet 3.0*, asked me to write something for the magazine to see if he could get it published. And indeed it was. Since that first article, I have written literally dozens of articles for *T-mag*, and I am thankful T. C. Louma allowed me to reprint them here.

It's difficult to explain my writings. I offer insights into literacy, systemic and systematic education, and the need to irrigate the nostrils. There are times when I read my articles and the advice I give and step back and wonder, "Why does anybody ask me anything? I don't say anything at all." Then, at the next workshop or gathering, someone will note that my basic mission is what makes the most sense. For years I have been preaching the following points.

1. The Body is One Piece.

2. There are three kinds of strength training:

> Putting weight overhead

> Picking it off the ground

> Carrying it for time or distance

3. All training is complementary.

As we weave through the following pages, you will find I am trying to map out these three points in everyone's journey to better health and fitness. As I encourage others with my work, please note the "answer" is probably right in front of you. Like Parsifal of the legend of the Holy Grail, the thing you search for is usually right there. I have traveled all over the globe only to discover the finest coaches I had were in that garage lifting the Sears barbell with me.

That's why I had to have this book. This book celebrates the journey from garage to platform to ring to gym to workshop and to this moment as I type this preface. Many of my mentors have passed over to eternal life and I worry the simple solutions — the gems — will be lost all too soon. Consider me just the storyteller. I dedicate this book, with these answers, to them.

And to you, my reader: Hold on to these lessons.

Dan John

One

Free Will and Free Weights

I've said it a million times: There aren't any secrets to training. I would've stood by that, too, until the single greatest moment in the history of strength training and fitness happened to me. I finally discovered the secret.

I tend to joke about secrets and gimmicks quite a bit. You know what I'm talking about:

- Lose ten pounds overnight with the diet of the stars!

- Instantly increase your arm size!

- Use psycho power to get women and money!

True, I bought all these products, and I decided to use them all at once. They all worked! I lost all my money overnight. Whoops.

No, I'm talking about a real secret here, the answer to a lot of the crazy issues that plague probably everyone. The funny thing is I'm serious.

There's something you have in short supply that you need to cherish. It's the difference between making your fitness, strength and body composition goals and not making those goals. Before I divulge it, let's look at a few examples.

New Year's Eve — A drunk walks over to you, spilling a glass of merlot down your arm and on the Persian rug. "You know what?" he slurs. "Tomorrow, I'm laying off the booze, going on Atkins, and I'm going to work out every day, just like I used to. Stopping smoking, too. This is probably one of the last times you'll ever see me smoking."

We all know what's going to happen. Most of us (raise your hands, please) have made a New Year's resolution that didn't exactly work out as we planned:

"I will eat low carb."

"I will work my legs first every workout."

"I will stop looking at internet porn."

What's strange is resolutions are usually good ideas. Let's be honest, saving the first ten percent of a paycheck, cutting back on carbs or sweets or whatever, exercising more, or being kinder to humanity are all pretty damn good things to try to do.

Next example: With my old job I did a lot of prison ministry. Prison is nothing like the movies or television shows, at least in my experience. Sure, there are deep dark bad places in every prison, but most of what I saw wasn't unlike hotels I stayed in while visiting New Jersey and Florida.

I sat on a couch once and had a long conversation with a very nice guy without any bars or guards nearby. I later found out he'd killed six people in one night... the last just to see someone squirm. He seemed like a wonderful guy.

One of the things people talk about is how buff prisoners are. "Ah, to have the discipline of a multiple offender," you might think. And there it is. That's the insight I had recently. All of the connections finally linked up and in a flash... I got it.

Got what? The secret to success in all of our goals. Don't laugh, don't undervalue, and certainly don't underestimate what I'm about to say: The secret to success is free will.

Free will? Sure, call it what you want: self discipline, habits, free agency, or my personal favorite, no other damn choice. Now listen, this isn't a religion discussion, but there's a great story that illuminates the concept. By the way, the story is absolutely true. I verified it.

There was a very religious man who lived in a flood plain. One year, a big flood hit and he stood on his porch watching the water go by. A neighbor came by driving a motorboat. "Hop on, friend, and I'll take you to safety!"

"No, thanks," the pious man said, "The Good Lord above will save me." Later, while sitting on his roof, the sheriff came by in a rowboat. "Here you go, hop in!" he said.

"No, thanks. The Good Lord above will save me," the man replied. As the water rose higher, a helicopter dropped a rope ladder down to him and offered him a lift off the top of his home.

"No, thanks. The Good Lord above will save me."

He drowned.

Standing in line waiting to get into heaven, the Good Lord walked by him. The man said, "Why didn't you save me?" The Good Lord answered: "I sent a motorboat, a rowboat, and a helicopter. What did you want?"

This is a true story and I'm standing by it.

What's the point? We all know we need to take the bull by the horns, pull ourselves up by our bootstraps, or add any cliché comment you were told as an adolescent to spur you to get off your damn computer chair and walk over to the gym and spend the next hour doing nothing but every exercise you hate.

Or, you can keep reading this article and eat some of those chips that are bad for you, but since they come from Hawaii must be pretty good after all, so eat a few more, then sneak over to those websites that have panting college coeds in pasties. Or whatever.

Every great motivational speaker from Napoleon Hill to Earl Nightingale to Anthony Robbins will always dedicate a large amount of time and energy to the concept of self-discipline. My college coach, Ralph Maughan, had a saying for his athletes: *Make yourself a slave to good habits.*

And you know, to a group of Division One track and field athletes who all have at least a 3.0 GPA, that's a nice bit of advice, certainly worthy of discussion. Of course, that audience was a little different than maybe most of us deal with during a typical day.

So, why does the guy in prison have a better body than you? It's because we have just a little bit of free will. How do I know? People actually research this stuff and then I steal it. Let me take a quick detour for a second and see if I can explain it.

I shave daily. I recently changed from shaving cream to shaving gel, but I'm going back to cream. Why? Well, with shaving cream, as you get to the bottom of the can, it splutters and spats and spits cream for about a week before it goes absolutely empty. The first time you get shaving cream spit in your eye, you mentally note, "I need to buy more shaving cream." In that week, you have three or four opportunities to get spat on as a reminder to buy more cream.

With gel, you're standing in the shower and you press the button and… nothing. Yesterday, a face full of gel; today you're trying to shave with Dial soap lather and all day your friends comment about your dry, bleeding face. Your coworkers might think you got into another bar fight, like you told them last time.

You see, free will is like shaving gel. It seems you have a one-can allotment and it just runs out without warning. Researchers did an interesting test on people: Everyone was asked to do a series of complex tests without any chance of success. They timed how long people would try the task before giving up — like maybe a Rubik's Cube that had been made impossible to finish.

When the next group came in, they offered everybody cookies. Those who said, "No thanks, watching my diet," or whatever, would quit the impossible task far earlier than those who said, "What the hell, give me a damn cookie."

Why? My friends, you basically have about one can of Free Will. If you use it saying no to cookies, you won't have any left for impossible tasks, quitting smoking, or whatever resolution you picked in a carb-induced haze sometime during the holidays. Sorry. One can.

That's why our friend in prison has a better body than you. When your alarm goes off, do you basically get up? Why? Could you miss class if you're a student? Maybe. Well, then, getting up out of your toasty bed will eat up some of your free will.

Can you miss work? Sure, but then, you know, something happens, like you miss the Henderson Report and the Dingwinglies fall off the Schimshank and whatever the hell else bad happens to you at work.

Do you have kids? Now we're really talking about losing free will, fast and furious. Children will drink every ounce you have before you send them off to school. Trust me, I don't have any personal choice at all!

Who makes your meals or chooses what place you'll eat? You. There goes some of that decision-making ability.

As decision after decision after decision hits you throughout the week, the reservoir of free will you'll have on hand to spend in the gym begins to fade. When I originally wrote my *Four Minutes a Day to Fat Loss* article, which you'll read later in the book, a number of people asked me, "If it's so good, why don't you do it every day?" My answer was always clouded: You do it and get back to me.

Why couldn't I do it every day? To push myself that hard after a long day of commuting kids back and forth to school, choir and volleyball, while the dog is puking next to the broken toilet, while the lady from the reunion wants to know if I can get there early to help hang crepe paper, after I get the truck back from getting new tires, before I mow the lawn, and while the boss still needs that report… I'm just happy to hide in the gym.

Lots of us know these workouts. We go into our gyms and hide. I call it arm day! Our buddy in prison? Does he decide when to go to bed? No. Get up? No. Eat three times a day? No choice. Meals? Not only no choice on what to eat, but usually our friend doesn't have to do anything to prepare the meal. Quiet time? I don't even know what that is.

Day after day after day, decisions I take for granted are just not a part of the prisoner's life. What does he have control of anyway? His workouts. That whole can of Free Will — literally bottled up inside of him for days, maybe even weeks, months and years in some cases — can be used for training. And train he does.

You decide on ten New Year's resolutions. Here's my unsolicited gambling odds: no chance. If you only make one resolution? Maybe you'll achieve it. It could happen, you know, with the right motivations.

Why am I confident you'll fail? My point: You have only so much in the can of Free Will, and most of us waste the bulk of our self-determination, grit, or free choice long before we can muster up the energy to deal with nicotine fits, carb cravings, and the three-minute wait to get on the treadmill.

Listen, it's easier to just eat the damn cookie. I know, I've been there. Hi, I'm Dan and I'm the guy who knows carbs are bad for me, but I eat them anyway so leave me alone in my corner to sob.

How can we save more of the can of Free Will so we can focus on our workouts or really push that diet? Let's be honest, look at Chris Shugart's *Velocity Diet*. Just look at it. Pretend for a moment you could do that for a month. Just pretend. I did and immediately came up with about 400 events I couldn't bring a protein drink to, even one mixed with flax seeds.

Here are three ideas to help you get more Free Will out of your can.

Number One

Camp. I'm serious. Each year, I spend up to four weeks in training camps. Somebody wakes me up, somebodymakes my meals, somebody else pushes me to work out, somebody else tells me when to put the lights out. You know, I work hard during those weeks.

How can I reinvent camp for my normal life? A couple of things leap out at me. First, if nutrition is so important, and it's my biggest trouble-spot, is it possible to sublet my meal planning? One day a week, should I do all the cooking and bag and freeze all the meals? Can I hire someone to do all the cooking? Should I buy a lot of pre-made meals? Or, should I just stock all my shelves with really good things, and only eat in appropriate places?

Really, none of these ideas are bad. Not great, but not bad either. In the area of training, we all know what the value of a personal trainer actually is: It's someone making sure you do something in the allotted training time. I'm not ripping on PTs here; I'm just pointing out the single greatest value of a personal trainer is someone else's will is replacing your will. That psycho, whistle-blowing high school coach you had might've been on to something.

Number 2

I'm working with a young woman, Edna, who recently did a pretty impressive thing: She quit smoking, lost a lot of bodyweight, stopped partying so much, and decided to recommit to her lifelong goals. As of this writing, she hasn't smoked in a long time, has lost a lot of weight, and is in the fog of love with a very decent guy.

Her secret? She took on one task at a time, but only with a large community effort behind her. What does that mean? It means she told everybody her goals. I mean that, gentle reader — everybody. Friends, people at parties, coworkers and people in the mall looking for a new microwave all heard the same chorus.

"Hey, I'm quitting smoking, so if I say I need a smoke, tie me down and don't let me smoke 'cause I'm quitting and I'm not going to smoke, so don't let me smoke." Hey, you aren't going to let that person smoke. Leave, yes; smoke, no.

Next, Edna joined Weight Watchers. She goes to the meetings. She talks about things. She talks to other people in Weight Watchers and she lets everybody know she's in Weight Watchers.

I'm telling you, you can save your precious free will by recruiting a vast army of people willing to give up their free will to bolster yours. How? Tell them, ask them, beg them for help. Does your family know your goals? Coworkers? Professors? Mailman? Start putting it out there.

There was a time in my youth where I could go to a party filled with booze and an assortment of products from Columbia and no one would offer me a share. Why? I was dumb enough to let everyone know I was going after something that drugs and booze would only hinder.

I was joking about the dumb-enough part. I'm damn proud of those decisions.

Number Three

I don't like this one, but it works: Whittle down your life a little. I've always told my daughters you can measure a good relationship by the way you expand rather than contract. What am I saying? Maybe you do too much.

I'm guilty; I love leaping into things. In fact, it's a rare fall that I don't have a conflict on a weekend between a Highland Games, a flag football league, and an Olympic lifting meet. To do all of this, something has to give. Usually, it's my skills at Highland Games, flag football or Olympic lifting!

Whittle. I was at a party recently with a guy who told me he couldn't get back into training. Six minutes later he asked me about a list of television shows I'd never watched, and a few I'd never heard of. By God, this guy watched *Joey*!

Whittle that TV habit and the time will appear for training. Don't TiVo a bunch of crap so you can watch it faster without commercials! When I was growing up, we never watched CBS; we didn't get the station where we lived. You know, I never missed a thing. Now, we have 10,000 stations and think there's always something better on another channel.

Whittle. Drunk all weekend and go to work hung-over? Whittle away a little there. Whittle away your workouts, too. Why does anybody do the innie and the outie thigh machines? Really, why?

There you go, friends. Once again, I offer some basic ideas, but the problem isn't so easy. Be very sparing with your little can of self-discipline, Free Will, or whatever word you want to toss around.

You have three options to help you make better choices:

> **One:** Be proactive and try to find someone or some way to cut back on the options, all those deadly choices and decisions… especially in nutrition and training.

Two: Bring everybody onboard to keep an eye on you. The more personal trainers, mentors, gurus, Yodas, and Gandalfs in your life, the better. Tell everyone you know your goals and watch how much easier it is to stay on track. The crazy lady on the 814 bus might be the one person who stops you from munching on that muffin.

Three: Whittle away at all the extras. Better yet, chop away. I'm not saying disconnect with humanity, but I'd like to see you turn off the damn television set. Chop. Chop. Chop.

Hey, like the knight in *Indiana Jones and the Last Crusade* said, "Choose wisely."
And not very often.

Two

The Rule of Five

I remember lying on the incline bench. It was an old-school incline bench: long, straight and red, with footpads at the bottom so I was literally locked in from heel to shoulder for every rep.

Normally I used it as a chair like I use most gym equipment, but in this case I was just holding on to whatever I could with whatever I had left. I stayed on it a long time as I worried about the ride home on my motorcycle. Leg cramps on a Honda 200 motorcycle are not advised.

What was wrong with me? In June of 1979, with a fair amount of dark Bavarian beer in me, I took a bet. It was a stupid bet in hindsight… and foresight. I took on the challenge to squat 300 pounds for sixty-one reps.

Now, go ahead, ask why.

You see, in the summer of 1978, we started a new club at the gym. The Pacifica Barbell Club had a bunch of little contests and we entered each contest merely by trying the event. Each contest became a club within the club. The list of names began with the original mark and we entered by beating the previous mark.

The list for the incline sit-up club, which I obviously never entered, had only two names, as the second mark was 1,400.

I decided to try the Squat Bodyweight for Reps club. I weighed 218 and piled on 225 — not exactly bodyweight, but everyone knows it's a pride issue to use the big plates — and squatted it fifty times. Every rep from twenty onward is virtually a max rep. The lousy part of this challenge is you can literally always do one more rep. Seriously. Each rep from thirty to forty was done with multiple breaths and lots of encouragement. And, of course, if you can get forty, why not go to fifty?

It was fun watching the pool of sweat on the floor grow as I hung onto the bar and worked towards fifty. I knew I couldn't let go of the bar, and since I had to keep focused on something, I watched my sweat pool grow large enough for the neighborhood kids to enjoy a dip.

There's today's mental picture for everyone trying to not snack: kids swimming in my sweat. Enjoy.

Obviously, then, sitting in a bar after a pitcher or three of Barvarian beer, someone commented, "Hey, what could you do if you trained for it?" My idiotic response was something like, "Well, 225 is too light; you'd need to push the weight up."

Surely I had some Newtonian explanation for this BS, too.

We drank and continued to up the ante, until I took on a bet to squat 300 pounds for sixty-one reps. I was allowed to train a few weeks first, of course.

That was a mistake. I should've done it drunk.

This all leads me back to the beginning, lying on an incline bench. My training that day consisted of:

- One set of thirty reps in the squat with 315

- Rest

- One set of thirty reps in the squat with 275

- Rest

- One set of thirty reps in the squat with 225

- Lie on incline bench for max rest

Which drops us where we are now. As I sat there sprawled across a device better suited for upper-pec development, I thought, "I've been here for two hours and I've done three sets. How can I top this?"

You see, I couldn't. True, within a few weeks my thighs had grown off the charts and I seemed to have dropped a keg of body fat, but I couldn't fathom continuing to train like that.

It's a profound issue and will be a factor in the training of every single person who ever attempts to push the envelope in training. How do I possibly repeat that effort?

Here you go: You can't.

Like the perfect moment, the perfect kiss, or the perfect date (see Bill Murray's *Groundhog Day*), the perfect workout is hard to repeat. What's perfect? It depends on who you are, but for most of us it might be that day when the weight on the bar, the number of reps, the number of sets, and the intensity of the exercise selection all combine to make whatever you write in your training journal literally stagger you a month or so later when you stumbled onto it.

Stagger you? Out of nowhere, you add thirty pounds to a max, deadlift another set of wheels, or complete some kind of mad challenge that still wakes you up years later, softly sobbing in the night.

I had a friend tell me about going to a world-famous gym and having a renowned bodybuilder ask to train with him. My friend did, and he went set for set with the best in the world. The next day he was unable to get out of bed.

That's staggering.

What can be learned from my idiotic challenge? First, a couple of general insights. I have a little formula concerning workouts that I call the Rule of Five.

In a group of five workouts, I tend to have one great workout, the kind of workout that makes me think in just a few weeks I could be an Olympic champion, plus maybe Mr. Olympia. Then, I have one workout that's so awful the mere fact I continue to exist as a somewhat higher form of life is a miracle. Finally, the other three workouts are the punch-the-clock workouts: I go in, work out, and walk out. Most people experience this.

In a hundred workouts, I'll have twenty great workouts. Of that twenty, a couple will be flat-out amazing. And in a thousand workouts, one is worthy of an article, or bragging to my buddies about. Once a decade, if I'm lucky, I have that workout.

Unfortunately, many people think they're undertraining all the time because they don't puke every workout, the world record doesn't fall during the session, or a swarm of reporters from *People Magazine* aren't taking their pictures. Really, I never understood this idea that every workout had to be life's best and finest training moment.

This brings to mind two things. Where else in your life does something become better and better and better every single time? Meals? Sleep? Work? Even sex can have highs and lows. (I was going to say ups and downs, but somehow even I can't handle that level of bad pun.) How can you honestly think training improvements are that linear?

Remember this: If you bench press a hundred pounds and add ten pounds a month, you'll bench 460 in about three years and 500 hundred in a few more months. How many of you with three years under your belt are pounding out 500-pound benches? You know… in the gym, not just on the internet.

In other words, give yourself a break emotionally and physically — most of the time. We should begin a conversation called Awful Workouts and share those wonderfully bad workouts one rarely admits having, and that we have all the time!

An example:

Today's Workout

5 minutes looking for training journal
Sat in chair 7 minutes reading *Seventeen Magazine*
Tried the exercise the girl did on the beach with her tote bag
Rubbed back for 6 minutes, injured by tote-bag exercise
8 minutes watching a hot girl on a treadmill watching *Oprah*
Did one pull-up and played with a plastic dumbbell
Hot tub and sauna

Actually, I've had worse workouts.

Occasionally, we'll hear someone argue we must always train harder and harder, usually quoting Arthur Jones. But you'll also notice rarely do we see people outline these kinds of workouts for more than two to six weeks. Why? Reality. And we all need a healthy dose of it now and again.

I've discovered I can push myself to press hard for three-week doses. I've also discovered week four better be light or even off; otherwise I'll be in rehab. I'm not urging retirement or sloth or a buffet of light workouts. My focus is on the reality of training.

1. We can all train really hard. Then, we have to plan to ease up a little bit. It doesn't have to involve higher math; plan a hard couple of weeks and toss in an easy week. Small wonder many of the classic training plans are three days a week with a heavy, a medium, and an easy day.

2. Redefine "easy" in your training, too. I like to use my easy days to try a new lift or perhaps even invent something new. The idea of doing snatches followed by sled pulls began on an easy day. I later moved that workout to a hard day.

3. Embrace lousy days. I've learned to remind myself easy days are part of the deal, and a great day is just around the corner.

4. Finally, don't let a great day destroy years of planning and training by thinking this is now the norm. Enjoy the day, but keep a little humility.

Oh, and the challenge of sixty-one reps with 300? Well, I failed to make it, but I gave it a try. Maybe it was just a lousy day.

Three

The Velocity Diet Experience

A few years ago, I woke up fat. The wonder of it all is I had been down this road before. How did I go from being in pretty good shape back to being fat? My first experience with fat loss had been a rousing success! What gives?

Several years ago I went into the men's room at the Catholic High School where I taught, and found on the wall a penciled graffiti: Mr. John is a fat a--hole. I could live with the a--hole part. Students often call teachers a--holes. It was being called fat that got my attention.

As an adolescent, I was quite skinny and the girls even snickered about my lack of muscles. (Along with zits and other adolescent nightmares, my teen years were as peachy as anyone's.) Twenty-plus years of weightlifting led me to the pinnacle of my game; I weighed 273 pounds and could out-lift most normal gorillas. Abnormal gorillas, no.

I looked at a picture of myself from my friends' twentieth wedding anniversary party, and noticed I had three chins. Then I looked down and saw my "ab muscles" frowning over my belt. I had a forty-two-inch waistline, although I also had big legs, a thick back, and no neck. But that men's room graffiti writer was right: I was fat. After three decades of lifting, I was strong enough to push heavy weights, but couldn't shove the chair from the dinner table.

To do something about the situation, my wife, Tiffini, and I began following the instructions of Ellington Darden. We did the whole Super Slow training, Slim Fast for breakfast, lots of water, sixty percent of the diet was carbohydrates, and microwave meals. Within two tough weeks, we lost a little bit off the various measurements. Let me tell you, those were wicked weeks, hungry all day, usually grumpy. But the research said it would work. Why then, a few weeks later, were all the losses gains?

Tiffini began talking to friends about her struggles; even a doctor kicked in with his opinion. All her friends, as well as the doctor, recommended high-protein diets. Everything I read and everything I heard said not to do this.

The popular opinion was a high-protein diet would give us stones, raise our bad blood levels, and — the kicker — all we'd really lose would be water.

While I did the research, Tiffini did the right thing: She didn't listen. As she pointed out, since the starvation diet didn't work, what did we have to lose? We decided to go ahead and try this insanity. We changed directions, cut out carbs and ate meat.

Once Tiff and I committed to eating like cave men, life became very simple. Almost overnight we both needed new wardrobes. I had to purchase new belts four times in a year. Tiff went through two wardrobes. She started in a size twelve; soon she could fit in sixes. But, of course, it was all water, or at least that's what people kept telling us.

The ironic part of this discovery was I used to eat this way; back in the 1970s, I ate a high-protein diet to get bigger and stronger. As a senior at Utah State, I weighed 218 pounds with eight-percent body fat, and threw the discus over 190 feet.

Then I got some advice from the people at the Olympic Training Center. I needed carbs, they advised, and lots of them. They pointed to the studies done on the American distance runners. I should have followed the logic: When is the last time an American distance runner dominated the world scene or even placed in a big meet? Take a moment to look at the high school men's running records — shouldn't it have bothered me that some of these records were older than the coaches? Being an idiot, I took the advice to eat like emaciated, overtrained sub-performers. It took years of high-carbohydrate grazing to learn the evils of this advice.

After the switch back to high protein, the hardest thing to get used to, besides buying new clothes and only having one chin, was how easy eating became. Meals were done in minutes; in fact, we often forgot to eat because we were still full from the last meal. Soon we simplified things even more: We ate meat, leaves and berries. In other words, we stocked up on fish, eggs, poultry, meat, salads, vegetables and fresh fruit. We avoided prepared food with the following insight: If it can sit on your shelf for years, it probably will sit on your hips and belly that long, too.

So, what happened? How did I let myself get overweight again? The following is all rationalization, but, let's be honest, this is life. First, I think 9/11 had an odd impact on me. Tiff was in Manhattan and saw the second plane go into the Towers. We couldn't get her home for over a week, and I was trying to deal with two kids who knew all too well what was going on. It was around then I started drinking a bit heavier, but it was no big deal, and I barely noticed the weight gain. The Nationals come around; I had added a few pounds and just barely missed making the 105-kilo (231-pound) class, to win the Superheavies. The next weekend, at the state meet, I broke my wrist. After two surgeries and a lot of rehab, I slowly rebuilt my left arm. I also refused to take pain medications. Why? I hated myself on the meds, but I self-medicated well with Scotch.

A few years passed, and in 2004 I decided to throw the discus far enough to qualify for the Olympic Trials. I didn't make that goal, but I really threw the discus far for a forty-seven-year-old. Who cares about bodyweight when you're throwing far?

More time passes, and I deal with tragedies and life and this and that happens, and once again, I look down and find a belly hanging over the belt. Let me explain it this way: In the *Brothers Karamozov*, a woman comes to the priest and says, "I have lost my faith." The priest asks how, and she answers, "Bit by bit." That is it exactly with fat gain: *You get fat bit by bit.*

I realized an interesting thing about this time. I knew I couldn't go on a gentle program to lose body fat. I don't know how I knew this, but it was time for something crazy. My friend, Chris Shugart, had developed a twenty-eight-day fat-loss approach I thought was stupid the first time I read it. When I looked at it more deeply, it looked even dumber. After listening to him present the diet in a Washington, DC, lecture, I was convinced it was crazy.

Here is a simple definition of the diet: Determine how many calories you need in a day. Consume that amount in at least five protein shakes made with added fiber every four hours. Take fish oil capsules. Once a week have a solid meal.

That is it. You should take a walk every morning, and lift weights three days a week. Food is a non-issue: You are not eating any!

I decided to try it. Let me say this: the Velocity Diet took every ounce of free will I could muster. But, it worked. In fact, it worked so well, it stunned my doctor. My body weight on day one was 249 and some change using the wrestling scale at school. On day twenty-nine, it was 226 on the same scale. My waistline on day one was forty-two inches and a little extra. On day thirty, it was thirty-seven inches.

That twenty-three-pound, five-inch loss wasn,t all water. My blood profiles from a week before the diet and a week after highlight the changes in my body.

Before:

Total Cholesterol: 255
Triglycerides: 182
HDL: 41.2
LDL: 177.6

After:

Total Cholesterol: 171
Triglycerides: 103
HDL: 46.9
LDL: 103

After the reviewing the numbers, Doctor Brunetti said, "I have never seen this! What did you do again?" This is fact. This is science. This is much better: HDL up, bad stuff down.

Later I talked with Chris Shugart and he asked why I started the diet. I told him, "This guy named Chris Shugart kept saying I was fat! Beyond the tears, I decided to change my life, and maybe love myself a little."

Actually, I'd had two disappointing competitive seasons back-to-back. I blamed job changes, kids, being an idiot. Eventually, I realized at my annual doctor's appointment I'd put on a lot of weight. And, dear Lord, there was a big fat guy in every one of my pictures!

Big deal, right? I wouldn't have changed, because as a strength athlete I'm allowed to not care about my physique. But I was beginning to drop in performance, and I started to get little injuries.

The thing about the Velocity Diet wasn't that I'd lose weight or body fat or whatever. I liked the discipline. I liked the jumpstart it would give me on my other goals.

Listen carefully: If you can do the V-Diet, if you can give up food and booze for twenty-eight days, you can go out and attack any other goals you may have rattling around in your brain.

It just came to me. I was sitting there watching my left knee oozing with infection after catching it on a dirty bolt in a throwing circle and wondering how to train for Pleasanton and it hit me: V-Diet. No kidding. And I have little memory of why that sounded so right. Part of me, the part who wants to be a monk, loved the idea. My favorite part of me, the party guy, objected. This time the monk won.

Chris has noted one of the reasons this diet works so well is it gives the person absolute control of a single part of his or her life. It's corny, but in a good way because it's true! There's an interesting thing with teenagers and their various eating disorders: It's the one area in their lives they can control. Maybe, just maybe, we all have a little place that wants control.

As a parent with all the various hats I wear, I often find something as simple as changing a thing in the yard brings me relief, some quiet or peace.

The biggest problem I had to overcome at first were questions about other things not on the diet. People would ask me, "Dan, how about Greens Plus, cottage cheese and cheap Scotch?" I'd reply, "No, Chris said to do this!"

I couldn't even entertain options! The plan took care of the food choices, and I just followed instructions. It was a great model for me.

Now, let's outline the diet. It begins with the alarm clock. *Briiiiiing, briiiiiiiiing!*

You have to be kidding.

That was what happened from day one of the diet to about day twenty. The 5:30 AM alarm. I would pee… again. I'd open my morning baggie filled with two Hot-Rox Extreme capsules, which is a thermogenic, swallow some water, get the dog leashed, and go walking.

The dog, by the way, looked much better after my diet, too. I did this for the dog.

When I got back, I drank some coffee, tried to read the local paper (it's awful), usually read a book, then had shake number one. Here's a good combo: a scoop of chocolate Metabolic Drive protein powder, a scoop of banana cream Metabolic Drive, and flax meal. Not bad really… considering.

School days were easy. I had two shakes in the morning between classes, then, at lunch, I had some fiber tablets, my multivitamin (I bought the Orange Urine Special it seems), two more Hot-Rox. That was it for supplements.

Before the end of the day, I'd have an additional shake, go home and train, then have my dinner shake and, later, the night shake of one scoop of protein powder with natural peanut butter. I ended up taking Flameout, a brand of fish oil, at night, too. I also took ZMA every night before bed.

I did the plan exactly as Chris outlined.

That's a big key: Don't start adding cookies, muffins, turkey, Alpo, or whatever. Follow the damn diet! "The V-Diet doesn't work for me. I ate five meals a day and six shakes and I didn't lose a pound!" That ain't it, folks.

At first I was just a sissy in my training; I was afraid to do anything. I was planning to do up to ten sets of three with the big stuff like deadlifts, squats, press, pull-ups and the rest, and six to eight of the single-joint moves. But, it was like I was waiting for a tsunami. When does it hit, the deadly bonk of no food and no carbs?

Never happened! After about week two or so, I started really pushing it, doing Olympic lift complexes or kettlebell work to get going.

This kind of thing:

> Power Snatch, 5 reps
> Overhead Squat, 5 reps
> Back Squat, 5 reps
> Behind-the-Neck Press, 5 reps
> Good Morning, 5 reps
> Row, 5 reps

This was all done with one light weight, and then I'd go back to back to back through the lifts. Doing all of that is considered one set.

I tried to do up to six of these, but usually had the ability to talk myself into three to five of the clusters. I'm good at talking myself into something easier.

The other thing I discovered was my squat wasn't too happy. I pulled out Dave Draper's Top Squat device to use with chains for reps of ten to re-groove my bottom position. After two workouts, I asked myself, "If I thrive on sets of ten in the squat, why don't I do them?" If I had the brains to answer that, I'd do much better.

I did lots of one-arm presses and added military presses with chains off a low box, and invented curls with chains, a great lift — there's no easy part with the chains.

I did pull-ups every workout, and the weight loss made these easier and easier. I also reintroduced sprints., doing up to eight sprints, bringing the speed and intensity up with each surge. I consider this and the complexes to be a good addition for most folks trying the V-Diet, but only after the second week.

I also started taking farmer walks seriously. My general physical preparedness (GPP) had gone bye-bye, and that had cost me in competition. We learn, again. I'm tired of relearning the same lessons.

I used some structure, but I kept things a little random; I can't do a workout without at least one experiment.

With my Olympic lifting, I noticed I was again smoother. What does that mean? I don't know, but I know I know it! Oh, and I broke the state record in the snatch at the Utah Recordmakers meet. My strength was fine.

I was also sprinting and walking and smiling and feeling good. I wasn't lying with all that "I feel very good" stuff throughout the diet. Not only did I look better, my joints felt better. Now, I still had some injury issues; throwing big stuff over the decades does lead to minor wear and tear, but overall, I felt great.

The one thing I liked best: I was much more athletic with the implements. I guess I knew the extra weight was a burden, but I didn't realize how much. The biggest factor was my right ankle didn't hurt so much — that's the turning ankle in the discus. That's big. Not being in pain when you train is bigger than one would think.

Of course, it wasn't all rosy and perfect. Seriously, one night I was craving roasted chicken as I tried to sleep, the same way a normal man thinks about womenkind. I just took my brother, Gary's, advice and thought, "Tomorrow, I'll break the diet and quit. Just not tonight." I woke up, walked, drank my shake, and I was fine.

That's a big one. You have to make deals with yourself all the time. That's fine. Every athlete does this: just one more hill, one more day, one more whatever. I thrive on it, but for me, it's one more decade.

The no-booze thing was interesting, too. I thought it would be hard, but it was quite easy. I discovered something I needed to know: Much of my alcohol consumption was just thirst. I never realized how thirsty I get at night.

All day, I coach and yell and teach, and I wasn't taking care of my water intake. At night, I found myself pouring three different beverages in my mouth and thinking nothing of it: water, beer and wine. Seriously. I dealt with the liquids issue and poof, much of the booze-drinking cleared right up. Funny. But, it could have ended up tragic without the twenty-eight-day test run.

Here's one more lesson: Quit BSing yourself about weight. I'm a 220-pound guy, and unless my lifts and throws really take off with each additional pound, it ain't quality weight.

I also think I didn't eat enough before the diet. Now, this is going to sound odd, but I noted the steady stream of protein and fiber made me feel good. I had energy; my joints felt good. I thrived!

The hardest part of living on six protein shakes are the questions. It was hard having women ask me about it: Oh, Danny, what's this diet I heard you're doing? Yeesh. "Oh, it sounds perfect for me! I have lots of self-discipline."

Right. You see, I don't. Really, I don't. What got me through the diet was a brilliant move on my part: I brought so many people into my story through the *T-Nation* forum that to fail would be a huge failure — in other words, a lot of public pain for me. People would question my will, my courage, my fill-in-the-blank. I put the price of failure very high! Look at all the email I received, the discussions, the phone calls. I put the price of eating a cookie beyond the taste of any damned morsel ever baked!

If you want to try the diet, let me give you a little advice: Be proactive. Day minus one: Organize all the baggies. Take every pill, every fiber cap, every whatever and put them into plastic supplement baggies. One grocery bag will hang in your bedroom for morning supplements; one is divided into a work supplements and weekend supplements; and a third is nighty-night supplements. Don't think at all once you start the diet.

Bring a blender and protein shake containers to work. Buy two bags of milled flax seeds, one for home, one for work, or school or whereever. You're going to go through a jar of natural peanut butter that month, one spoonful at a time. Buy a good one.

Invest in some special bottles of water, too. Tap water is fine, but at night a glass of water with some lime or mint will give you a moment of formal relaxation. I know it sounds goofy, but it'll make sense on day two.

Finally, continue to join your family for meals. Cook the meals! Yes, the world needs martyrs, but not on this diet. Converse, enjoy, relax, entertain, and try to see the world through a new lens: You are in charge of your eating.

When it's time to transition off, let me give you some advice: Shop wisely. On Alwyn Cosgrove and John Berardi's advice, I went shopping. The day after the diet, I brought to school:

A case of albacore tuna
Three pounds of spring salad mix
Two pounds of snap peas
Three pounds of broccoli
A container of hummus
A bunch of limes for my water
A case of diet iced tea

I couldn't make bad lunch or bad snack choices. I also started each day with two eggs and a whopping seventy-calorie can of green beans. One of the best lessons of the V-Diet: Veggies can be made to taste like candy just by not eating whole foods for twenty-eight days.

Finally, the summation of what I learned: *Fat loss is an all-out war.* Give it twenty-eight days — only twenty-eight days. Attack it with all you have. It's not a lifestyle choice; it's a battle. Lose fat, and then get back into moderation.

There's another one for you: moderation. *Revelation* says it best: *You are lukewarm and I shall spit you out.*

Moderation is for sissies.

Four

The Rest of the Story

Paul Harvey made a career with the statement, "And now, the rest of the story." I think most readers will recognize the phrase and perhaps, like me, they've leaned in to hear the interesting turn the story they'd been hearing was about to take.

When the Beijing Olympics ended, a lot of people came up to me and asked, "Do you think the Jamaican sprinters are using drugs?" When I caught my breath after laughing for a few minutes, I agreed there may be an outside chance one or two athletes somehow slipped past, and, just maybe, a sprinter may have beaten the tests.

But I also know that soon we're going to hear the rest of the story. It might be something new in the world of training, or something spectacular we've all just missed. Most likely, the answer will be more clear than we all think.

In one of my favorite books, John Jerome's *The Sweet Spot in Time*, the author makes a wonderful, but naive, point regarding the East German swim team at the 1976 Olympics:

"Observers maintain that the East German breakthrough, if any, is not in basic science, not in physiology of training, but in development of the computer programs that can plan workloads with such precision.

"For the East German women, who dominated swimming for a period of years before and after the 1976 Montreal Olympics, the method seemed to work, at least for a while. For the East German men, interestingly enough, it did not."

Well... I'm sorry... but it might have been something else. Computers helped a little, but essentially turning women into men helped even more.

That's the rest of the story, and the longer I play in this game called strength, fitness and health, the more stories I hear.

Years ago, I had a great interview with Dick Smith, the master of functional isometric contractions (FIC), a training trend that swept the world in the early 1960s. One pushed and pulled against immobile objects until muscularity and fat loss happened.

That was almost fifty years ago, so nearly all of his method is lost, but I have dozens of articles cataloging football teams that "won overnight" by pushing and squeezing for a few minutes a day. As a coach, I can tell you any program that promises instant strength increases in minimal time will get noticed, and it won't disappear.

Later, of course, writers such as Terry Todd and John Fair opened the door that anabolic steroids were the rest of the story.

Those pink pills, the original steroids, were touted as something to help the athlete digest protein. Through the 1960s and 1970s, many writers, including Vince Gironda, emphasized digestion as the missing link in superior muscularity and size. Papaya extract, HCL pills, and a plethora of awful metallic-tasting things were sold to mimic the effects of drugs.

In any case, the verdict on isometric training was that it didn't work; the steroids made the lifters improve. But, the story continues. Three points.

Number One: Functional Isometric Contractions

A few years ago, I had trouble standing up with cleans at a weightlifting meet, so I called Dick Smith. His advice? Get in the rack! First, Dick emphasized I should clear the bottom pin in rack work. One didn't need to use static things, like door jams or his or her other limbs. He emphasized using maximal weights in the rack.

The perfect weight is one that all you can do is clear the weight off the rack and hold it for all you've got. I took Dick's advice and found the human body can clear a lot of weight off a rack.

Second, he was very clear one quickly overtrains in the rack, but at the same time doesn't notice this overtraining. I found this to be true. In 1991, I went on a serious imitation of Bill March's program, one of the original experimenters in isometrics.

I got very strong... then I pulled my right trap. My friend, Paul Northway, commented, "You jerked 315 off the rack without any warm-ups." I got seriously strong and badly overtrained mixing programs, and I wrote in my journal, "This stuff works!"

Later, after talking with Dick again, I began my dead-stop front squat program to cure my sticking point in the front squat. The best thing I ever did for my front squat strength, which is a basic indicator of total leg strength, was to purchase an inexpensive set of sawhorses. I could've purchased a rack for $2,000, but those sawhorses were about 70 bucks. I got them adjustable, to set at my exact sticking point.

I packed on a lot of plates and squatted from the dead-stop, bottom position. It worked wonders!

The term "dead-stop" explains having no rebound or bounce on a lift. This works for the bench press and military press, too.

In just a few weeks, I fixed a serious issue. Here were my observations.

- Six singles, max! I believe I'd argue for fewer now; after a couple of warm-ups, maybe two or three total-effort reps. Dick wouldn't agree with this, but I don't just clear the bottom position, I stand right up, so the weight would actually be less.

- To warm up, I like two sets of five with fifty percent of the estimated max in the full motion. For example, 165 times five sets of five, if using 330. I tried doing dead-stop front squats cold (no warm-ups at all) and it works, but my hips and psoas killed me the next few days. Of course, I'm a geezer. Young bucks might not need the warm-ups.

- I'd agree with some who argue one day a week is good, and you could do three if you're only doing one movement in the rack. This is going to be an experiment of one — what works for you with your weak points.

I did three days a week for about two weeks, then I started hating lifting (again) and I stopped improving. Two days, at the most, would work for me... I think.

The rest of the story is, yes, isometrics work. FIC — rack work— could be the answer for those with sticking points in any basic anti-gravity lift. The deadlift from the floor is certainly a dead-stop, but raise the bar up in the rack and see how much you can pull from just above the knees.

Number Two: The necessity of abdominal training

If you want to show off your abs... or core... or whatever you call it, go on the Velocity protein shake diet and call me in twenty-eight days.

Someday you're going to pay for the 10,000 crunches you were sure would build a six-pack. Instead, those built a bad lower back. Ab work does absolutely nothing for you. Just ask any long-time strength trainer.

And now, the rest of the story. I've been in touch with Dane Miller, who has been training with Dr. Anatoli Bondarchuk. Bondy is a legend in strength training, and Miller changed the way I'll look at abs forever. Imagine a mathematical formula as a template for your training program.

A+B+C=D

D is your goal. It could be an athletic performance or a certain amount of lean-body mass.
A is an upper-body movement, let's say the bench press.
B is a full-body movement, like the deadlift.
C is abdominal work.

When I increase B, either by max lift or increased volume, I've noticed D improves. Therefore, dropping B is universally bad. No matter what your goals are, you should keep deadlifting, or squatting, or whatever. Generally, increases in A have some effect on D, but it's more difficult to see the value.

Which leads us to C. Increasing ab work doesn't seem to help us with the goal. I've seen guys using ridiculous weight on forty-five-degree abdominal boards. What's the point, besides back surgery before you're middle-aged?

Why do abs? According to Miller, when you drop C, A and B go straight to hell, which we already know is going to impact D so fast it'll make your head swim. In other words, abs support your training goals as much as they support your internal organs! You have to do abs, simply to support the whole training system.

That's the rest of the story with abs. Working your abs won't help your six-pack, but it will support all your efforts to be able to show off your six-pack.

Number Three: Fat loss is about intensity

It's official. I've received my 10,000th email message asking about the fat-burning miracle that is high intensity interval training (HIIT), or the Tabata protocol.

A while back, I bored the world with my article on the Tabata Method. As a reminder, take ninety-five (or a humble sixty-five) pounds and front squat for twenty seconds. I'd expect, and demand, between eight and fourteen reps. Rest for ten seconds, then, without reading *War and Peace*, do another set of twenty seconds. Continue this cycle of work twenty, rest ten, for a total of four minutes.

Ever since, I've had dozens of emails from people who did Tabata sit-ups and got none of the pain about which I waxed so eloquently. My friends... never compare sit-ups to front squats.

It's like comparing your neighborhood street football game to the NFL. Yes, you got a stinging two-hand slap from 'lil Timmy down the block. That doesn't quite compare to being manhandled like a puppy's favorite chew toy.

The HIIT workouts I hear about offer the same idea. One guy was pouring the coals to a vigorous interval treadmill workout... thirty seconds of high-intensity jogging with five minutes of easy walking. (For the record, I have no idea why people email me about anything beyond lifting and throwing.)

I decided to figure out just what HIIT was. The best material I found was a summary from Dr. Tom Fahey: *HIIT - High-Intensity Interval Training Workout: A Time-Efficient, Low-Volume, High-Intensity Training Strategy for Building Cardiovascular Endurance.* Tom, an old friend and a great discus thrower, summed up the basics of HIIT very clearly, but I needed something more.

At a Highland Games fundraiser, we once sold attempts at a farmer walk with 105 pounds per hand. To keep the event going, I had to jump in every few attempts and take a thirty-second walk to reset the weights. The next day, and for several days after, Fahey's insights suddenly made sense.

Listen, would you rather do a thirty-second treadmill jog or would you rather march around death-gripping heavy dumbbells? I'm only allowing one answer. For your HIIT workouts, strap on a heavy sled, or grab two heavy dumbbells, and crush yourself into fat-burning mode.

This idea is a work in progress, but before you know it, you'll hear the rest of the story.

For those who missed the points:

- To fix a problem, consider a short experiment with dead-stop FIC movements exactly at your sticking point. Don't do a billion reps, just a few.

- Ab work won't give you a six-pack. It will, however, be the best support work you can do for your entire training regimen.

- Instead of embarrassing yourself on a treadmill, burn fat using a barbell or dumbbell with either Tabata front squats or a HIIT version of farmer walks.

And that's the rest of my story.

Five

The One Lift a Day Program

When I was a teenager, I turned from comic books to men's magazines. Not just the notable one with Hugh Hefner at the helm either; I also began to thumb through fitness magazines. At the time, there was *Strength and Health*, the old (and always bizarre) *Ironman*, and an assortment of pure bodybuilding rags.

In the last decade or so, a whole new fitness genre has appeared, as well as men's magazines with attitude, which usually means one paragraph of writing for every three near-nude women holding chainsaws. Call these Strength Lite, if you will.

I admit these magazines are the best airline flight reading I've found. Turn one page and you have thirty bulleted items detailing everything from quick fixes for spills to how to care for a pet.

One that caught my eye recently was a very interesting article about casual wear for men... written by a woman. It wasn't the suggestions that stopped me; it was something else:

Shirt: $245
Pants: Flat front and sexy, $210
Belt: $105
Socks: $29
Shoes: $285

This is casual wear? I buy my socks in bags bundling six pair, my suits cost as much as this guy's shirt and I'm not sure I've ever bought a belt — don't those come with pants?

After flipping a few more pages, I found the Training Program of the Month. Forget squats, rows and presses. This article was all about Reverse-grip Rubber Ball Axe Twists combined with Hungarian Cross Leaps. I have no idea what these exercises are in the real world, but the guy modeling them seemed to be getting a workout.

I don't think I'll ever make a living selling exercise programs. Why? Because the single finest training system I've ever used continues to be the only training program I can recommend. The problem? Well, the problem with this training program is it's really hard. No, really.

It's really hard, but really simple. Still, a fitness magazine would never run it because the average reader would never even try it. Will you? We're about to find out.

I call it the One Lift a Day program. Its roots are in the dim past of Olympic lifting, and it cuts past all the BS of modern training. It's so simple it can easily be overlooked. It cuts gym time, but increases recovery time. It may also cause you to miss work.

First, let's discuss why anyone who tries this is going to hate it. I'd bring this up later, but there are some subtle and not-so-subtle issues regarding the One Lift a Day program. The biggest issue for most people trying this for the first time is hard to fathom: You don't get to spend a lot of time in the gym… because you *can't* spend a lot of time in the gym.

The other issue is closely related: Since you're only doing one exercise, you can't slip away from squats to the leg extension machine to convince yourself you're working your legs. If you're only doing squats, you do squats. If you're only doing chins, you're going to chin for forty-five minutes!

Doing just chin-ups might have sounded like a grand idea in the car on the way to the gym, but I guarantee after about five sets you'll be looking around for the relief that changing exercises brings to the body and the mind. On the One Lift a Day program, you just aren't going to get that relief.

The biggest problem is there are no excuses. If you choose to do squats, it's a squat day. There's no place to hide in this program. You can't convince yourself you had a good day because you did forty-one different lifts or a lot of volume or you did a lot of abs after blowing off the stuff you hate.

It's as simple as this: Pick one lift each day and do it for the entire workout. The first advantage, obviously, is the simplicity: You don't have to bring in a computerized printout of all the exercises, seat positions, alignments, tempos and order of lifts. You do one lift for an entire workout. It sounds easy, doesn't it? Yeah, it can be deceptive that way.

Before considering exercise choices, let's look at approaches to reps and sets. One thing that may help when attempting the One Lift a Day program is to look at the training week a little more globally than most trainers view a typical week or month. One idea is to cut volume by half each successive week simply by changing reps and sets.

Week One: Seven sets of five

This is a tough workout for any lift, but when doing big lifts like squats, benches, deadlifts, presses, snatches or cleans, it will be exhausting. Through a little trial and error, I discovered a simple wave with the weight selection made for a better result:

>   Set One: 225 for 5
>   Set Two: 245 for 5
>   Set Three: 265 for 5

Set Four: 275 for 5
getting tired, tough lift, might not be able to get another set
Set Five: 235 for 5
nice refreshing drop in intensity
Set Six: 255 for 5
nice, challenging set… but not hellish
Set Seven: 275 or 285 for 5
depending on spotters and energy

Another idea that works well for bench presses (if you have great spotters) and squats (even better spotters) is to use max weights. Lower the bar on your own, but have your spotters help you through the lifting to insure a smooth rep. After finishing the five reps, rack the bar and perform eight to ten quick jumps for height if squatting, or eight to ten explosive push-ups if benching.

This is the workout that's caused more days lost from work or school than any workout I've ever recommended. Seven sets of five max squats followed by jumps seems to burn every fiber of the legs. My athletes in some cases literally can't get out of bed the next day.

I know of only two athletes who've ever done the seven sets of five with jumps and made it to work or school the next day. But, as I tell everyone, one day you'll thank me. Today is not that day.

Week Two: Six sets of three

At eighteen reps, this week is basically fifty percent of the volume of week one (thirty-five reps versus eighteen). Repeat the exact same weekly format of week one, but try to go a little heavier. After the volume of week one, week two seems rather easy… on paper.

Week Three: Five, three, two

This may be my favorite sets-and-reps selection. Basically, we're considering the double as a max. Like many coaches I learned, all athletes lie about max singles, but seldom do we find fuzzy logic with doubles. One thing you can generally count on is whatever someone can do for a double, they can usually do for a single.

Trust me, athletes and coaches lie about maxes all the time. Go to any college football locker room in America and ask for numbers. Recently a college football player claimed a 540 clean as a max. The American record in the clean and jerk is 517.

Week Four: Off!

On paper, the first three weeks look so easy. When you look at this week, many people scoff at the idea. "A week off! I scoff at thee!" Try the One Lift a Day idea, then get back to me. If the week off sounds wrong, I'm willing to bet you didn't push the big exercises.

Exercise selection should match your goals. It should also match your life. If you like to hit the bars or go dancing on the weekends, slide those squats away from Thursday or Friday. You literally won't be able to move from one leg to the other. Come to think of it, that's how I dance anyway.

For a powerlifter or someone who uses a power bodybuilding approach, this One Lift a Day program could be perfect. Consider a weekly approach like this:

> **Monday:** Bench Press or Incline Bench Press
> **Tuesday:** Row or Row Variation
> **Wednesday:** Squat
> **Thursday:** Off
> **Friday:** Military Press
> **Saturday:** Curl, Deadlift, whatever

I can hear some of you already: What about abs? What about serratus? Trust me, a forty-five-minute workout of military presses will work the abdominal muscles as well as any machine advertised on late-night television.

The One Lift a Day Program is really hard. Certainly, it's the most productive program most people have ever tried, but it's simply too hard. It isn't fun, except for your buddies who laugh at you as you try to walk after the squats. You probably won't even complete the whole month. Is that a double-dog dare? Yeah, I think it is.

Interested in trying it? Think about a few things:

- Big weights, short workouts. It's hard to go heavy for a long workout. If you don't believe me, enter a Strongman contest or a Highland Games and see how the day goes.

- If the whole idea sounds crazy, just try an occasional one-lift-only day. It certainly breaks the mold of what most trainers do, and is actually fun.

- One Lift a Day might open up a new training paradigm for many lifters: *Core exercises are core and assistance exercise assist!* In the past decade, many trainers have forgotten this basic truth.

- The worst thing that can happen from squatting once a week is your thighs might outgrow that $210 pair of pants that are flat front and sexy.

You've been warned.

Six

The Tabata Method — Fat Loss in Four Minutes

A couple of years ago, a company came out with an exercise machine that guaranteed results in only four minutes a day. The main problem? The $12,000 price tag. My car didn't cost that much. I'm not sure I've ever spent that much on anything, including my education.

I'm going to save you a lot of money today because I'm going to show you how to do the same thing without an overpriced machine. This top-secret training method may do more for you than all your other training combined, and still leave you with twenty-three hours and fifty-six minutes to live the rest of your day.

But there's a price to pay. Think exhaustion, vomit and pools of sweat.

Tabata is the name of a Japanese researcher who discovered an interesting way to increase both anaerobic and aerobic pathways at the same time. It's one of those strange training programs that seems to fit across disciplines: It's excellent for bicyclists, speed skaters, Olympic lifters, or the person looking to lose fat quickly.

This training method is so simple, yet so incredibly difficult, athletes try it once, acknowledge its greatness, and vow to never speak its name again. What is it? Nothing to it: Take one exercise and perform it in the following manner.

1) For twenty seconds, do as many repetitions as possible.
2) Rest for ten seconds.
3) Repeat seven more times.

That's it! You're done in four minutes! Oh, and that thing you're trying to brush off your face? That would be the floor.

Eight sets of as many reps as you can get, followed by a brief ten-second rest… simple and effective. The two best exercise options for the Tabata method are the front squats and the thruster, which I'll describe in a bit.

It helps to have someone record the reps of each set for you because, well, you won't remember after you pass out. I use the lowest rep number of any of the eight sets as my measurement to compare workout to workout. If you go too heavy, that number might be two. If you go too light, you might find yourself getting fifteen reps or more.

Before we talk about the exercises, let's take a moment to be perfectly clear about what we're doing. This isn't eight sets of eight, although the goal of doing eight reps in each of the twenty-second clusters is about right. Instead, it's as many reps as you can get during the twenty seconds, followed by a ten-second rest.

And by the way, ten seconds is not racking the bar, getting a drink, talking to the cute girl on the bike, looking at the clock, walking back to the bar, chalking up, adjusting your belt, talking to a friend, then doing the next set. Ten second is ten seconds! *No cheating!*

You need to choose an exercise that uses a large number of muscles. I suggest the front squat. You may argue, why not the back squat? Because it's hard to dump the bar quickly into the rack with back squats, while with front squats, you can just fall into it and start your ten-second rest.

With something like a military press, you won't be using enough muscles to allow you to survive in the last minute; you might only get one or two reps with your shoulders on fire. Deadlifts have been tried, but most people get a little worried about injuries doing them Tabata-style.

The front squat might be the single best Tabata lift. Having said that, if you don't know how to front squat correctly, the Tabata method might teach you to lift better than a thousand coaches could. In the four minutes, it's easy to get sixty-four to seventy reps, which teaches the nervous system better than any two-hour PowerPoint presentation.

The bar will be held in the front of the body, with the fingers relaxed, the elbows high, and the bar resting on the clavicles. Sit down between the legs. This actually gets easier in the third and fourth minutes as you just start to drop back through. As you rise up, you don't need to lock out the knees; in fact, don't even think about it. Just get up and go back down.

Weight on the bar? Let's just say this: A guy with a 465-pound front squat puked with only ninety-five pounds on the Tabata front squat. Generally, I urge people to go light, like sixty-five to ninety-five pounds the first time. There are those who've gone up to 155 pounds and have still gotten eights in the last twenty seconds, but they are very rare people.

The other great Tabata exercise is the thruster. The thruster is one of the greatest lifts rarely seen in the gym. Take two dumbbells or kettlebells and hold them at shoulder height. Squat down, keeping the 'bells on the shoulders or the kettlebells in the rack position. As you rise up, press the 'bells to overhead lockout. You can either press as you rise, or use the momentum to help kick the bells overhead. I find I do a little bit of both in the four minutes.

Thrusters do things to your heart rate and breathing that I honestly can't describe. Go light! A thirty-five-pound 'bell in each hand is a very difficult thruster workout. Check your ego at the door for the first two minutes.

You need to be able to see a wall clock with a secondhand during your four minutes of fun. Stop at twenty seconds, rack the bar (assuming you chose the front squat), rest ten seconds, grab the bar and go again. Watching the clock seems to help with the focus.

And remember this: You really shouldn't consider doing much after a Tabata workout. Your lungs will be going like a locomotive. Go ahead and plan anything you like, but don't be surprised if it just doesn't happen. I keep the family dog nearby to chase away the carrion birds while I rest on the sidewalk.

The hardest thing about this workout is staying focused for four minutes. Don't let your hands leave the bar or dumb-bells if you can help it. After you put the bar in the rack during the front squat, stay right there, an inch or two back from the bar, and stare at the secondhand of the clock.

If you do thrusters, put the 'bells on a bench and watch the clock with your hands ready to grab the handles. This little trick of staying with the weights seems to help make those ten seconds seem like, well, not much, really. But at least you don't have to move much to get the weights again.

I do either Tabata front squats or Tabata thrusters about twice a month. I'm sure someone will comment, "If it's so good, why don't you do it every day?" Go ahead, try it and report back after the second day.

Why should you do this workout? The Tabata program might be the single best fat-burning workout I know. It may only be four minutes, but I keep sweating and breathing hard for a long, long time afterwards. Moreover, it seems to teach the body the proper method of squatting far easier than all the instruction in the world.

One other thing: Tabata truly teaches a person the mental focus needed to push past pain to reach other body comp or athletic goals. It'll save you 12,000 bucks, too.

Seven

A History of Dieting

A couple of years ago, I was asked to speak to a group of high school students. I said no. I was asked again and I said no again. The third time something in my guilt-ridden conscience made me say yes. I regretted it as soon as I found out the topic: moderation.

I instantly realized I'd been conned. Nobody wants to stand before a group of teens and talk about *Just Say No*, or discuss death and dismemberment from drinking and driving. I needed another focus, one that would make the same point without having a roomful of adolescent faces glaze over like this morning's doughnuts.

Fortunately, a friend of mine, Kathy, had just told me about her current three-day diet. It was called the 7-7-7 Diet. On day one she ate seven eggs throughout the day. That, by the way, was all she ate. On day two she consumed seven oranges and on day three, she ate only seven bananas. According to Kathy, on day four she was supposed to wake up seven pounds lighter.

I didn't have the heart to tell her this, but any period of starvation will cause weight loss, but by day four she'd probably wind up fourteen pounds heavier with less lean muscle tissue. Kathy's wonder diet (you wonder why she does it) was the perfect inspiration for the topic of moderation. During my research I also came up with a few truisms about weight and fat loss that seem to hold the test of time. Here's what I learned.

As you wander around the grocery store, you'll notice yesterday's diet crazes are today's staples. Oddly, some of the oldest diets were designed to battle not only corpulence, but also immorality. The remnants of these diets can be found on grocery store shelves even today.

In the 1830s, Reverend Sylvester Graham believed gluttony was the gateway to lust. Any such venereal excess was deemed evil. Graham thought men should remain virgins until age thirty, and then should only have sex once a month after marriage. Masturbation was off-limits, too, that particular act leading to a body full of disease and mental illness.

To get rid of hunger, both sexual and nutritional, Graham prescribed a vegetarian diet that included a biscuit he'd created, which later became known as the Graham Cracker.

Within a few decades of Graham, another noted dietician and full-time undertaker, William Banting, lost fifty pounds on lean meat, dry toast, eggs and vegetables. "Banting" became the verb for dieting in America not long after his book, *Letter on Corpulence*, became a bestseller.

At the same time, Dr. James Salisbury proposed a high-protein diet of ground meat patties and hot water. He preached against starches, stating these would turn into poisonous substances during digestion. The solution was ground meat three times per day, with limited amounts of vegetables, fruits and starchy foods. Today you can still order Salisbury steaks in most family restaurants.

The most noted of the pre-1900 health enthusiasts was the enema enthusiast, Dr. John Harvey Kellogg. Yep, the same guy who basically invented cold cereal and whose name probably appears on the cereal boxes in your cabinet. Kellogg invented Corn Flakes and an early version of granola to reduce sexual desire and curb the epidemic of masturbation.

He also recommended that small boys be circumcised without anesthetic so they would forever associate the penis with pain. Women should have their clitorises treated with carbolic acid to prevent what he called abnormal excitement. Yes, Kellogg was a real winner.

Kellogg's regimen of vegetarianism and colon cleansing were lampooned in the 1994 film, *The Road to Wellsville*, with Anthony Hopkins portraying the good doctor.

Hopkins also portrayed a carnivore in *The Silence of the Lambs*. The Doctor Hannibal Diet will not be discussed here.

So, Graham Crackers, Salisbury steaks and Kellogg's foods were at one time the cutting edge of nutritional strategies in America. Moreover, we also have one of the most interesting relationships in understanding weight and fat loss: the role of money.

My personal favorite ad campaign for weight loss came in the 1920s when Lucky Strike cigarettes were promoted as a fat-loss tool: *Reach for a Lucky instead of a sweet*. Lung cancer seems to be an effective weight-loss program, although I wouldn't recommend it.

Certainly, a quick look through the back pages of women's magazines, especially those in the 1950s, would provide plenty of insightful ways to lose weight, including creams, lotions and, of course, the famous tapeworm-infested diet pills, although I still think this is more urban legend than truth.

The three basic diet methods are categorized as follows.

- **Food sorting or combining diets:** These methods have been around a long time, as some argue the Kosher food laws are dietary magic for weight loss. Basically, it's the idea certain foods or combinations of foods are good or bad.

- **"More" diets:** Whenever you see the word "high" in a diet, it's probably part of this group. Usually a diet like this encourages the consumption of more of a certain macronutrient: carbohydrates, protein or fat. These normally appear after a period of something else being high. For example, higher fat diets followed the low-fat-diet craze.

- **"Less" diets:** These would be recognizable with the word "low," but I include various starvation diets with this idea, too.

Food sorting or combining diets have a certain appeal to me on a basic level. It isn't the fact that I drink a six-pack of beer every night that makes me fat; it's the darn peanuts I snack on with the beer. It's the combination that causes the gut, not the calories. Whew, what a relief! Now I'll just drink the beer.

Pavlov, of dog-drooling fame, had a theory that combining protein-rich foods and carbohydrate-rich foods was the greatest problem in digestion. Chiropractic doctor Phil Maffetone developed this concept in a series of books, with my favorite being *Everybody is an Athlete*. Basically, eating a piece of salmon is fine, but adding noodles would be an issue for the body. A few hours later, though, that bed of noodles with a tomato sauce would be fine, too; just don't add a steak. Uh huh.

Being the star of the sitcom *Three's Company* developed Suzanne Somers into a diet expert and household name. No, really. She has a series of books that deal directly with this concept of food combining. Fruits eaten alone is the bedrock of many such food-combining programs.

Besides Pavlov, there are other food-combiners before Somers. In the 1920s, Dr. William Howard Hay thought blood pH was the key to health, and one of the factors was not combining starches, fruits or proteins at the same meal.

People also needed to have daily enemas and slow down chewing, a very popular early twentieth-century idea for health known as Fletcherizing. Horace Fletcher came up with the idea of chewing food until it was liquefied in the mouth before swallowing. This was still being discussed as a proper digestion tactic during my high school years.

Judy Mazel may be the most famous food-combiner before Somers. Her fruit-heavy diet was the rage in the early 1980s with the publication of her book, *The Beverly Hills Diet*. I clearly remember women eating forkful after forkful of spaghetti, certain the mango, papaya or pineapple they ate after the meal would ensure no weight gain.

This diet highlighted a major diet fad during the eighties: the brand name issue. *The Cambridge Diet* was not from Cambridge, but was written by a doctor working there, using multi-level marketing (legal pyramid scheme) to sell a protein drink. The Beverly Hills or South Beach names seem to sell better than the Ozark Mountain Valley Diet. Funny that.

About this same time, Dan Duchaine and Dr. Mauro DiPasquale concomitantly began writing about longer periods of food combining. Mixed with specific training for specific days in the cycle, one could go five days of high-fat and high-protein eating with practically no carbohydrates. This was followed by a two-day carbohydrate feast. The original diets, *BodyOpus* and *The Anabolic Diet,* have become very popular among strength and power athletes in the past dozen years.

Recently, guys like Dr. John Berardi have been advocating diets where you try not to mix too many carbs and too many fats in the same meal.

The upside to these plans is no macronutrient is considered evil. You get to eat protein, carbs and fats, as long as the timing or meal combinations are addressed. The simple idea that a dieter is forced to plan eating might be the secret weapon in the success of these diets.

Most people recognize the "more" or "high" diets as the last few decades of diet books have emphasized one heroic macronutrient battling to the death with another evil macronutrient. Fats are bad, eat more carbs! No wait, carbs are bad, eat more fat!

Historically, some single foods have been the secret of becoming lank, as was the goal in Dr. George Cheyne's works in the late 1600s when he told his followers to increase the amount of milk they drank.

The advent of the first high macronutrient diets didn't really show up until the early 1960s, although writings from *Strength and Health's* Bob Hoffman had been encouraging high protein for decades. In Herman Taller's book, *Calories Don't Count,* Taller pushed the high-fat, high-protein, low-carb diet. Quickly, several books appeared including Stillman's *The Doctor's Quick Weight Loss Diet,* rich in meat and cheese and, a decade later, Dr. Robert Atkins' first book on the topic, *Diet Revolution.*

Since the mid-1990s, the lower-carb, higher-protein diets have taken center-stage. In fact, one could argue we've just seen a paradigm shift in diet thinking in the past few years when the shift of evil macronutrients went from fat to carbohydrates. Barry Sear's book, *The Zone,* gave rise to the 40-30-30 phenomenon and shifted many away from thinking protein and fat were evil.

Sugar Busters, Protein Power, The Carbohydrate Addict's Diet and the various paleo diets have all been accepted as a mainstream style of eating today. Mention "I'm eating Atkins," and a waiter will know exactly what and what not to serve you.

It's obvious now even to researchers the two-week Atkins induction seems to really make a change in weight on the scale for many people. Increasing the fat in the diet also reminds people what it feels like to be satiated after a meal. Again, the reason these kinds of diets work might be because the dieter has to plan a meal or, at the very least, limit choices at a meal.

The "less, low and no" diets can be traced almost directly to 1910. The concept of calories had emerged and with that, Gustave Gaertner invented the food scale. His mantra for weight loss was, "Without scales, no cure." Within a decade, Dr. Lulu Hunt Peters offered her lifelong diet plan: Begin with a fast; fletcherize your food; and limit yourself to 1,200 calories a day for the rest of your life.

Of course, soon 1,200 was considered too high. Diets began to recommend 600 calories with the famous Hollywood Diet of 585 calories a day for eighteen days. The staples of this diet — grapefruit, eggs, oranges and melba toast — became the iconic foods of diet perhaps even to this day. Ask Grandma about diet advice and she might give you that list.

Later, diets of 400 calories a day were recommended by some doctors to eliminate obesity. By the 1950s, a whole new market developed for dieting cookbooks that now stuff entire sections of your local bookstore.

In the late 1970s, Nathan Pritikin decided eating fat was the cause of being fat and wrote *The Pritikin Program for Diet and Exercise,* which advocated a very-low-fat diet. Dr. Dean Ornish added to this a decade later with his book, *Eat More, Weigh Less,* emphasizing a low-fat vegetarian diet for weight loss and improved blood profiles.

The "fat makes you fat" issue is still popular among most people interested in fat loss, which leads to a lot of diet failures. All too often, in a carbohydrate-friendly environment one stops eating only when all the chips are gone.

Floating around the diet world during the 1960s and 1970s were also several liquid-protein diets based on gag-inducing products made of liquid cow skin, as well as Herman Tarnower's *Scarsdale Diet* that allowed only 700 calories a day.

The advantage of these kinds of diets is the rabid, warrior-like mentality that clinging to them seems to develop. Unfortunately, especially with ultra-low-fat diets, blood profile tests don't improve very much. In fact, many meat- and cheese-eating Atkins dieters find their blood work superior to their old rabbit diets. Maybe the lesson is to eat the rabbit, not the rabbit's dinner.

What do we take from all of this? First, when you review diets in books or articles notice most still discuss weight loss, not fat loss. Wanting to lose weight has practically no meaning. Certainly, an accident with a lawn mower would cause weight loss, but is that our goal? Second, study this stuff enough and you'll notice you'll soon become a prophet of sorts by guessing the next great diet wave.

The most concrete advice I culled from all of this revolves around one basic issue, your food choices. The key here is to prepare yourself on a daily and weekly basis to be able to make good food choices.

Years ago at a workshop we were asked to keep a food journal for a few days and list the foods we ate. Not the volume, calories, protein, or anything like that, we were merely asked to make a column of the foods we ate during that time. The point was simple: Most people eat about ten to twenty foods a week. Don't believe me? Keep the journal.

If those foods are:

Eggs	Salmon
Tuna	Oatmeal
Blueberries	Almonds
Chicken	Apples
Grapefruit	Cottage Cheese
Vegetables	

… you probably didn't need to read this section.

Some quick ideas:

Never shop or go out hungry. That's right, eat before you go out to eat. Not only will you save money, but you'll make better food choices. Eat before you go food shopping and you won't buy stuff that will end up as another chin.

You must have a shopping list. I have one at work, one on the refrigerator and plenty of extras in a drawer. Take a few minutes to make sure you have what you think you have. Stick to the list!

Buy a lot of the stuff you're planning to eat. If you decide to eat four eggs a day and you buy a dozen eggs, your new-found enthusiasm will end in three days. Then you'll likely eat something you hadn't planned to eat.

Snacking on fruits isn't a bad idea. Try to eat a bowl of apples. It's really hard to do. I've found almonds or apples to be ideal snack options. Keep 'em handy and you won't be so tempted to pull into a fast food joint.

Finally, really strive to make good food choices. A woman once asked me if I knew a diet where you could eat anything you wanted. I said yes, but first she'd have to eat two pounds of salmon, three cups of oatmeal, a cup of blueberries, two bowls of mixed vegetables, and a carton of cottage cheese. After she finished that each day, she could eat anything she wanted.

In short, focus on good foods and the rest will probably take care of itself. Just think, it only took us a couple of hundred years to figure this out.

Eight

The Classic Top 10 Tips

Years ago, I offered this list of tips for athletes:

1. Use whole-body lifts; rarely isolate a muscle.

2. Constantly strive to add weight to the bar, and move it faster.

3. The best anabolic is water.

4. Did you eat breakfast? If not, don't ask me anything about nutrition.

5. If you smoke or don't wear your seatbelt, please don't tell me the quick lifts are dangerous.

6. Go heavy, go hard.

7. Keep it simple. Less is more.

8. You have to put the bar over your head.

9. Put the bar on the floor and pick it up a bunch of different ways.

10. Know and love the roots of your sport.

I still stand by this list. However, the past few years of coaching and working with athletes have taught me a few new lessons. The first three contain warnings, the second three are the hard-won lessons, and the last four are the tips that work in life, in love and in lifting, but not in that order.

The Warnings

1. Beware of anything that makes no sense.

Okay, everybody try this: Breathe through your eyes.

"I'm sorry, Dan, I thought you said to breathe through my eyes."

Yes, yes I did. Now, imagine yourself as a fetus in the womb of the universe.

"What?!?"

Exactly.

My first tip is to beware of anything that makes absolutely no sense. If you're at the local nutrition store and the assistant day manager begins to spout about how the regression of this or that can be subdiverted by the axial dynamic of a bottle of stuff costing ninety-nine bucks, back away slowly. My favorite new thing in the nutrition stores is the locked glass cabinet. Certainly, something that has to be locked behind glass must be worth more than I make in a week!

Breathe through your eyes takes on many variations. There's nothing worse than when someone takes a community education course and becomes an expert on how yoga is the best way to burn the visceral fat that's housed deep in your abdomen. Breathing deep will flush it out. Well, doesn't that make sense? You have fat deep in your belly, so to eliminate it you do deep belly-breathing and the air will carry the fat out.

If someone tells you lifting slow makes you fast or jolting your abs with an electric shock every few seconds will carve out a six-pack, try to breathe through your eyes. It'll bring clarity.

2. Beware the real estate professor who doesn't own real estate.

Several years ago I asked my buddy, Jerry, how he became so rich. (Jerry has some serious money.) He told me a very simple story. He'd gone to the local university and started taking courses to become a successful businessman. During the first week, a student asked the professor in the real estate course about the professor's holdings. The professor's answer? He didn't own any.

Jerry dropped out of school that day and took up a career in real estate. He said, "If this guy's students are my competition, I should be a millionaire in no time." Jerry was right.

No, a guy doesn't have to be Mr. Greater Westphalia to be an expert in nutrition or in training, but he needs to look like he bumped into a weight sometime in his life!

Generally, I find I learn the most from people from other disciplines. I've heard great advice from ballerinas, martial artists and monks on things that have done wonders for my training. The point is this: If somebody is telling you to radically change your training merely on a whim or unsupported opinion, ask him to try it on himself first. Beware advice from somebody who doesn't put the advice into practice.

3. Beware of overkill.

Here's an example of overkill:

"If jumping off a small box helps my vertical leap, jumping off a building will help that much more."

Whenever I think about this, I'm reminded of my uncle who survived a fall of thirty-nine stories off a building. Unfortunately, the building was forty stories. Get it? He was fine for thirty-nine stories; it was the last one that did him in. Of course, my uncle was an optimist. At the twenty-sixth floor a lady leaned out the window and asked, "How's it going?" My uncle answered, "So far, so good!"

Okay, sorry, enough of that. This little warning illustrated by the statement above is perhaps the most ignored in most people's training programs.

"If two sets of curls make my biceps pump, I'll do twenty and the pump will stay with me until the lights come on at the club at three in the morning."

Well, the pump doesn't last that long and what are you doing at a club that late anyway?

Basically, I'm talking about overkill here. You shoot the deer, then pump it full of twenty more shots just to make sure. It's the most common error in sports.

"Sixty grams of fiber a day is what some guys take to cut fat, so I'll take in 160."

"The Bulgarians train six times a day, so I'll train twelve!"

"Arnold got up to 240 in the off-season, so I'll get up to 480 and be twice as big!"

You've seen it. You've done it. We all do it. Stop doing it.

4. Everything works.

Everything works for about two weeks. Nothing works after about six weeks. I love books that promise "Titanic Triceps in Two Weeks." Of course, the *Titanic* sank — didn't you know?

Things need changing. You don't have to throw everything out, but as Pavel Tsatsouline says, you must change things so you do the same, but different. When you change a program after two weeks, you must learn the most unused concept in training: Be subtle. Don't use a sledgehammer; use a touch of variation. Change your grip, change the angle, add a little to the rest period or cut a little off, change the order of exercises. Change it up, a little.

It's possible your training program does need a complete makeover. How can you know that? Read number five.

5. Build a foundation of basic strength.

Generally, if healthy and fit, you should be able to do a double-bodyweight deadlift and a bodyweight bench press. I won't say you need to military press bodyweight, but that's what I insist on.

Why? A double-bodyweight deadlift means the posterior chain has been built up enough to begin the process of adding something to the rest of the frame. The bodyweight press is just something that's cool. I wish I had more to say about that, but that's just the way it is. If you can't bench your bodyweight, don't ask me about all the other stuff until you can.

If you're not yet at this level, you need to get there. All the excellent supplements available and all the great training programs you read won't put Humpty Dumpty back together until you're at these basic levels. I've worked with many people who suddenly thrive when they get their basic strength levels up to these marks.

You need to have some basic strength to support advanced training. If you don't have it, get it!

6. Commit this to memory: It is your parents' fault.

There. Something every daytime talk-show host blathers about each afternoon is finally true. Yes, blame your folks.

You're hamstrung by your genetic capabilities. I have a friend who played for the Utah Jazz and stands seven-foot, four inches. His wife is six-two. They have three children. Do the math: Will their children have a leg up (more like two feet) on you in basketball? Yes, because they will be taller than you!

The problem with genetics is this: Exactly what have you been dealt in the gene pool crap shoot? You can't find out if all you do is bench press and curl. You may be standing on the finest legs since Tom Platz or Cory Everson, but if you don't ever get off the pec deck, you'll never find out the truth.

I've always wondered if I could have been an Olympic champion in kayak, fencing or team handball. Without any exposure to these events, is it possible I was a natural in saber?

Once again, I can blame my parents for not exposing me to each and every athletic competition the world has to offer. I could've been the best cow-chip tosser in world history.

Now, shake your fist at the universe and blame everything else in your blame pantheon. Do a good job; don't forget your third grade teacher, too.

Done? Good. Now, get back to work and forget about all of this because there's nothing, and I mean nothing, that can be done about it! You can stop blaming your parents now and get back to the workout.

7. Stand on the shoulders of greatness.

Guess what? Whatever you're striving for has been done before.

I've had the unique opportunity to talk with most of the elite discus throwers from the United States, including those from the 1950s, 1960s and 1970s. I sat in the stands with former world record-holder Fortune Gordien, who told me, "When you get stuck in practice, either do throws with iddy-biddy footwork or throw with no reverse." It's a gem I still use, and I still call these iddy-biddy drills.

The road to leanness can be studied by looking over the books by Clarence Bass or Vince Gironda. Interested in starting training as a teen and following it through adulthood? Read Arnold's book. The web is loaded with books and information from strongmen from the 1890s to the present. Certainly, you'll need to discern some of the information, but don't reinvent the wheel.

Generally, I avoid clichés like the plague, but reinventing the wheel is the greatest mistake most trainers make. Learn from the greats!

8. Train outside.

What's the one thing missing from most modern trainers' quivers? They need to go outside and train more.

I'm famous for my hyperbole, but in this case the following is true: You will never reach your potential if you stay in the cozy confines of your gym. Why? First, you'll never ever see anyone except those in the cozy confines of your gym.

If you're the biggest guy at the spa with your guns measuring fifteen inches around, you might never be inspired to go beyond your current regime of bench, curl, bench, curl, bench, curl. Recently, I saw a young woman do twenty-one straight pull-ups and immediately decided I had been dogging this exercise.

But when I say train outside, I also literally mean go outside! Get off the treadmill and run in a park. Dump the lat pulldown machine for a set of monkey bars. Drag your bar out into the field and work out. Make a picnic and eat between sets of deadlifts. Carry a loaded bar for long distances. Breathe fresh air for a while and click off your DVD, CNN, iPod and CDs.

One-dumbbell training is perfect for training outdoors. Grab a dumbbell or kettlebell, put it on the floor of your car, drive out to a nice spot and simply invent a workout. Lift the thing as many ways as you can imagine, and do as many reps as your body will allow.

I spend the majority of my workouts outside. Certainly, rain makes it difficult with iron, but I've trained in snowstorms and torrid summer days. I keep a towel on the bar so I don't burn my hands when I grab it, but it's well worth the effort. Besides, why go to a tanning bed when you can get a golden tan while performing multiple clean and jerks?

9. Have some fun!

I have a workshop that emphasizes balance. In it, I outline four terms: work, rest, play and pray. (Pray can simply be alone time. I'm amazed at how many of my college athletes literally have no alone time. They're always surrounded by roommates, teammates and mate mates.) The harder you work, the bigger the other three components have to become in proportion to your added level of work.

Fun has disappeared from the strength world. I don't mean dinking around with someone while they squat 700; I mean training that's fun. I was raised in the gym with goofy contests like max sit-ups on the steepest inclines, jumping up on things and trying to leap up and touch something with the most weight. (Use dumbbells, by the way. Trust me.) No, they had no medals nor trophies or award ceremonies. It was just fun.

You need to work hard. Okay, I agree. But we have nearly forgotten the fun stuff, like training outside or competing at some silly game, and the joy of the opportunity to lift weights. This isn't the same as making fun of someone while lifting (that can be anywhere from juvenile to deadly), I'm talking about having a great time training. It's easy to measure: If you're doing something that seems like five minutes of work but it actually lasts an hour, it was probably fun.

When in doubt, listen to one of my mother's mantras: Go outside and play.

10. Have some passion!

Passion is a word that doesn't mean what you think it means. It means to suffer. Now, that may not be how we use it today, but that's what the root of the word means, at least in the dictionary. Let's define it this way: *Passion, to suffer for love.*

I think greatness comes to those willing to go past the sweat. I hear it all the time, "Look, see, I'm working hard. I'm sweating." Yeah, well, you'll sweat in a sauna, too. It doesn't mean nothin'.

You have to go past the hurt, too. The hardest thing to teach young men in football is the difference between being hurt and being injured. Injured means out; you're done for today, this week, this season. Hurt means you've just moved beyond the pain. Winners learn to live with hurt. In life, you're going to be hurt a lot. Bosses don't always care about your inner child when you blow a sale or ram an oil tanker into a dock.

Passion is learning to push beyond all of this in the pursuit of your dreams and goals. Your goals are going to cost you in every nuance of the word: physically, emotionally, financially and all the rest of the 'allies you can find.

I was once asked how to generate passion in an older athlete, one like me. I wrote:

- Travel to a lot of meets.

- Hang out with your competition for long periods afterwards.

- Read everything and watch everything you can about your sport.

- Travel some more. Hang out some more. Learn some more.

- Spend your money on your sport!

- See number four above!

Simple, huh?

Nine

Systematic Education for Lifters

It happens every time I write an article or give a workshop. Someone asks me, "So, uh, Dan, do you think I should do it five times a week or should I do it twice a day?" It doesn't matter what "it" is — one-arm lifts, Tabata front squats, Olympic lifts — I always get the same perplexing response.

I understand perplexity. As the father of two teenagers, being perplexed defines most of my life. Only recently have I understood the issue from both sides of the question. Responses like the above mystify me because I've been training since 1967, and I can therefore discern whether or not something works. Perhaps more importantly, I understand the steps needed to take to add something (an exercise, a training protocol, a supplement) to my training.

Some people have no idea how to do this. If you're one of those, let me give you a hint: You must begin by understanding how we learn.

Imagine asking a five-year-old to figure out how many square yards of burnt-orange shag carpet would be needed in a room.

Issue One: This five year-old still counts "one-two-free-four-five-uh?"

Issue Two: Not only does this young scholar not know what a yard is, but he thinks a foot is only made for kicking a ball.

Issue Three: Sure, it's a simple issue of length times width. Says the kiddo, "What's 'times'?"

To learn math, we follow a progression we call systematic education. Math skills are based on first learning the numbers in the correct sequence. (This doesn't apply to me when I'm doing high-rep squats. I count by fives when I get tired.) Next, we might approach adding two numbers together to get a sum. I have thirty-three-inch arms, for example.

After learning addition, we learn subtraction, then multiplication. Finally, we learn about feet and yards so we can figure out our carpet problem: Take the width and multiply it by the length to discover they no longer sell burnt-orange shag. However, they do have a lovely lime green on sale.

See, systematic education is the best way to learn anything. But how the heck does this relate to chunking weight around in the gym?

Pick up a bodybuilding magazine off the rack in any grocery store. Open it and find Mr. Great Galaxy's official training program and supplement schedule. Let me say this for you: Yeah, right. Having said that, let's move on.

So, young Billy, who wants to impress his fourteen-year-old female classmates, buys this magazine, takes it home, drags his older brother's weights out from under the bed and tries to follow Mr. Great Galaxy's training program. In a few years, he's done every curl imaginable and performed so many skull crushers that his I.Q. has dropped. (Note to Billy: These aren't designed to be a bouncing, ballistic exercise.)

He then joins the local fitness center and discovers bench pressing five days a week, and the indisputable fact that squats hurt the knees, which, of course, is quite disputable. By this time, Billy has also joined an internet forum and is an expert on biochemical reactions inside the human body, trash-talking beginners' questions, and making fun of old guys who Olympic lift.

Then, Billy goes to a workshop or, worse, reads one of my articles. You see, Billy doesn't have a systematic education. He never learned to squat correctly, deadlift correctly, nor learned the basics of the sport. He doesn't eat breakfast because he's on the Warrior Diet; he drinks five Super Huge Gulps of cola a day because he heard that was the best way to get creatine to work; and he thinks the only way to get a bodyweight bench press is to be on drugs.

At the workshop, he hears someone like Mike Burgener discuss the Olympic lifts. Mike breaks down the lifts to the key points and hammers them over and over while the group does the lifts with PVC pipes. The next presenter might be someone like Coach Christopher Sommer discussing the one-hour warm-up he has his young elite gymnasts perform each workout. Each drill is amazing, and certainly would fit into any athlete's program.

And maybe they ask me to speak at this workshop and I explain the joys of sprinting with heavy boulders, tossing long wooden poles end-over-end, and mixing chains, rocks, thick bars, kettlebells and isometrics into one exercise. Young Billy stares up at the ceiling after the workshop. He just doesn't have the time to train on the Olympic lifts two hours a day, train to be an Olympic gymnast, train to become a Highland athlete and a terror in the neighborhood, and continue training for the Mr. Great Galaxy contest.

You see, Billy doesn't have the background to discern what to do and when to do it. He "knows" a lot, but he can't sift through the process. Billy is right: He *doesn't* have the time to do all the things he learned at the workshop, nor should he attempt it. What should he do?

The problem with systematic education is it takes a long time. Now, the fact that you can read this shows the value of the process, but unless you had an extraordinary elementary physical education teacher, opportunities to train in a wide variety of sports, an elite-level high school program, and the finest coaching in the world in college, it can be difficult to pick up all this information in the typical gym.

For the adult learner, especially those who use my articles as their on-going lifting education (college credit should be given, by the way), I propose another method.

Systemic education is based on understanding a simple model. You can use the image of a ladder as a basic model, but as the cliché goes, be careful when you get to the top of the ladder because you might have it on the wrong wall. In systemic education, we use the image of a tree. If you don't know what a tree is, move out of the city.

You are the tree. The seed you came from is your genetic inheritance. Some of you are oaks, others are cedars, and a few of you are Bonsais and for that I am sorry. The soil can be considered the environment in which you grew up. If you grew up in a town with phenomenal success in wrestling, you might be a wrestler.

I don't want to beat the model to death, but the tree rings represent your years of experience. Like many of us, I have some thin years and some thick years, years that went bad and years that went well. The key to this model is this: Your continued growth relies on the previous rings!

Let me cut to the point: You go to a workshop and hear about a wonderful new supplement. What do you do? This is the core of systemic education. When you add something to the soil, you need to test it by the fruit it bears. The problem? When you go to a workshop you tend to add fifty new things to your training and you can't measure what worked and what didn't work.

When young Billy reads an article or goes to a workshop, he's enthused beyond anything he's felt in years. He begins to take twenty fish oil capsules an hour, depth-jumps off the boxes with the bar in the overhead squat position, sprints like a Canadian Olympian, performs ring work, eats extra chocolate protein Wizzbangs, and snorts six hits of sugar-free psyllium every hour. Within days, he's a mess. What happened?

If you have a tree and add ten ingredients to your soil, nine of them good for the tree and the tenth poison, how will you figure out which one is which? That, my friends, is the issue. When I'm learning all these wonderful new things and ideas, how do I discern what works and what's killing me? You need to do it systematically!

This is how I approach new training ideas. First, I immediately fall back on one of two workouts. I have two basic workout models I've used over and over and in which I have a feel for what's going on with the balance of training load and recovery over a few weeks.

The first standard workout I use is the Transformation Program. Don't worry about the name; basically, it's three days a week of lifting, with one day devoted to pulling movements, one day to pushing movements, and one leg day. I only do two exercises, and keep the rest period at strict one-minute intervals.

Generally, I like three sets of eight, but any reasonable rep-and-set combination will work. One other day a week, I do a few hill sprints (very few) and on another day I do a fun activity like hike, bike or a team sport. This is an easy program to manage and I know my joints will feel good; I'll have a lot of energy and I generally look okay doing this program. The other standard workout I may do is the One Lift a Day Program. I might even simplify the workout a bit by just doing a push day, pull day, squat day, and whole-body day, say, snatch and clean and jerk.

By choosing to train in a program that basically covers everything at a very-easy-to-moderate level, I'm pretty sure I'm ready for the experiment. The experiment? Yes, now I add the new groovy thing I learned at the workshop. If, after two weeks, my knees hurt so bad I can't use the gas pedal, deem this a failure. If, after three weeks young supermodels are throwing themselves at me (again), something good is going on and I'll keep doing this new thing.

You know, it sounds so logical, so simple, but very few people do this. If you learn five new things, it might take a few months to run these through your training program to figure out whether or not they work for you. Keep testing the fruits of your labors, not the hype in the advertisements.

Let's review.

Number One

Set yourself up with a basic training routine you can count on to keep yourself fresh, but in shape. What in shape means to you might be different than what it means to your training partner, but I like basic lifting measurements or throwing distances. It could be a ratio of upper-arm measurement to waist measurement. My long-term plan is to have a one-to-two ratio in the arm to waist. I just need to get my arms to twenty-seven inches.

Number Two

Add new lifts, variations, or ideas to your training program one at a time. I bought a set of chains a year ago and I only used them with front squats for the first month. The next month, after discovering how excellent these chains were for acceleration, I tried them with deadlifts. Now I use them for all squats, deadlifts and presses, but I might not have realized their benefit if I'd added a bunch of things at the same time.

The next idea is this: Some things only work for a short period of time. I use the word quiver to describe all the lifts, exercises and routines I can draw on through a training year. For example, thick-bar deadlifts have a real value sometimes. Still, you don't want to constantly train with oversized bars because even though your grip gets better and better, you never truly push your posterior chain.

Number Three

Some great ideas work sometimes, but not all the time. In fact, I keep a chart of all the training tools at my disposal and reread this list anytime I feel like having a little instant variation.

In nutrition, the formula is a little harder. I live by this two-part mantra: If it works immediately, it's illegal. If it works quickly, it's banned. Again, I'd recommend setting up a standard eating plan. These days, you have the advice of lots of people brighter than me, so read up on diet. A couple of things I insist upon for the standard diet:

- I like my athletes to eat three meals before they train with me: breakfast, lunch and a snack. This almost instantly helps most modern teens.

- Eat protein at every meal. I like the simple rule of at least a fistful.

- Water should be your base beverage.

Once you're doing this consistently, try to add the magic food. I did this a few years ago with fish oil capsules, and became an instant missionary for this cheap, wonderful supplement. Again though, think systematically.

In dietary changes, you may not notice any difference. I look for improvements in blood profiles (I get an expansive, yet inexpensive blood profile done once or twice a year), skin health (less acne, more glow, better elasticity) and, sometime a hard one to recognize, moods. Ask your friends about your moods. If they all smile and back toward the exit, it isn't a good sign.

You have to learn what works for you through personal experience. It's not perfect, but find a basic training regime you can count on for a few weeks and a basic approach to diet you can live with for a month or so. Then, add the magic, add only one new thing at a time, and see what happens.

After that, of course, you can pester me with questions about whether doing the clean and jerk with 400 pounds will build your biceps.

Ten

5 X 5 Variations

One of the great lessons of life is to ask follow-up questions. When you're in college and meet a lovely young lady at a party, you may ask something like, "So, do you have a boyfriend?"

Of course, she'll answer yes. She's good-looking, after all. What, do you think you're the first guy to notice she should have fold marks on her photographs? (Think that through.)

She said she has a boyfriend, now what do you do? Most freshman would immediately say, "Gotta get another brewski," and leave. Bad move. What you should do is ask a follow-up question: Is your boyfriend here?

Smooth. If she answers, "He's back home," you've determined a key principle to further communication. There may or may not be a boyfriend, but you're allowed to remain close to her, purchase her drinks and make an attempt to get even closer. If she responds, "Yes, he's standing behind you crushing stones with his paws," my best advice is to say, "What a coincidence! My boyfriend is here, too, and there he is!" as you rush away.

The follow-up question is one of those odd little things that brings clarity not only to college parties, but also to the world of lifting, sports and body composition.

Recently, I had a young man email several questions about a previous article of mine. He was baffled by what I consider one of the pillars of lifting, the Five by Five workout.

But then he asked me a follow-up question: How do you do it? Thanks to his follow-up, I realized I knew literally dozens of variations of the five-times-five workout and, well, they all work. His question led me to consider how a simple workout (and five times five is about as simple as you can get) can lead to years of subtle variations to keep pushing you to the top of your game.

Okay, what is it? It's simple: Pick an exercise and do five sets. Each set, perform five reps. Rest between each set. At the completion of the fifth set, you're done. Now, why is there confusion?

This young athlete's follow-up question drew me back through my years of lifting and reminded me how something as basic as five by five can be as complicated as... well, trying to explain to someone why you called him your boyfriend at a party.

I'm sure when I say a "five sets of five reps workout," you know what I mean. Well, maybe you don't. I once found myself pushing my bench press up to my annual attempt at 400 pounds. A fellow at the gym recommended I really increase my max by performing five sets of five reps with my max five! At the time, I could bench press 365 for five. So, this workout called for:

> 365 x 5... Rest
> 365 x 5... Rest
> 365 x 5... Rest
> 365 x 5,,. Rest
> 365 x 5... Check into hospital

Moreover, I needed to warm up to this 365 for five. I like to ramp my bench press warm-ups (benches are the only lift I really warm up for on a consistent basis), so I'd also do:

135 for five or so
225 for three
275 for one or two
315 for one or two

Now, we're up to nine total sets. Some might argue I should do sets of five to warm up, but let's be honest here, this is going to be a long workout. I doubt this would be a repeatable workout, too. This isn't going to be the kind of workout done three days a week for a couple of years.

There are other, better, five-by-five workouts out there. Let's take a look at five of them.

Variation One: The John Powell Workout

My buddy, John Powell, is a former world record-holder in the discus. He had an interesting yearly variation on the old five-times-five workout: Each year he'd set a goal of doing a weight for five sets of five. Yes, we all know that, but his variation was unique. If he chose our 365 as his target weight, he'd plop down on the bench once a week and test himself.

365 for 4
365 for 3
365 for 1
365 for 1
365 for 1

He'd then add up the total reps of the workout, ten in this case. As the weeks and months progressed, he'd slowly work up in the teens, then the low twenties. With a serious enough weight, it could take months to build up to the full twenty-five reps of a five-by-five workout.

The upside of this workout may not be obvious; it allows us to use heavy weights and slowly, steadily build the volume. Don't worry if the fourth set has more reps than the third set or if it takes months to get that fifth set to come around. We're focusing on the big picture here.

Variation Two: What most people really do

Yeah, I know the truth. Most people do the five-times-five workout with essentially four slothful warm-up sets and one work set, like this:

135 for 5
145 for 5
155 for 5
165 for 5
365 for 5

They then brag to all their buddies about their five-by-five workout with 365 pounds. They don't mention only one set was performed with this weight, but they're sure their buddies think that… if nobody asks any follow-up questions.

There's a lot of value in this workout, albeit with more logical weight choices on the first four sets. There used to be a school of thought that argued, "last set, best set." Whatever weight you finished your workout would set your muscle memory somehow. I realize this may be akin to voodoo for some, but I know guys who swear by the idea the body remembers only the last set. Hey, it might be true.

Variation Three: The Wave

Whenever I see crowds performing the wave at sporting events, I keep reminding myself the song Y.M.C.A. causes everyone in the same stadium to stand up, spell out letters and boogie. I refuse to boogie.

That's not the wave I'm talking about here. It's simply the idea of increasing weight over several sets, dropping back for a set or two, then going back up. Here's an example following a normal warm-up.

315 for 5
345 for 5
365 for 5
335 for 5
355/365/370 for 5

Note how we dropped back on set four, then finished big. The upside of this workout is we get a lot of volume with the big weights, but we also get that nice light set where the weights seem to just fly up. If the weights aren't flying up, maybe you need another variation.

Variation Four: The Wave II

Maybe you need a few lighter sets, but still want to push the bigger weights. It helps here to have a thorough training log. Where do you seem to be at your strongest during the five sets? If you find yourself at your best on set three, try this:

345/355/365 for 5
315 for 5
365 for 5
335 for 5
345/355/365 for 5

In this scheme, you have two back-off sets. Rarely does a person peak on set five, but if you do, use variation three. If you peak on set two, try this:

335 for 5
365 for 5
315 for 5
335 for 5
345/355/365 for 5

For sets three and four, you're trying to hold on to finish the workout; a few relatively easier sets will prep for a big finish.

Variation Five: Dropping back

There are those in this world who have one good set in them. Others may also like this variation as it gets the hard set in first, then blows through the volume part of the workout. It could be as simple as:

365 for 5
335 for 5
315 for 5
295 for 5
275 for 5

This is a great adaptation for people who train in a situation where they can't always be sure about spotters, not just the home-gym trainer, but people who train in gyms where consistent, competent spotters can't be found. I never count on spotters in any place that has a step aerobics class or a rule against using chalk… or a gym with more than half the men wearing Lycra pants.

Whatever variation you pick (and let's be honest, there are plenty more of them), I suggest the following rules.

Number One

The most important: Strive for the same rest periods between the sets for whatever variation you pick. I recommend chosing either one minute, three minutes or five minutes, but stick to it. Judging improvement is crucial, but you need to be honest about the rest periods.

Number Two

Rarely do you want to do an entire program of five sets of five reps. You certainly could do it: squat, deadlift, bench press, row, military press and curl. The problem would be you'd be doing some seriously heavy lifting, plus a surprising amount of volume. Now, if you choose Swiss ball hand-chop cross-body L-raises, that's another story.

Number Three

Get out a calculator and figure the weight times the reps and add them up over the five sets. That number is a nice measure of progress. As the number goes up in any of the variations, you're getting stronger.

Hopefully, I've armed you with some new ideas for five-times-five training. If you have any follow-up questions, I'll be around to answer them.

Just don't ask me if I have a boyfriend, punk.

Eleven

Three Mentors, Lifetime Lessons

I discuss training a lot, and the same basic questions keep surfacing. The thing is, my answers don't seem to change much.

"What works?" I'm asked.

"Everything," I answer, "well, everything for about two to six weeks."

This leads to the follow-up question, "What do you do when things start going wrong?"

That's the real question.

I've slammed my head against the wall enough times over the last four decades of strength training to learn, well, slamming my head against a wall hurts. Therefore, I recommend everyone stop doing that. I also wouldn't recommend the way I learned my greatest lessons in sport, allowing surgery to tell me I need to slow down.

As I review the journals I've kept since 1971, what I discover are the best lessons of my career come from odd little meetings with mentors, my own little cadre of Obi-Wan Kenobis, who have taken me aside for a few minutes and summed up their athletic experiences for me to try on for size.

Let me share with you an amazing one-month experience when I literally bumped into three of the greatest names in sports… and built a career on a paragraph worth of information.

In 1977 I had one of those outstanding months that still impacts me three decades later. I met three people — three very famous people — and came away from the conversations with insights about training and life that still shape me today.

In a three-week period, I had conversations with arguably the world's most famous basketball player, a world record-holder and Olympic medalist in the discus, and one of the greatest bodybuilders the world has ever seen. For my part, I just bumped into each of them. Fortunately, I was too dumb to ask any questions, so all three gave me answers to questions I didn't even know to ask.

In late May, just as the college track season started to wind down, I was invited to throw in the Mount SAC Relays. At the time, it was the hottest track meet in America, maybe the world. I was the lone freshman in my division and, to paraphrase my dad, I looked like I was standing in a hole when they introduced me. I took my first warm-up throw and it skidded far into the field.

As I walked out into the field, I noticed something very odd: The man bringing me the discus seemed to be getting larger and larger. And larger. It occurred to me as we got closer this wasn't an optical illusion; this guy was enormous. He was as big as Wilt Chamberlain… probably because he *was* Wilt Chamberlain! Turns out the NBA legend was a fan of track and field.

Wilt literally reached down to hand me the discus and said, "Nice throw, looked good." I realized at that moment the role of genetics is key in athletic success. Wilt was immense. Huge. He blocked out the sun.

As I turned to walk back to take my second warm-up, I heard a voice say, "Go get 'em, bum." I looked over and saw my dad, just outside the ropes. I found out later Wilt asked my dad to come out with him in the field. Both he and Wilt stood out in the sector for the next few hours watching the discus and talking about track and field. (For the record, my dad never mentioned basketball, a good lesson really. At parties, a doctor doesn't want to hear your symptoms, an accountant doesn't want to hear about taxes, and Wilt doesn't want to talk about center play at a track meet.)

I placed. All in all, a pretty good effort when you consider during the warm-ups I was the worst thrower by quite a bit. My dad offered me his hand in congratulations. Wilt smiled at me as he put his hand on my shoulder. "Yep," he said, "Practice is practice. Warm-ups is warm-ups. You gotta do it in competition." He noticed I lost the warm-ups and did well in the meet.

Wilt's advice is worth considering for every effort in your life. All of us have a friend or two who mastered all the intricacies of high school or college life, but failed miserably in the real world. At the local gym, we all know somebody, call him Spandex Guy, who has the iPod cranking, the doo-rag going, the wrist straps, the big belt and knee wraps, as he sits on the leg adductor machine.

These people are mastering the warm-ups and losing the competition. Think about it.

One week later, I was back down in Southern California for the state meet. I fared well for a freshman… the only freshman. At the end of the competition, I came up to sit with my mom and dad in the stands. My dad leaned over to me and said, "Hey, this guy knows something about the discus." I turned back to meet Fortune Gordien, former world record-holder in the discus and multiple Olympic medal-winner. Yeah, Dad, I think he might know something.

Fortune gave me a piece of advice, "When things go bad, and they will, either simplify your footwork doing 'iddy biddy feet' or stop reversing when you throw. The key, though, is when things go bad, simplify."

I don't want to worry anyone about the technical aspects of the discus. The gem here is this: *When things go wrong, simplify.*

Most of us, of course, do the opposite. When we get in trouble with a little fat gain, we go over the top with excessive cardio, insane dieting, and massive increases in workload in the weightroom. A few weeks later, depressed and hungry and walking around with less lean muscle mass, we wonder what went wrong. We didn't simplify.

I always like to remind people when they ask about cardio — or jogging, as we used to call it — that John McCallum, author of *The Complete Keys to Progress*, encouraged people to jog. It's true. McCallum told his readers to try to run a quarter of a mile and, if possible, build up to a whole mile over the next few months.

One mile… built up over a few months. That's not much, folks. Simplify.

Toss out the extras.

With the season over, I jumped right back into training, but it was obvious I needed a break. I needed some sun. I needed the beach.

My friend, Howard, had to go to Santa Monica for business, so I hopped in the car with him and went to Muscle Beach. It was all there: the original Gold's Gym, the original World Gym, Franco, Lou and all the rest, topless girls on the beach, and all the crazies lined up outside the doors. I paid my ten bucks (in 1977!) for my day membership and went into Gold's to train.

In the back, they had a nice little platform with a great barbell, so I started off my workout with power cleans. It was one of the best decisions of my life. Robby Robinson, The Black Prince, came over to compliment my form. He said, "It's nice to see a young guy who knows how to work out." Robby, like all the greats, knew the Olympic lifts and the powerlifts.

Now, at ten bucks a day, I decided to train several times. As I walked down the beach after my first workout, a rather big human in sweats ran past me from the opposite direction. Then, I heard, "Hey, hey." I turned, and it was Robinson.

"You're the guy who was doing cleans," he said.

"Yeah," I said. I mean, what else do you say to one of the greatest bodybuilders in history?

We walked for about a mile together talking about training. Not gear, not theory, but good old-fashioned "this works, this doesn't." I'm amazed at how much of it I still use. Robby believed his best workouts came when he tossed out all the extras. Basically, his best workout came down to two cycles or supersets:

Bench Press
Pull-ups

He'd do set after set after set of these and he told me he could feel his whole upper body grow.

For his lower body:

Front Squats
Straight-legged Deadlifts

Again, set after set after set until his legs blew up.

For fat loss, he only recommended one thing. There was a flight of steps down on the beach, maybe 200 steps. He told me to sprint up to the top of them.

"Try it. Then, after a couple of weeks, try to do it a couple of times."

Ever since that day, the first thing I look for is a hill or flight of stairs to train. I walked with Robby and went back into Gold's Gym. I started doing front squats; he headed north toward the beach and I never saw him again.

There you go, a handful of advice that continues to shape my training each and every day:

- First and foremost, it's what you do in competition that you measure. Warm-ups are fine, but they mean very little. Base your practice sessions around your successes in competition. By the way, that's an easy thing to say, but very difficult to chart.

- When trouble arises, simplify. Cut back, toss something out, eliminate the extras. Simplify.

- Just because it's simple doesn't mean it isn't hard. Learn the difference.

I'm lucky I didn't have any questions when I met these three guys, or I wouldn't have gotten the right answers.

Twelve

Geezer Wisdom

Somewhere between high school graduation and age thirty-five, an interesting thing happened: Your life doubled.

Somehow, you turned age eighteen so you could vote, age twenty-one so you could drink, and age twenty-five so you could rent a car. During this time, going out to play took on a radically different meaning. Summer vacation used to last forever in the fourth grade; now your two-week vacation (okay, maybe one week) means you only check email twice a day.

Inevitably, we pick up baggage during these years. I've been working with a young woman recently who's thinking about getting married again at age twenty-nine — her fourth marriage, three kids so far, one from each marriage. That, my friends, is baggage.

Sure, we pick up that kind of baggage, but we also pick up other kinds. Drive to your old high school sometime and run up the flight of steps you used to sprint to get to class on time. Did you find yourself out of breath? Baggage! And it's usually the kind that jiggles around your waist.

Hey, I'm not saying being over thirty-five is bad at all. In fact, I'll argue over and over life is better after thirty-five. In fact, our lives are much better than those under thirty-five. What surprises most people is I think the athlete over thirty-five can beat the under-thirty-five crowd, and not just on the athletic field, either. For the record, how many lovely young women really find the puking frat boy attractive, anyway?

The first thing we need to do is make an assessment of what we have going for us. Advantages to being over thirty-five? Oh, dear Lord, yes!

First, you don't sound stupid. Usually. By age thirty-five, you have some level of what we in education call Party Knowledge. This, of course, is the great dirty secret of American education: We teach people simply to get jokes at parties. You know, if I tell a joke about someone treating his wife like Henry VIII treated his wives, you realize she isn't being treated well. Nothing can prepare you for a Dennis Miller rant entirely; that would be like asking Warren Miller to film Euripides' *Iphigeneia in Taurus* for an Aspen homeless shelter fundraiser... but, I digress.

With apologies to Jeff Foxworthy, you might be over thirty-five if:

- When you talk about Arnold, you mean the body-builder... or the owner of the restaurant in *Happy Days*, depending on what you were doing in the 1970s.

- When someone asks you about the highlight of high school, you remember the time forty kids started punching and swinging away at a pizza parlor and a bunch of cops showed up and nobody really got hurt, but it was really cool because there ended up being more cops than kids. Compare this to your neighborhood teen who told you his highlight was when he got to level fourteen on some violent game on his computer.

- When you talk about things you hated in high school, you mention the rope climb in P.E. class because it made your biceps ache for five days. Today, the wise leaders of our youth have banned rope climbing in many states because it's too dangerous. Guns, drugs and bombs seem to make it onto the high school campus, but rope climbing is dangerous. Go figure.

Let's talk about our real advantages now. There are a couple of obvious ones, but let's look at some of the less-obvious advantages.

Advantage One: Experience

When we were in high school, every P.E. class began with two laps and an obstacle course. All of us would run 800 meters, climb over various walls, monkey crawl down a series of bars, hit the dip station and sprint to the teacher. That, my friends, is more work than most internet forum participants do in a week!

We were also tested three times a year and graded on pull-ups, push-ups, sit-ups, six-minute runs, shuttle runs, and a host of other tortures I don't remember. Then, only then, did we go play the sport of that particular six-week session.

How's this an advantage? Somewhere in the deepest hole of your brain, the one scientists are now referring to as the geezer brain, there are memories of running, jumping, catching, throwing, biking, hiking and training. Hard to believe, but it's true: There are people you interact with daily who have never had an organized physical education class.

I work with adolescents daily who can't throw a football. Why? I was told by one young man, "My coach said I was a lineman." I responded, "You never just played football?" He hadn't. He never learned to throw a football because he never just played — no street football and very little playground ball of any kind. Baseballs break windows, basketball invites the wrong element, and don't even get me started on the political incorrectness of hide-and-go-seek.

See? You have an advantage many of the younger gymrats lack: You've actually done something physical in your life without wearing spandex pants, headphones, or shelling out $500 for a personal trainer. Your personal trainer was called Coach and always smelled like locker mold.

The advantage goes to the geezer. You probably have a wealth of experience in all this stuff, but you forgot about it.

Advantage Two: Time and future vision

My brother, Gary, and I talked about this a while back. Gary's son had taken up discus throwing and, as is the course of these things, Gary found himself interested in throwing himself. After a long, successful career as a runner, he discovered the odd magnetism that throwing stuff far seems to hold for human males. Gary began competing and finds himself in the midst of his third year as a discus thrower.

Our discussion summed up the best thing about being a master athlete. If you start today, in four years you'll have as much experience in your sport as any high school senior. In eight years, you could be as accomplished (and as good as) a collegiate athlete.

And if you don't start today? In eight years you'll be eight years older than you are today. Sounds stupid, I know, but you can choose today to be at your physical peak in a few short years. Trust me, the years are going to be here much faster than summer vacation lasted in the fourth grade.

The second advantage of being a master is time. Time works the same for all of us, yet after thirty-five we don't have peer pressure or some foul-smelling guy named Coach blowing whistles and forcing us to get off the couch. We have "me." You're the reason for getting back out there. So go!

Advantage Three: Money

My favorite advantage: my wallet. This may not be universally true, but generally we're starting to get settled by thirty-five. Those wonderful little plastic cards in your wallet, that number on your paycheck, and those marvels called investments all come together for a geezer athlete to provide something called money. Ah, money.

In high school, if Mom didn't buy those chalk-tasting "protein" supplements, we didn't supplement. In college, the choices were beer or B-15. (I chose beer). The geezer jock can do something amazing: Go to the supplement section of an online store, click the Buy button, and have quality stuff delivered to his door in a day or so. Magic. A miracle. Or, as I like to call it, money.

And it's not just supplements. You can also buy equipment. You think chains might help? Buy some and try it out! I never have to worry about crowds at the spa because my gym is open twenty-four hours a day. I own it, in my home, with nobody else's butt sweat on anything.

Don't ignore this advantage!

Advantage Four: Focus

Finally, here's the big one... seriously. If you love to ski or lift weights or do whatever, you probably own a lot of magazines, tapes, DVDs, equipment, clothes and general stuff related to your passion. Your competition, that hot-dogging nineteen-year-old, might flash past you on his snowboard, but give it a day. The total lack of focus isn't all Jamaican weed; it's his worldview.

Recently, a buddy of mine helped me with a project at my house. He said my bicycle was really heavy when we put the odds and ends back away after we finished. In fact, he made some rather cruel remarks about the seventy-dollar bicycle I bought at a local store with "Wal" as part of its name.

"My bike," he said, "weighs a lot less than this."

So I asked, "What did it cost?"

"$1,800."

"Wow, how often do you ride it?" I asked.

He changed the subject. You see, as I discovered later, he never rides it. He has an expensive snowboard he never uses. He has everything he needs except focus. He has a lot of toys and things he bought with his variety of interests... but no focus. Maybe he will when he reaches age thirty-five.

By thirty-five, you should have made some decisions. If you're thirty-five or older, you already know the decisions. Hopefully, you and your buddies have decided your garage band isn't going to make it big. You probably know wine is better with a cork than a cap. And, like fine wine, age can do wonders.

I have a ninth grade daughter and she has a buffet table of life spread before her this year: She can do drama, dance, discus, lacrosse... the choices are endless. By her senior year, the choices will be narrowed. After college, they're cut drastically. After marriage and a few kids... well, you know. None.

Use your advantages to rekindle the fire in the belly. Use these four advantages — your past experiences, your vision of the future, your lovely wallet filled to the brim, and your sense of focus to go beyond what you ever thought was possible.

Thirteen

The AIT Formula

As I get along in my athletic career, I'm starting to understand more and more what Yogi Berra meant when he said, "The longer I've been retired, the better I played."

It's true, you know. I coached high school football for a long time and I never failed to get at least one dad who'd tell me, "Yep, I was All-American in high school." Clearly, the child inherited none of this talent. And I usually had doubts about the actual truth of the story — there just can't be that many All-Americans in one small corner of the country.

The mistake I made was never quitting sports. I can only be as good as the weight on the bar or what the tape measure tells me. I guess I can't wait to quit just to discover how good I was, if you don't mind a Yogi-ism. What keeps me going? I keep learning so much every year I can't wait for the next season! And the reason I keep learning? My approach to training is designed to keep expanding.

The AIT Formula

Over the past few years, I've become infamous for two heretical beliefs:

1. I don't believe in peaking.

2. Connected to that, I don't really believe in periodization.

It's true there are people who've peaked. I'd argue, however, there are far more people who've trained to peak and failed. For proof, just look at the Olympics. It isn't uncommon for an athlete to have his worst performance in years at the Olympic Games. One can argue it's the pressure, and I'm fine with that insight. I believe, however, the pressure is caused by the imagined need to peak, the change in training to allow a peak, and, ultimately, the pressure to respond to the need to peak.

As for periodization, my argument is simple: By the time you finish with all the charts, graphs, percentages and number crunching, the athlete can barely load a weight on a bar: I need to do six reps with eighty-three-point-four percent of my four-rep max in a nine-three-two tempo and a twenty-six-second rest between sets for maximum hypertrophy. The math alone will paralyze the lifter.

True, I exaggerate, but not by much. So then, gentle reader, you may wonder how I train athletes. Years ago, I came across a simple formula that has elements of peaking and periodization, yet also allows for the natural fluctuations of this thing I call life.

Life? Yep, think it through: How many times have you finally put together an ideal training program and training environment, only to have some life just sneak up and clobber you? You know, sick kids, sick dog, broken car, best friend's bachelor party, that job thing, and just plain life.

This formula I came across is simple and natural. It works in three parts:

1. Accumulation
2. Intensification
3. Transformation

For those of us who grew up during the Vietnam War, AIT meant Advanced Infantry Training, but here we'll be using AIT to focus on training for life and lifting. We'll break that down.

Part I: Accumulation

If I could highlight the single greatest error most lifting enthusiasts make, it would be this: They have no variety. I'm not talking about using the decline rather than the incline for your pec development. I'm talking about doing nothing save going to the gym, walking on the treadmill, hopping off and doing a set of benches, playing with a machine or two, and hitting the steam room.

This is far from an overstatement. The first part of the AIT formula is accumulation, and doing just a few exercises a year is the antithesis of what I'm hoping you'll adopt.

Accumulation is actively seeking and learning new sports, lifts, moves, ideas and games. One literally accumulates a number of new training moves and attempts a low level of mastery of each.

Growing up, we did this naturally. In school, we'd play basketball or touch football during recess. During P.E. we played kickball. After school we'd hit the local playground with its monkey bars, swings, tunnels and a variety of other dangerous contraptions I'm sure have been banned from most of America today, and eventually we went home to breeze through whatever school work was left.

Then, as fast as we could, we'd regroup and play street football, baseball, basketball and a variety of games like tag, hide-and-go-seek, and one-foot-off-the-gutter. By the time I entered organized sports, I'd probably been fouled ten-thousand times, caught hundreds of touchdown passes, and, for the record, ran into one truck that was still moving.

In school physical education classes, we had speedball, volleyball, dodgeball, wrestling, basketball, crab soccer, soccer, swimming and a host of other classes. In addition, I competed in several sports at the interscholastic, community and church levels. Like all my friends, I was exposed to a myriad of sports experiences and soon discovered the tricks in one sport often worked well in another.

You get the point: We need to add some variation to our training. But, that isn't the entire point. The idea of accumulation is to actively seek out new training concepts — not only to add variation, but also to challenge our long-held notions of strengths and weaknesses.

The general idea of variation

1. I'll add wide-grip bench presses in addition to my normal-grip bench presses.

2. I'll do decline bench press in addition to…

The general idea of accumulation

1. I'll enter an Olympic lifting meet.

2. I'll enter a triathlon.

By taking on the challenge of Olympic lifting, certain things leap out immediately: Do I know how to snatch and clean and jerk? Am I flexible enough? Are my legs ready for all of this? Do I know how to use the hook grip?

After these simple questions, another layer of questions emerges concerning registering for the meet, registering as a lifter, buying a singlet, buying lifting shoes, finding a place to train, and on and on. Taking on a triathlon at the same time would probably be too much, but let's look at a few of the questions: Can I swim? Let's just stop there.

Years ago I injured my back. I'd like to tell you it was on a triumphal third attempt at the Olympics, but what really happened is a secretary at school asked me to move her typewriter (an ancient device that made words appear on paper), so I leaned over, picked it up, my back spasmed because of the odd position and I had a back cramp that laid me up for months.

I got some good advice: I should lose a few pounds, ride a bike daily, and learn to swim bilaterally. Bilateral breathing is taking in air from both sides in the freestyle. Like most right-handers, I only breathed from the right, and it took a few weeks to train myself to be a left-breather.

Since I had to do this for rehab, I thought, "Hey, I'll do a triathlon!" I bought a triathlon suit, had my bike tuned and, literally, jumped in.

I learned an instant lesson: Triathlon swimming has nothing to do with what I learned in the pool. With about fifty people thrashing and kicking all around me, I quickly discovered my nice breathing pattern in the pool meant nothing when I attempted to breathe with someone's foot kicking me in the face. I accumulated a lot of knowledge in just a few strokes.

I ultimately entered three of these things. One thing I learned: I'll never do this again. But I came away from my triathlons with some insights about training that stay with me today. Clearly, the greatest lesson I learned was the more time you swim, bike or run, the better you are at swimming, biking, or running.

If you come into triathlons as a champion biker, you'll dominate the bike phase probably your entire triathlon career. In other words, throwers throw, bikers bike and lifters lift… and if you want to play in another person's game, you might get whipped merely because they have more time in the saddle.

When my back healed, I went back to throwing stuff and lifting. I noted immediately I could train longer. It wasn't that

I had more throwing endurance or anything like that, but after sitting on a bike for up to ten hours, hanging around a nice field tossing stuff didn't seem so boring. My boredom index had been expanded by all those hours in the pool and in the saddle.

That's the goal of the accumulation phase. You take on a new challenge, do your best to learn and master what you can, then apply the lessons in your chosen field. Some of the results may shock you.

I noted, as have other former lifters who've moved into endurance events, my body fat went up. True, I lost weight, but my body fat percentage went up, which led me to believe a high-carbohydrate endurance diet mixed with an enormous volume of low-intensity training doesn't lead to fat loss, but merely weight loss. The numbers didn't lie.

The Rules of Accumulation

- Try something new. Join a team, a club, a sport, or take up a new hobby. Meet new people; learn some new skills and have fun.

- Continue your chosen sport or continue working on your body composition goals. Monitor your progress in all the usual ways: before-and-after photos, body fat measurements and athletic achievements.

- Through the lens of your new endeavor, rethink and re-imagine your primary goals. This, of course, is the key to the whole process.

I applied the third rule to my discus throwing a few years ago. I played in the Fast Action Five on Five football league and I was losing a step. I was also forty, but my numbers in the weightroom were excellent. Then it hit me: I'd been doing hill sprints regularly for nearly a decade, but had recently changed training facilities where there was no hill. Sure, my lifts were good… but I was lacking my two days a week of charging up the hill.

I bought a sled and starting madly sprinting in the area behind my home. Within two weeks, I found my lost step. Without the football league, I might have missed an obvious omission in my training. I'm always amazed how easily we lose sight of the big picture when we keep a single focus. Open your eyes by opening up to new opportunities.

Part II: Intensification

The second part of our formula is intensification. Throughout your career, keep adding new ideas and challenges to measure, as well as keep you interested. There does come a time when we need to ramp up to the next level. Everybody knows this; it's as old as Milo and the calf. But, I bet the bulk of the people you meet in a typical gym never ramp it up.

The training focus I use with the athletes I work with comes from the Olympic wrestling champ, Dan Gable. Dan said, "If it's important, do it every day. If it isn't, don't do it at all." I have to leave it to each and every person to decide what's important, but this statement certainly is a challenge.

I always use a brief question to clarify the answer to what's important. Let's say, for some reason you find you can only train for a total of forty-five minutes a week; maybe you become a political prisoner or something. You'll only be able to get in three workouts of fifteen minutes each. What will you do? Think this through — this is going to be the core to the intensification program.

Would you:

Train your core on a large inflated ball?

Be sure to stretch all your muscles so you don't strain anything?

Walk on a treadmill and slowly let your pulse climb?

Be sure to leave plenty of time to cool down?

If you answered yes to any of these questions, I suggest you not read any more of my work.

Obviously, with only three fifteen-minute workouts, you're going to cut to the core of what you need. Here's the key: Whatever you answered to the political prisoner question is what you need to focus on during intensification.

Yes, that can be hard. If your answer was front squats (not a bad answer, really), you're telling me you need to take front squats seriously when you train from now on. Certainly, doing front squats three days a week is a challenge.

When I discuss this with throwers, very often they realize throwers need to do full throws, yet when they look over their training journals, they notice very little of their training is dedicated to the full movement.

I asked a famous basketball coach this question a few years ago and he instantly answered this ties into what he thinks wins games:

1. Free throws when you're tired
2. Transition defense — I have no idea what it means, but he nodded really hard.
3. Make lay-ups

Then, after saying this, he smiled and said, "You know, I know this, but I don't think my athletes do."

Let's put this into practice. Here's how.

1. You can do the old Arnold trick: Work your weaknesses first each workout. In this example, do the most important thing for your training first. Perhaps twice a week do nothing but whatever lifts or exercises you chose in the political prisoner question. My wife, Tiffini, has a one-line time-management system: If you have to eat a plate of frogs, eat the biggest one first.

2. Measure your workouts only by how you answered the political prisoner question. All the extra stuff is great, but it's only the icing on the cake.

3. Using the lessons from some of the information you gathered during the accumulation phase, try to see if you're making improvements in the areas you found in need.

There's only one rule in intensification: Do what you say you need to do. Good luck.

Part III: Transformation

The final part of the AIT formula is transformation. I like to think I'm a master at coaching athletes in this phase. The transformation program is taking all the skills, lessons and progress made through the other two parts and then — be careful with the following, it could hurt — using what you've accumulated and intensified toward your goals.

I don't think anyone has ever said that before: Your training should, in some manner or form, lead you, at some level, to achieving your goals. Sorry, it's true. Your training should lead somewhere — ideally, to your goals. All too often, most people's training has almost nothing to do with their goals!

Hey, if you want to meet a nice churchgoing girl, you might not find her on ten-cent-wings night at the strip club. I'm not casting stones; I'm just putting out a discussion point. Most people train like that; they want to be Mr. Universe, but please pass the keg, the bong and the chips, thank you very much.

Here's what I discovered while working with athletes for several decades: You need to back off and let success happen. (Caveat: You, of course, need to have done a little accumulating and tapping up the intensity). Everybody knows this.

One of the things we began to notice years ago is our peaking athletes were getting a little pudgy, a tad bit soft. We also began to see that without a lot of direction, the athlete who'd trained so long and so well began to play pick-up basketball games and lose the season to an ankle injury, volunteer for the couple's dance in the school production, or find some other way to destroy a few years of work.

This observation led to the transformation program. We drifted back in time to the most basic program we could find, three sets of eight with one-minute rests. We decided to move to the weekly format of push-pull-squat, too. The best decision was to take all the best stuff we'd learned through the year and keep those new toys, skills, or drills as part of our package.

We also chose to keep a weekly game day, realizing our athletes needed a low-key competition as well as some fun. Soccer and flag football are the best choices as they included a lot of running, yet little contact. Indoor games with big, powerful athletes are not a good choice. Trust me.

A typical transformation week

Day One: Push Day
We assume some skill and tactical work every day. Body composition people can work on details.

Military Press: Three sets of eight with one-minute rests. Judge weight by the last rep of the last set. Don't be too gung-ho the first set.

Power Curls: Three sets of eight with one-minute rests. Again, judge the weight by the last rep of the last set. The power curl is basically a power clean with a curl grip and you can use some seriously heavy weights. This isn't exactly a push, but it works well with the press.

Isometric ab work: I'd recommend hanging from the pull-up bar with your knees folded up to your chest for as long as you can.

Day Two: Leg Day

Same three sets of eight with a minute rest for everything, but today is leg day. This will look easy on paper, but beware:

Front Squats: 3 sets of 8

Overhead Squats: 3 sets of 8

Assuming you do skill work every day in your given sport, do two hill sprints. Two sled pulls would be fine, too. That ain't much, folks, but it keeps you going.

Day Three: Games!

Have some fun playing ultimate frisbee or flag football.

Day Four: Pull Day

We found the best of all pulls for the peaking athlete is the clean-grip snatch. We also included the whip snatch, a wide-grip snatch that starts almost upright with the bar in the hip groove (the crotch).

Clean-grip Snatch: 3 sets of 8

Whip Snatch: 3 sets of 8

Day Five

A nice full warm-up, whatever it takes to get you loose and feeling warm, then go home.

Day Six

A couple of easy hill runs. Works like a charm to prep for a contest.

Day Seven: Compete

That's it — compete. Go do your thing.

You can shift the days around to fit any order you like, but the principles are the key.

- Stay tight on the diet and keep the workouts fast to keep some of the pudge off.

- Don't go crazy and try to make some massive leap overnight. Enjoy the benefits of all the work up to this point.

- Have some fun; enjoy yourself. Reap what you sow.

What you actually do here doesn't matter. The key is to you keep yourself in shape and not give away all your hard work by blowing an ankle in a pick-up game on the schoolyard. You might find, like I have, the rewards of achieving your goals may outweigh winning a casual game some afternoon over your buddies.

Summary

1. Be open to new ideas and new experiences and don't be afraid to plug in fresh approaches to your training.

2. When you learn something new, check to see where you struggle. It might be a hint this is an area to look into for your biggest progress.

3. Take time to think about the political prisoner question. What's important?

4. When you do decide to test yourself, ease off. However, continue to keep an eye on your waistline and your general fitness levels. Also, keep an outlet for your new levels of energy. Don't blow all your hard work on a lay-up on a school court.

Fourteen

Self-Evident Truths

We hold these truths to be self-evident.

Thomas Jefferson was onto something with the *Declaration of Independence*. There are self-evident truths in the world of fitness and strength training, too. Here's the problem with them, though: You knew them once, but forgot.

Seriously, you did.

Everything I'm about to discuss is information you once knew, but somewhere along the line, someone convinced you it was wrong, usually with slick marketing involving a lovely young thing in a bikini and lots of posing oil.

Hey, we've all been there. I remember spending a lot of hard-earned money for a training program and a couple of cans of stuff that contained virtually undetectable amounts of amino acids. It only contained tiny amounts because the aminos were supposed to work synergistically. Uh huh.

The training involved working out only after a fourteen-hour fast (so the body would be primed for an anabolic environment) and a quick boost from Miracle Fuel 5000 or whatever. The program involved four or more circuits of four or more exercises using drop-down sets, where we were to keep taking weight off the bar so we could keep going. The program promised steroid-like results in only thirty days.

I gave it my best shot. I'd squat like a demon from hell on crystal meth, drop some plates off, give it another go, pull off a few more plates, squat again, then leap up and try to touch the ceiling for as many reps as I could get. Instead of resting, the instructions were to stretch vigorously between sets to allow more growth.

Good job. One set down, three to go… then three more circuits. Hey, I bought it. I tried it, I hated it, and I quit it. The money-back guarantee worked like this: If you could do that for three months and not make gains, you'd get your money back. But, what person in his right mind would do that to himself?

I promise you one thing about the self-evident truths that follow: They'll save you time, money and embarrassment. I can't promise miracles in thirty days (my miracles take about ninety days), but I can promise you'll feel smarter and realize you can train longer… not just in minutes, but years.

First Truth: It's just a workout.

You are just working out or playing a game. You aren't scaling K2.

Why do I say this? Go to any gym and look at what people are consuming. We have pre-workout drinks (900 calories), an oxygenated power drink to swallow while treadmilling (300 calories), an instant gel to sustain the first set of walking to the water fountain (500 calories), a candy bar and a power drink to survive the lat pulldowns (900 calories), and a post-workout drink to get anabolic (1200 calories). Total caloric intake: 3800 calories. Calories burned during training: 211.

A few years ago, my daughter, Lindsay, played soccer in the county rec league. I'm actually thankful for the experience as Lindsay developed a lifelong loathing of anything related to this sport. Here's a nod to bad coaching and crazy parents. The thing that drove me mad about this particular team was the parents and the coaching staff spent the bulk of our time at practice and parent meetings organizing the food and drinks.

I'm not kidding. We had rules, contact sheets, telephone lists, back-up parents, and probably twenty pages of information regarding food and drinks. The athletes consumed two or more fruits each game, a plethora of sport drinks, and finished with a treat. Again, they consumed far in excess of any calories they could have possibly burned off on the field of play. Usually, at least two of the girls sat on the field and picked petals off the dandelions.

Reconsider your intake. Do you really need to be sipping carbs while treadmilling? It's a warm-up, right? Do you need a sports bar (read: candy with protein) after doing a set of benches with ten minutes rest between sets? No, you don't.

There are a lot of us who used to train in the summer twice a day with a psycho coach who screamed, "Water will make ya a pussy!" Twice per day, three-hour practices, ninety-degree weather, full pads, no water. That's one extreme. Don't go to the other extreme, either.

Second Truth: Follow Mom's rules first.

Here's my ultra-secret training diet regime:

1. Eat breakfast every day.

2. Be sure to eat three meals a day.

3. If you're hungry an hour or so after a meal, you didn't eat enough protein.

4. Water should be your major beverage.

5. There's nothing more fiber can't cure. (I might be betraying my age on that one.)

You've heard it all before from Mom. She was right. Do you follow it? I'm serious. Recently, I had an athlete pass out during one of my workouts. In fact, anyone who works with teens will tell you our next generation of warriors doesn't last as long as their age would indicate. When the man-child came around, I asked the question, "What have you eaten today?"

It was two in the afternoon and he answered, "I had, like, five fries at lunch."

"Five servings?"

"No, just five."

No breakfast, no lunch, no snack, and no protein. And the young lad shows up to train with me. Mom wouldn't have allowed that!

Here are a few more rules:

1. The hours you sleep before midnight are better than the hours after midnight. Sounds odd, but it's sure true. My mom once said, "If it hasn't happened by ten o'clock, come home because it isn't happening." (I was afraid to ask what she meant, because I knew what I was thinking.) Try to get the bulk of your sleep while the sun is down.

2. Don't take supplements if you don't buckle your seat belt. Think this one through from a cost-to-benefit perspective.

3. Be careful what you wish for, because it might come true. You want to put on fifty pounds? Just wait. The last time I visited the mall it seemed everybody had figured out how to put on fifty pounds.

Third Truth: There's pain and there's injury. Learn the difference.

I have a sliding scale concerning pain. Just about everyone I know has had this happen: You get up in the morning, walk around, and catch one of your toes on a chair leg. Your eyes roll back in your head, you drop F-bombs like a B-2, and you can barely focus on anything but the blinding pain. A minute later, you're fine.

It's the same with a brain freeze. As teenagers, we used to go over to a little place named Carl's and order something called a slush. It was filled with tiny ice balls and imitation flavoring. When we heard *Go!*, we raced to the bottom of the cup. (Yes, we were stupid, and we were also bored.) Halfway down, I'd become incapacitated by a brain freeze and try to soldier on. Ah, youth.

Folks, that's pain. It comes in all forms. Recently, I worked with a young man who went to a therapist the morning after a high school football game. He was informed he had some kind of "serious blood contusion formenting the rheonarcissism of the conobal antordia."

"What?" I asked.

"Well, it seems I have some blood in my muscles," he said. I silently thought this would actually be a good thing.

Another coach and I examined him again. By Zeus, he had a bruise! What a champion! Fortunately, modern medicine has been able to solve the great mystery of sports: Getting whacked by another human (or anything else, really) leads to a bruise. Do nothing to it for a few days and it'll magically disappear. I'll send my bill.

Injured is different. I sometimes joke surgery is nature's way of telling us to slow down. Injuries require medical attention, often medical intervention. Soreness, some bruising, and scraped knees dictate the following medical procedures: Do what Mom used to tell you to do. There's going to be some pain on the journey to reach your goals.

Back to our sliding scale of pain. Often, a sign there's an injury is when the athlete actually feels nothing. I was once the first person to arrive to help a guy who'd been driving a bullet bike at extreme speeds. He ran into the rear wheel of a car and did his best imitation of the ski jumper on the *Wide World of Sports* opening. When I got there, I noticed he was in shorts and a tank top. He no longer had kneecaps, shoulders, elbows, and the bulk of his blood. Don't worry; he looked up and told me he was fine.

Often, one of the big signs of injury is that it doesn't hurt — it doesn't hurt *right away*. Rule one: Stop what you're doing. Rule two: Go see somebody who can help you. Rule three: Do what he says.

Fourth Truth: That's not what they meant.

We rarely get the real story. The best example of this is aerobics. The first thing to remember is Dr. Ken Cooper invented the word in 1968 to mean, well, whatever it means to us today. Unfortunately for American health, the jogging wave that emerged from the book also coincided with the high-carbohydrate diet craze, and Americans are proudly fatter than any generation in our history.

In Cooper's defense, the original program suggested building up to a quarter-mile run/walk over a few weeks. Getting up to a mile might take you the better part of the year or longer. You see, Cooper was talking about one thing, but what most people heard was something else.

He later came out with books — largely ignored — advocating supplements and lifting weights. Your crazy neighbor who wakes up every day to stretch out for the better part of an hour, then runs a half-marathon and finishes up with several bowls of cereal and a soda is a far cry from the original teachings of Cooper.

The same truth can be found in bodybuilding. I had the great opportunity a few decades ago to train in the same room

136

as Robby Robinson, Lou Ferrigno, Danny Padilla and a host of other bodybuilding legends. One of the small truths I picked up that day is none of them were doing anything remotely like what was seen in the magazines... especially the mag with masthead with the publisher's head stuck on top of a statue of Robby Robinson's body.

I mean, the guys trained... normally. Lou was in the corner using half of California for calf raises. Padilla was doing a bunch of variations of rows, but nothing like the magazines claimed. And Robinson? He was working out like everybody else I'd ever seen.

Yet when the muscle magazines reported their training if not just made up from thin air, it usually reported last-minute detail work for a major competition. The bulk of the top bodybuilders' training, as Robinson told me, was getting the big lifts done and striving for more weight and more reps with more weight. I know this is true.

I can't tell you how many young Highland Games athletes have asked me, "Waddaya bench?" Calmly, I tell them they need to do this and that to become a better Highland Gamer. "Do you ever bench?" they ask. Well, sure, I tell them. The next day it's posted on an internet forum: Dan John sez all you need is bench, bro.

In other words, it's always worth getting to the source before you run a marathon carrying a barbell while wearing jump shoes.

The Fifth Truth: I can tell everything about your training by what you do first.

There are a few things I guarantee will lead to achieving your goals. First, keep a food log of everything you eat and drink in the next month. Figure out your calories, your carbs, your fats and your proteins. Be honest.

The second thing is this: Work your legs first the whole month. It's that simple. Squat deep or do deadlifts or realistic variations like front squats the first thing for a month. Unfortunately, many of you will nod about the food diary, agree it's a grand and glorious idea, then forget it. It's the other idea, working your legs first, that we might be able to pull off.

Throughout my time in coaching and training, no other observation has been more important: What you do in the first ten percent of your workouts will determine your level of success for the long haul. Honestly, can you even imagine the Arnold of *Pumping Iron* hopping on a treadmill with a carb drink and a headset cranked to Brittany Spears?

Well, I can't. Get in the gym and start doing front squats. Give it an honest five sets of five with the weight rising each set. Then, do whatever you like. Really, it won't be long before you find the quality of your workouts and your body improving before your eyes.

These are the self-evident truths. These are ideas that are so dull and boring, we like to ignore them. But, they're also the pillars of elite training. Following the self-evident truths might prevent you from being the person in the spandex pants gumming carb gel while peddling three miles per hour next to Grandma on the stationary bike.

Fifteen

What You Know Versus What You Do

There's a movie, *Office Space*, that didn't do very well when it first came out, but became an underground success on DVD. The reason most of us like the movie is because, well, it describes our work day.

Hawaiian Shirt Day, endless weekly birthday parties, and all the paperwork for a meaningless job seems to define some of us. But there was one thing missing: They forgot to discuss lunch at work.

Lunch at work could be a movie itself. I've had the following scene happen literally dozens of times. I sit down to eat lunch. I'd appreciate little or no conversation. By God, I just want to eat my damn tuna fish, shove down my salad that was a good idea four hours ago, and eat those two pears I swear were yellowish green when I put them in my lunch sack.

As all of us know, my hope of little conversation ain't gonna happen. "You know, if you substituted yogurt for mayo on the tuna fish, you could save thirteen grams of fat," says the co-worker on my right. Across from her, another one chimes in, "But then you have to be careful with the carb count. That's why I toss in a bit of sour cream with the yogurt and add spices."

For some past sin of either omission or commission, I've been sentenced to eat every meal with a fat-counter and a carb-counter. Ah, each of these ladies has locked into her brain volumes of information concerning every food and possible way to prepare each, and every food and the corresponding fat and carb grams associated with said foods. I'm just trying to eat my damn tuna.

Later that day, during the afternoon break, we celebrated (for the fourth time that week) another staff birthday. Out came the goodies, treats, and cake, plus the vending machine was opened up so we could enjoy cold beverages. As usual, I was offered a piece of lard with sugar and politely said, "No."

My two coworkers who argued for the better part of forty minutes about prepping tuna fish with sour cream versus yogurt versus imitation sour cream and yogurt, well, they consumed pieces of cake (the lard and sugar confection) large enough to be declared sovereign states by the United Nations.

Here's what I've discovered about most of us: If we were given a thirty-question test about nutrition, most of us could correctly answer questions regarding vitamins, minerals, and amino acids. Hell, we could answer questions on Vitamin C use in barometric chambers!

And there's the problem. Take the same person who fully understands amino-acid barriers and ask him to go into his kitchen and make a good breakfast and you might find him lost. Hint: Grab the eggs and a little cream, whip them up, and have some scrambled eggs.

The same exact problem hits most of us with our training. With the modern issue of the big-box gym, where you're literally in a facility that houses perhaps a hundred machines and countless dumbbells, bars, spinners, climbers, walkers and rowers, you might find yourself like my two officemates: You know what to do; you have the info, but you end up eating cake and drinking soft drinks each workout.

You know what to do in terms of strength training, body-composition work, fitness improvement and fat-loss techniques.

But, you can't apply this knowledge because:

1. Your machine doesn't look like the machine in the picture in the magazine.

2. When you're trying to do squats mixed with jumps, by the time you get back from the water fountain someone has taken all your weight off the bar and is staring at his guns while doing curls in the squat rack. Oh, he's also wearing a doo-rag on his head, fingerless gloves, a weight belt, Spandex pants, a muscle shirt and is cranking the tunes on his iPod… while curling forty-five pounds.

3. You like the workout you saw a few pages ago, but you don't know how to do _____ (fill in the blank). It could be Romanian deadlifts, clean-grip snatches, reverse batwing flying Hungarian side twists… you know the issue.

4. You're convinced if you could just afford _____ (again, fill in the blank), you could make progress.

I've been there. I remember nearly quitting lifting when the Nautilus machines were first advertised in massive spreads in athletic and bodybuilding magazines. Some of the ads were over a dozen pages long! As a kid, how could I argue with such overwhelming evidence? All these ads said I must purchase a full line of machines to train on every third week, otherwise I'd never achieve any success!

Let me suggest a few ideas to help out. First, and maybe there's no second, is to do something I've been doing since I was just a lad. Ready? It's this:

Write down your training assets. What? All I'm asking you to do is to write down what you have to train with in your home, your neighborhood, and your place of lifting worship.

Do you remember that ab roller you bought from the late-night girl in the Lycra tube-top on television? Write it down. Doorway chin-up bar? Write it down. Track near the house? Park within walking distance? List what you have.

If you take the twenty minutes to do this, you'll be well on your way to begin the process of applying what you know. Within walking distance of my home and work, I have three par courses available to me.

The concept of combining basic callisthenic moves to walking or running (I almost said jogging, please forgive me) began in the 1970s. It's a wonderful idea: Walk for a hundred meters and then do dips. After that, saunter over to do pull-ups, push-ups, bar jumps, squats and a host of other things.

Here's what's wrong with it: It's free, open twenty-four hours a day, never crowded, a great workout, a wonderful way to train, and probably one of the best ways to burn fat.

Now, you may ask, what's wrong with that?

Well, you don't have the guy in his doo-rag doing curls with a weight a ten-year-old girl tosses around in her purse. There might not be one hot babe doing steppers either! And no one to hassle you about lifetime memberships or the rules that don't allow you to use chalk in the gym.

In other words, you might have some great resources for your fitness goals passing you by each time you drive to the gym. Listen, I think many of us think this way: If it's free or simple or easy to understand, it can't be as good as something that's expensive, complicated and difficult to figure out on your own.

After reviewing the neighborhood, look at what you own. About a year ago, I went to a discount store and bought a storage box for lawn tools and put a lot of my stuff in it. Why? Because the moment I saw what I had lying all over the place and put it all in one spot, I realized just how good my home gym had become. Not including my weights, bars and various lifting pieces, this twenty-four-dollar box contains:

1. A set of farmer bars
2. A set of thick-handled farmer bars
3. Cones
4. Volleyball net
5. Soccer balls, footballs, volleyballs
6. An assortment of medicine balls
7. A huge array of throwing implements
8. A couple of kettlebells
9. A sled for dragging stuff
10. An 85-pound stone for carrying and throwing
11. A 150-pound backpack for lugging around
12. Pieces of PVC and broomsticks for whatever

Here's a great workout: Empty the contents of the box and do everything at least once and make up a couple of combinations of things, like dragging a sled while carrying farmer bars… and call it a day. This, in fact, is one of the reasons people fly from all over the place to train with me. I show them how to piece together a workout with practically anything they can find.

Not convinced? Try this workout, a typical workout my athletes perform about three times a month: Do fifteen overhead squats with only PVC. Upon completion, sprint 200 meters. Repeat three to five times, finishing with a final set of overhead squats.

Overhead Squat
Sprint 200 meters
Overhead Squat
Sprint 200 meters
Overhead Squat
Sprint 200 meters
Overhead Squat

I've had elite level athletes go quite pale with this quick workout.

Somehow, this combination seems to make the legs and cardiovascular system stage some kind of rebellion, even without the guns and rum. The PVC barely registers during the first set, but by the last set it seems too much to ask.

I've also found I can get a great workout by playing with my gym toys. Sure, just by doing pull-ups, some kettlebells swings, some one-arm lifts, and some deadlifts you can get a fantastic workout.

A year or so ago, I decided to push the idea of gym toys a little farther. I decided to train for an Olympic lifting meet by organizing my toys. At the time, I owned a thick Olympic bar, a good standard Olympic bar, one set of chains, and a nice box, the kind you find in powerlifting for box squats. I designed this simple program:

Day One

Snatches (a power snatch followed by an overhead squat followed by a hang squat snatch followed by a full squat snatch): 8 sets

Front Squats with chains: 8 sets of 2 with a reasonable weight

Day Two

Thick-bar Deadlifts: 8 sets of "as many" with a good solid weight

Military Press with chains, seated on the box: 8 sets of 5 — Note: If you don't sit on something, the chains don't really work; they just swing back and forth.

Now, don't worry about the exercises or how to do them. Focus on the concept: I was training in my garage with a minimal investment in equipment, but having a cutting-edge workout. In other words, take what you spend on your spa membership and buy stuff for your home gym.

Taking an honest look at your local free fitness assets, combining them with what you already have around the house, and making a thoughtful investment in training equipment might be the single best thing you ever do for your training.

The second bit of advice is something I've wanted to shout for years: Write down the list of lifts you've mastered. When I say mastered, I have some funny thoughts this would include certain lifting standards to go along with it. For this assignment, I'll give you one or two examples of the standards.

Do you know the Olympic lifts (snatch, clean and jerk)? Variations of these lifts? The powerlifts (squat, bench press and deadlift)? Classic bodybuilding lifts? Classic bodyweight exercises like pull-ups, burpees, push-ups? You know, gym class. How many kinds of squats and deadlift variations do you know?

This is just a rough list, but very helpful. I think mastery would be a double-bodyweight deadlift and a bodyweight press as a simple standard. Certainly it can be more than this, but you get the idea: Don't critique the world record-holder if you can't lift the PVC.

One of my favorite workouts is to list these exercises, then do one of those lifts each day for a few weeks. Oh, and by the way, don't dismiss doing only pull-ups for the better part of half an hour. Try it. Wait, before you do, get a buzz-cut haircut. You might not be able to reach up to comb for a few days.

My final piece of advice to transform what you know into what you do is to reread your favorite strength articles, your favorite magazine training programs, and perhaps your favorite training program books, looking at them through the lens of our first two points.

- Do I have this equipment or environment available to me?

- Do I know how to do the exercises and movements involved in this training program?

Environment is extremely important. Quality football players come from Texas and Florida year in and year out because of the expectations and amazing level of competition. Like it or not, your chances of making the NBA from a small town in Utah are rather low unless you're sneaking up on eight feet in height.

In fitness, California seems to have certain built-in benefits for bodybuilders. Beyond the beach and quick access to Mexico, there's no question the worst bodybuilders in some gyms in SoCal are far beyond the best in most parts of the world.

As you review your classic favorite programs, I suggest two directions. If you find a recommendation for a piece of equipment you don't have, substitute something else for it. Sure, the glute-ham raise is a cool thing to have, but reverse hypers are pretty good, too. No reverse hyper? Do Romanian deadlifts.

If you don't know how to do Romanian deadlifts or any other exercise on your favorite program, I'd first argue: Learn the lift! The time spent learning a new lift (or even a new sport) will be an investment in pure gold over the course of your training or athletic career.

Certainly, you can modify, but the discipline and skills learned in mastering a new movement will provide amazing benefits throughout your life. For example, once you push bodyweight over your head, it's a breeze to bench press the same amount.

To summarize, I don't want to appear anti-gym. I'm not. I'm not anti-fitness magazine, either. What I want you to learn is how to apply this knowledge into your training. How?

- Make an honest assessment of the tools you have available to you. You might be amazed, as I was, to find you have accumulated a small fortune in training equipment. Use it in fun and creative ways.

- Make an honest assessment of what you know how to do. If you have serious gaps, like you don't know how to squat and deadlift, take care of that first. Try to learn a new lift or a new sport at least once every few months.

- Finally, after making these two assessments, review the articles and training programs that mean a lot to you. Challenge yourself to not only master these programs, but to improve upon them.

Oh, and if I'm wrong, I'll eat my words. It seems if I mix sour cream with yogurt…

Sixteen

PVC and Presuppositions

I recently started a new job at a high school. In my first few minutes on the job, it all made sense. What made sense? The reason people are herded to the treadmills, steppers and cycles for twenty minutes to warm up; the long stretching periods where hyperflexible Barbies stretch beyond what anything in real life could ever demand; the whistle blowing coach who announces, "Two laps!"

You see, class had started for me for the first time in a decade. Taking roll ate up about a minute and I was left with an hour and twenty minutes to eat up time with sixty-five students. Sure, half the class were varsity football players with years of perfect technical training and a wealth of knowledge about all the particulars of lifting and training. At least, that's what I was lead to believe.

But what about the freshman girls who were also in the class, and the ten international students who were on exchange and spoke as much English as I spoke Korean, Croatian, Japanese or Chinese?

In that moment, nothing would've been easier than to have them all lumber away for a few laps of joint crushing and fast-twitch-fiber-sapping jogging, followed by a half-hour of injury-inducing overstretching. It would've been so easy.

Six weeks later, I walked into the same room. On this day, all the students were holding four-to-six-foot lengths of PVC pipe. The room looked like a scene from *Revenge of the Sith*, except, you know, interesting. Nobody, however, will practice their light saber skills. That is being punished. Being punished is bad.

After roll call, *"Sticks up!"* The whole room grabs the PVC pipes with a snatch grip and everybody does three sets of eight in the overhead squat. The *"Down on a knee!"* command orders the class into a hip-flexor stretch.

"Up position!" readies everyone for push-ups, clapping push-ups or push-ups with feet elevated on a box. Again, three sets of eight before we move on to pull-ups (three sets of eight) and medicine ball abdominal throws (one set of twenty-five).

Ten minutes after taking roll, we have a class of sixty-five warmed up and ready to go. This, my friends, is the warm-up. It's more work than most of my athletes usually do during their practice sessions. Now, we begin!

Great, you might say, but how will the organization of some high school weightlifting classes help me? I have a simple, albeit clichéd, answer: paradigm shift. Let me just say this: Having a roomful of people stare you in the eye with a look that says, "Okay, what's next?" makes you reconsider everything you know about strength training.

The world-changing paradigm shift: I realized certain aspects of my training are comfortable. Certainly, they are hard; no question about that. Pulling a loaded sled with a 150-pound backpack while holding two 100-pound dumbbells is hard. Just getting the stuff going is one step from sticking your hand in magma.

Yes, it's hard, but I became very comfortable with my presuppositions. (My toilet paper with the big word of the day printed on the sheets comes in very handy at times.)

Here are some of my presuppositions.

1. When we move from the front squat to an upper-body exercise, the athlete will have an incredible cardiovascular hit.

My athletes: What's a front squat?

2. The snatch and clean and jerk are both essential lifts and fundamental to athletic success.

My athletes: What?

3. The athlete needs to eat fiber and protein at every meal and supplement with fish oil capsules.

My athletes: Coach, what foods have protein? I couldn't find any on the side of the bag.

Folks, I'm telling you, this is the reason your personal trainer tosses you on a treadmill, makes you do the abductor/adductor leg machine, and insists on twenty minutes of stretching before and after anything you do. There's a lot of teaching that needs to go on before you can even begin to train. Yet, both the coach and the athlete want results now, not some basic beginner-level introductory BS they're well past because, well, damn it, they're special!

What I'd like to challenge you to do is to begin rethinking your presuppositions. On the internet, you can literally scan hundreds of articles in a few minutes and look at dozens of workouts and training ideas. How do you apply these ideas? I have three areas I want you to address:

1. How do you approach learning a new lift, exercise or sport?

2. How do you gauge the intensity of all your training?

3. When we talk about nutrition, do you think supplements, diet and food or is whatever set before you what you'll consume?

Let's look at a typical workout from my facility.

Warm-up
Overhead Squat (with PVC pipe): 3 sets of 8
Hip-flexor Stretch
Push-ups: 3 sets of 8
Medicine Ball Ab Throws: 1 set of 25
Pull-ups: 3 sets of 8
A minute or so to stretch anything tight

For time
Dumbbell Squats, 10 reps
Swings (with the same dumbbell), 10 reps
Dumbbell Squats, 10 reps
Swings, 10 reps
Dumbbell Squats, 10 reps
Swings, 10 reps

Workout
Front Squats with Chains
Bench Press with Chains
Pull-ups
Box Jumps (a variety of boxes used)
Deadlifts

We do these in conga-line style; one athlete starts at the front squat, then over to the bench, then pull-ups, then box jumps, then, finally, deadlifts. Once the first athlete finishes the front squats, the second starts front squatting, then follows the first athlete through the workout.

The reps are: ten, nine, eight, seven, six, five, four, three, two, one. We have five squat stations, five bench stations, seven places for pull-ups, about twelve boxes, and nine deadlift options. The front squats and bench presses are loaded up to ninety-five (not including chains) on the heaviest station and the heaviest deadlift bar is 185.

An athlete can change lines to increase or decrease the load, and the loads are as light as thirty-five pounds on the easy station. To finish off this workout, we do an isometric abdominal hold on the floor and a walk with dumbbells.

The number of skills required to do this simple workout is larger than you might first think. Note this: We don't have snatches or cleans or overhead presses on this day; this is considered a volume day. The teaching progression needed to teach the quick lifts takes coordination, foresight and patience by the coach.

The warm-up alone will confuse many people. I answer dozens of emails a month about the Olympic lifts and the biggest stumbling point is the overhead squat. Yet my athletes have learned them in just a few weeks. Why? We do them every day! Everybody does them.

I tell the students this, "Look around. If everybody is doing one thing and you're doing something else, maybe you got it wrong. Fix it!"

Lesson one about presuppositions

You might have been wrong the first time. The tenth time, too. If squats make your knees hurt, maybe what you're doing isn't squats, but your own version of knee-ripping knee bends. Stop. Relearn.

Lesson two about presuppositions

If a world-class athlete is doing a drill, lift, exercise or whatever, and you get nothing from it, consider two things. One, see the lesson above. Two, and more important, maybe you aren't doing it at a very high level.

True, you can get a whale of a workout with PVC pipe. Doubt me? Do this:

Take a PVC pipe to an outdoor track. Do fifteen deep overhead squats. Sprint a lap. Repeat this five times and finish with fifteen deep overhead squats. If you don't walk at all and honestly run, you should finish this under ten minutes, maybe nine. Do this and learn the power of PVC.

Back to lesson two, though, maybe you aren't doing it at a high level. My first day with my varsity football athletes I tell them this, "I expect everyone on the field to be able to bench press 200 pounds and deadlift 400. By the way, whatever you bench, you should front squat and clean, too." So, day one the prospective football player looks at this list:

> Bench Press: 200
> Front Squat: 200
> Clean: 200
> Deadlift: 400

Every time I post strength standards, I always get at least one fretful email: Danny, I'm an adult and I can't do these lifts! This will be followed by a seven-page description of the guy's current training protocol including the letters "A" and "B" and several mentions of cadence and joint-rehab work.

My answer: You're too damn weak. Toss out all that crap and add some plates! Which leads us to the next presupposition…

"I think I'm advanced."

Have you trained more than a year?

"No."

Not advanced. Can you bench bodyweight?

"I'm working toward it."

Sorry, not advanced.

To me, an advanced lifter:

1. Has competed in one of the strength sports: body-building, Olympic lifting, powerlifting or Strongman

2. Doesn't get his information from magazines at the airport

3. Can look at one of my typical workouts for high school athletes and complete it without trouble

4. Has at least pressed bodyweight and deadlifted double-bodyweight

5. Understands food and supplements are partners in diet, but one can't live on creatine and beer alone

Give me four out of five, at least, before I consider you advanced.

Let's review the three presuppositions concerning learning new stuff.

• You might have been doing it wrong since the first time you tried something. You've simply been repeating "wrong."

• You might be doing something right, but at such a low level you should consider not doing this anymore.

• You might think you're advanced and able to skip the beginning steps, but really you're just beginning. Beginners, by definition, should start at the beginning. I'm not making this up.

With this in mind, here are some suggestions to consider over the next few workouts, weeks and months.

Using the presuppositions list, let's review these:

1. How do you approach learning a new lift, exercise or sport?

2. How do you gauge the intensity of all your training?

Presupposition One

Is it possible my technique in lifting is truly wrong or simply really bad? You know, it took breaking my wrist into a lot of pieces to make me reconsider how I do the Olympic lifts. As a fairly successful lifter, I relearned the lifts and discovered a terrible truth: I could've been very, very good if I would've relearned the lifts when I was younger and healthier.

For those of you who carry the flame of train-to-failure, how do you really determine failure? I've been involved in an interesting challenge several times in my life, to squat bodyweight for reps. Simply slap on bodyweight, do as many squats as you can, then put out a number.

I was thinking I was great at twenty reps until a buddy of mine did thirty. At the next contest, I did fifty to win (ultimately, I did fifty-one with 225). What was the difference between failure and failure? Someone else doing more.

Presupposition Two

I knew some guys once who won the local church league basketball tournament. They were watching the video of their game at the same time they had the Utah Jazz game on television. One guy said to me, "You know, we thought we were great, but we were so slow and so bad compared to the pros we had to turn the video off. It sorta ruined the party."

Wise man. These guys, in their defense, were doing a lot right, but at a low level. It could apply to you, too. I had illumination simply by sitting at a local Olympic lifting meet as an eighteen-year-old. After seeing real lifters lift, I knew being the strongest kid on my block really didn't matter that much. Short advice: Get out there and compare.

Presupposition Three

Occasionally, restart your training with the Zen notion of the beginner's mind. Find a book or training article that has a two-week beginner's program and follow it. Have a buddy watch your lifting technique, and allow comments. Hey, here's one: During a pull-up, go from straight arms to chin over the bar. Really, try it that way. It's called the Right Way.

Now let's look at our presuppositions list with nutrition.

Nutritional Presupposition One

You might have been doing it wrong since the first time you tried something. You've simply been repeating wrong.

The great example of this is guys who try macro-diet cycling — you know, five days of zero carbs, two days of high carbs or whatever. During those days of zero carbs, they drink protein drinks twice a day that include massive amounts of sugars carbs. A total disconnect that never seems to conncct!

Oh, I could go on forever: People who eat fruit for protein, avoid fiber because it's starchy… don't get me started. Take five minutes to read a high school health textbook on diet and get the basics squared away.

Nutritional Presupposition Two

You might be doing something right, but at such a low level you should consider not doing it anymore.

This is more common than you think. Somebody goes on the Atkins diet and has one egg for breakfast. Lunch is a piece of string cheese. Dinner is nine pizzas.

Hey, if you're going the low-carb route, gorge yourself on bacon and eggs, cheese, duck, chicken, tuna, steak and a celery stalk, then worry about hunger after six o'clock! If you're going to eat, eat.

Nutritional Presupposition Three

You might think you're advanced and able to skip the beginning steps.

My universal short list for all dieting advice:

1. Eat protein at every meal.
2. Eat fiber at every meal.
3. Take fish oil capsules.
4. Drink a lot of water.
5. Eat at least three meals a day, never missing breakfast.

Yep, beginner stuff. Which of the rules do you break daily? Take a few honest weeks of following the basics of diet and you might be amazed at your results.

You could argue this is just another one of those back-to basics articles and ignore some of these simple tools that can revitalize your training. Just don't let your presuppositions strangle your career.

Seventeen

The Litvinov Workout

An amazing thing happened in 1983. I went on a date. Okay, that was a joke, because everybody knows during the '80s I was covered with black and blue marks from being touched with ten-foot poles.

Actually, the World Championships of Track and Field began in Helsinki, and the list of winners is a *Who's Who* of the sport. You'll find the names of Carl Lewis, Mary Decker, Edwin Moses and Sergei Bubka littered among the gold-medal winners.

It was also the year of an important failure. John Powell, who'd led American discus throwing for a decade, failed to make the finals. Powell came away with two important lessons and inspired a generation to rethink training from his observations.

1. The discus trials were at nine in the morning. Powell had never trained to throw at nine in the morning — not ever. He thought he could just walk out and throw the qualifying distance.

He learned after the competition it took him a lot of time in the morning to get the snap he had in the mid-afternoon. This is a good lesson for a lot of us who take performance for granted in life and sports.

2. When Powell looked around to see how the rest of the world was training, he noticed his training hadn't advanced much, if at all. Throwers from the rest of the world were leaner, faster and more muscular.

Especially impressive was the young gold-medal winner in the hammer, Sergey Litvinov. If you're interested in becoming leaner, faster and more muscular, keep reading.

From Powell's observations of Litvinov, I put together some training ideas that completely reshaped my approach to training athletes and it completely reshaped my athletes. It's such a simple training idea you may discount it at first. Let's start by looking at what Sergey Litvinov was doing that awoke Powell's imagination.

It's truly a simple workout. Litvinov, a five-foot, ten-inch, 196-pound hammer thrower, did the following training session.

Eight reps of front squats with 405 pounds, immediately followed by a seventy-five-second 400-meter run. Repeat this little combination for a total of three times and go home, thank you. Let's just stop here and marvel at what Powell observed. A 196-pound man front squatted 405... eight times!

"Dan, do you have any advice for my quad development?"

"Dear reader: Front squat 405 eight times. I'll now debit your account for this expensive advice."

Moreover, Sergey racked the bar and ran 400 meters... then did this two more times.

After listening to Powell's story, I invented a workout combining front squats with running. Let's look at the basic workout, The Litvinov.

Perform any big lift and then drop the bar (gently) and run. My charges and I have used the following lifts:

Cleans
Clean and Press
Clean and Jerk
Deadlift
Front Squat
Overhead Squat
Snatch

Any and all variations of snatches and swings
with kettlebells and dumbbells

Over time we discovered the 400 was far too long a run
for the needs of my athletes. But, if someone really desires a
fat-loss blast, by all means run the 400!

I found strength athletes weighing in the mid-200-pound
range just didn't recover very well from the full 400. I have to
ask myself: If the world champion weighs 196 and my chubby
body weighs 260, how does that extra sixty-four pounds help?

The devil is in the details with this workout. Back squats
don't work because racking the weight and running away involve way too much care and planning. We also discovered
even our lightest racks were a hassle to pack up into the bed of
a pickup truck and haul to a place where we could combine
the lifting and running.

Also, I hated having my bar, weights and rack outside in
lousy weather collecting rainwater and mud. Then I got tired
of burning my hands on the hot plates in the summer sun.

Some lifts don't work very well. Yes, we tried other lifts
like military presses and one attempt with the bench press, but
it seemed foolish — lots of work and set-up for not much of a
return on the time and effort. The clean and jerk never seemed
to work right, either. The lift has to be easy enough to push
quickly with little mental effort. So, the best lifts are:

Front Squat
Overhead Squat (if you're good at them)
Snatch
Swings with kettlebells or dumbbells, but
really knock up the reps, like 30 or more

Soon, the Litvinov became re-imagined as the LitviSprint.
As we played with lifts and distance, we found ourselves one

day with a kettlebell and a hill. We discovered the speed and intensity of the run had a bigger impact on the workout than the lift itself.

Kettlebell swings followed by a hill sprint of thirty yards seemed to leave the athlete burning oxygen for hours after the workout. Moreover, massive amounts of meat and analgesic liquids (beer) did little to revive us.

Once again, the most obvious lesson of my coaching life has been reinforced. The more intense you can train, the better. Yep, you knew that. So did I. Why, then, don't we follow the rule?

A nice little spin-off benefit began to emerge from LitviSprints: If the athlete is learning a lift, very often the overhead squat, doing the sprint after the lift seems to speed the learning process. Why? I have two ideas.

1. When most people try to learn a new skill, they think too damn much. I'll show someone how to snatch or clean at a clinic and the questions just keep coming:

"Where do I put my thumbs?"

(Um, near your fingers.)

"Where do I put my elbows?"

(Between the upper and lower arm.)

Making the new lift even more complex by adding sprints, the athlete stops with the questions and just does the movement. By magic, it looks okay.

2. Moreover, they attempt perfection on the new skill the first time they try it. I've probably squatted near 100,000 reps and I still learn new things each time I read a Dave Tate article. Ain't gonna happen on the first set, people. The challenge of sprinting seems to get the athlete to forget perfection and focus on completion.

There's a lot to be said for this workout.

One, you can bring a single piece of equipment outside, or if you're lucky and have a gym with a nice area to sprint next to your weights, just get going. You'll get an unusually demanding workout with a minimum of mental effort.

Two, and this is the interesting part, as you finish the lift and attempt to sprint away, you'll instantly understand how well this workout will impact your overall conditioning. Usually, the first two steps feel like running in waist-deep water as the legs send up this response: Could someone please tell us what the hell is going on?

Third, I contend this combination is the single best crossover training idea ever from the weightroom to the sports arena. Athletes who do LitviSprints note the improvement on the field, track and court within a few workouts. Something is different and performance improves.

Not content with leaving well enough alone, I began experimenting with LitviSleds. There are some equipment issues here. Beyond the bar or kettlebell or dumbbell and the need for an area to run, you'll also need a sled and a harness.

First, choose the lift you'll be performing before you start dragging the sled. I'd cut your list down to these basic moves:

> Front Squats
> Overhead Squats
> Swings with kettlebell, T-handle or dumbbell

The reason why you have to simplify is you hook yourself into the harness before you lift. You're hooked to the sled when you lift so you can drop the bar and sprint or drag away.

A caveat: Lift to the side of the path of the sled. Obvious, yes, but more than a few people have started their drag, snagged the weights and been yanked to the ground. It's funny to watch, but it may also really hurt. I'll still laugh at you, but you will be hurt.

I have no idea how much you should load on the sled. I've found hooking a seventy-pound kettlebell so it drags is about right for most people. The drag is nice, but don't overdo it like many who think you need to pull a building. What's important isn't wallowing around like a pig in slop, but flying away like an athlete. So, less wallow, more speed.

I also encourage my athletes to go for about five seconds and not worry about distance. Otherwise, you lose the quality of effort almost immediately.

Litvinovs, LitviSprints and LitviSleds are very simple ideas. The quality of effort is far more important than the quantity — a concept that'll be missed by many. Don't do twenty-five-pound squats, then hop on the treadmill for a four-minute walk while watching *Oprah* and consider this Litvinovs.

To summarize

You may find this the fastest workout you've ever done. Don't be surprised if the workout seems too light or too easy at first. Judge the workout on the last set, not the first.

- Pick a lift you know. Hit eight good reps with it, then sprint away for five seconds. Rest and repeat this two more times.

- Next time you try the workout, try another lift and maybe go a bit longer on the sprint.

- Do this easy progression about twice a week. If you choose to make this your whole leg workout, you've chosen wisely. If you're preparing for an athletic competition, see if this workout carries over to your field of play.

- Don't measure rest periods the first few workouts. Let yourself recover fully. As the weights go up in the lift and the sprint gets around ten to twenty seconds, try to zero in on three- to five-minute recoveries. You'll need it.

Oh, one final note. Four years later, at the 1987 World Championships in Rome, John Powell — noticeably leaner, faster and more muscular —took second place in the discus. He was forty years old, ancient in track and field, and this accomplishment is still considered one of the most amazing feats in track and field history.

Eighteen

The Gable Method

It turns out I've been using a training secret. One of my friends, Ben, came out to spend a week under my guidance — another way of saying hang and work out — and he pointed out one of my Top Secret Training Protocols is truly unique, so unique it must be shrouded in science. Unfortunately, this secret is just one of those things I figured out along the way.

Sometimes I think I've been coaching and training so long I just take for granted this thing called experience. As an athlete, I always felt we wasted up to an hour of practice doing this thing called a warm-up. If you ever had a P.E. course, you know what I'm talking about:

Two laps of a jog
Jumping Jacks (smartly counting out every fourth rep)
Cherry Pickers
Yoga Stretches
Hula Hoops

…and on and on and on.

The jog had little to do with anything, save to train you for taking last place in a race, and the rest of it had little to do with Jack, cherries, yoga or Hawaii. At the end of the warm-up, I always felt tighter and less ready to practice.

Why? Because practice never related to anything we did in the warm-ups! I'm going to let you in on my little secret. Ready? Here it is: *The warm-up is the workout.*

In 1982, the school where I was working hired Chris Long to be our wrestling coach. We soon discovered both of us shared a hero, Olympic gold medalist and wrestling coach, Dan Gable.

Chris shared Gable's coaching method with me: *If it is important, do it every day. If it's not important, don't do it at all.*

You know, it's hard to argue with this… but we all do anyway! I've spent the best part of the last three decades asking coaches from every discipline this question: What are the three keys to winning in your sport? I have yet to find a coach who can't name the three. From "making free throws when tired" to "turn the right foot," coach after coach after coach has had a clear vision of what it takes to win.

Then I ask two follow-up questions:

1. Do your athletes know this?
2. Do you practice these every day?

Never, not even once, has a coach answered yes to both. It's not that the coaches are ignorant of this little paradox (this is my formula for winning, but nobody but me seems to know it), rather, they're stuck finding a place or time in practice to ensure the keys are addressed.

It's true with everyone. The person interested in losing body fat or gaining muscle deals with the same issues: I know I need to [*fill in the blank*], but I don't have time to deal with it after my forty-five-minute treadmill walk watching Oprah discuss Katie and Tom, my Pilates class, and then working my abs on the Ab Blaster 2000.

Time to look at warm-ups in a whole new light. Using Dan Gable's paradigm, I'd like to suggest three ideas — levels of implementation, if you will — I've used for the past few decades. Remember, if it's important, do it every day.

Level One

The first level of implementing this idea is rather simple — so simple you might ignore it. You decide you're bad at pull-ups. How do you know? You can't do twenty perfect pull-ups. Why twenty? Well, in the ninth grade that's how many you needed to max out the test. Why perfect? Why not?

Each and every training session from now until you get twenty, do pull-ups. Yes, every workout. You can do one set of "as many," a couple of sets, or what I have my athletes do every day: three sets of eight. It's a program as old as the hills and it seems to work.

Can't do three sets of eight? Do three sets of what you can do. In a few months, you'll amaze yourself with your progress. Do the rest of your arm swinging and treadmilling and stair-stepping and whatever you call your pre-workout stuff, then do your regular workout.

I did this a few years ago with front squats. At Olympic lifting meets, I'd snatch well, then go into the clean and jerk and get two attempts, only to get buried in the bottom position on my third. So, I decided to front squat every day. (The front squat is how you recover from a heavy squat clean.) *If it's important…*

I used 165 pounds and did two easy sets of five. Every day. For about two months, I kept my bar in my garage loaded at 165 (I only had a bar, two thirty-fives and two twenty-fives; I was poor) and no matter what, I did my two sets of five. I don't have the science to explain it, but after that I never missed recovering from a clean again. How did this work? I don't know, but if it's important, do it every day.

Do this with a weak body part, a weak lift, or something you're trying to learn. Don't force it, just keep banging away day after day and soon the body is going to grant your wish; you're going to have some level of success here.

Yes, it's that simple: Do something you think is important every day. Oh, the other hints:

- Tell those significant people in your life you love them every day.

- Spend less than you earn every day.

- Eat fiber at every meal, eat protein at every meal, drink water, sleep nine hours, take fish oil capsules, and exercise every day.

I know you know this.

If you like the first idea, you might want to try the second. I've been a fan of Percy Cerutty for years. Cerutty was an Australian track coach/guru/fitness buff/nutcase who coached some of the best middle distance runners in the world in the late 1950s and early 1960s.

Some consider him a nutcase, but rarely have I found normal people to have all the answers. If you strive for normal, spend an hour at a Las Vegas casino and take inventory on what normal is in America today.

Why was he crazy? He told runners to:

- Run up hills

- Lift weights

- Eat odd foods like oatmeal, vegetables and fruit

Before I was born, he insisted all athletes do the big five lifts:

1. A deadlift

2. A form of pressing — Cerutty liked a lift called the bench press. I'm not sure if it ever become popular.

3. An explosive full-body move — He chose the heavy dumbbell swing.

4. A form of pulling — Cerutty called for pull-ups and cheat curls. Cheat curls are like a power clean with a curl grip (power curls), or that bouncing heavy bar curl you see every gym-rat in the world do when he gets tired from strict curls.

5. An abdominal exercise — If deadlifts make you go one way, the ab exercise should strengthen you in the other.

After going heavy on these lifts with two to five sets of two to five (save for swings and abs where the reps go fairly high), hang from a pull-up bar and stretch for a few minutes.

Recognize it? I think I've recommended this workout for thousands of people, after I, uh, invented it.

Level Two

My second recommendation for expanding your notion of warm-ups is this: Look over your plan for the day and add two sets of the big five lifts for whatever you're not doing that day.

During an old-fashioned arms day of biceps and triceps work, toss in the deadlift, the swing and the ab work, and let the press and pulls get dealt with by the skull crushers, Zottman curls, hammer curls, and masticated rear triceps squeezes or whatever. You can add to Cerutty's five with the inclusion of squats and rotational work, but I begin to worry when my training starts to get over 200 core lifts in a week.

The idea here: Keep your specialized training, but continue to keep in contact with the big general movements each workout. It's an easy way to have each workout become a full-body session with an emphasis on a body part. Don't go crazy on variations; keep pounding away on the foundation. From a strength coach's perspective, you'll get stronger and stronger in these basics, which can't help but make a difference in your other long-term goals.

Level Three

Finally, we can think about the approach I've begun to use with my athletes: The warm-up is the workout. I've been using two- to six-week short cycles of only two lifts. We max at the end of the cycle… within reason. Pick two lifts:

Bench Press and Front Squat (a great pair)

Bench Press and Deadlift (the answer to the question, "Am I getting stronger")

Military Press and Snatch-grip Deadlift (odd combo, but amazingly insightful for pointing out weaknesses)

Or, anything you choose.

If you work out twice a week, have one day be the fast day, where the bar comes down slow and up fast with very reasonable weights. The other day is a max of some kind, either a variation (off boxes, boards or whatever), or a rep max (fives, threes, doubles… you know the drill). If you try this three times a week, think fast on one day, max on another, and a nice medium workout on the third, whatever medium means to you.

Those two lifts come at the end of the warm-up. The warm-up is this:

1. Overhead Squats, three sets, with either a light bar or PVC pipe

2. 40 meters of Rock Carries

3. One-handed Overhead Carries, 40 meters

4. Waiter Walks, each arm. Lock the weight out overhead and walk as far as you can, like a waiter. Those funny muscles around your waist are called obliques. You may not have noticed them before.

5. One-handed Side Carries, 40 meters

6. Suitcase Walks (each arm)

7. One-handed Overhead Carry and One-handed Side Carry (opposite hand, of course), 40 meters, then switch hands

8. Farmer Walks with heavy load, 40 meters or until done

9. Sled Drags, 40 meters

10. Sled Drags with Farmer Walks, 40 meters

11. Sled Drag with Rock Carry, 40 meters

12. Pull-ups, 3 sets of 8

13. Push-up Variations or Dips, 3 sets

14. Medicine Ball Throws from the Sit-up position, 25 reps

15. Swings for one minute (I recommend doubles, one kettlebell or dumbbell in each hand)

16. Weighted rotating sit-up (clockwise with a small circle, bigger circle, huge circle, then opposite), 3 sets

You can include anything else, everything. I like to note, "Hey, we're done with the warm up!" as my athletes fold over and look forward to something fun like max front squats and bench press.

What? Yes, the warm-up is the workout.

I've just sketched out some ideas here. To review:

• Try working a weak exercise, lift, or body part each and every workout as part of your warm-up.

- With a body-part workout, add a few sets of a few reps with whole-body lifts you won't be targeting.

- Put together a series of walks, drags, carries, lifts, moves and exercises that challenge you in a variety of ways, but are still doable, and toss in a workout as a bit of dessert at the end of your training day.

This is a paradigm shift for many lifters. What am I saying? *If it's important, do it every day.*

Nineteen

Strong Eye for the Weak Guy

There I was sitting at breakfast during discus camp when a very nice guy tells me his son wants to write a book called *Getting in Shape for the Martial Arts.*

I'm always cranky before my third pot of coffee, so I blurted out, "The market is saturated. Charles Staley put together an all-encompassing Western-style book; Pavel has a bunch of stuff from the Russian perspective; some other guy has a bunch of bodyweight exercise books; and there are dozens of sites on the internet where you can pick up a couple of million other books, too."

"Oh," said the dad, and then I felt bad. His kid had a goal and some goon in a tank top gobbling eggs and coffee shot down the dream.

I felt horrible, so I softened things, "You see, he'll need to add a fresh new perspective, something that will grab people, something that'll get them to his website."

"He doesn't have a website," said the dad.

"Okay, his articles."

None.

"Okay, his school or training hall."

None.

It was time to leave. I had to work out, but I offered this, "Tell him to drop by the cottage tonight; a group of us are meeting to talk about strength stuff."

About eight hours later, this young man appeared at the guesthouse, or The Cottage as we like to call it. Let's call him Doug, which isn't his real name, but it sounds like a nice name. If your name is Doug, you know for certain I'm not talking about you in this article. If it isn't Doug, just keep reading.

For years, Dr. Tom Fahey and Pavel Tsatsouline corresponded by email. And Pavel and I had been talking for a few months about meeting together during discus camp and sharing some ideas.

Pavel, if you don't know, is an expert on strength training and flexibility. Tom is probably someone you know, but don't know you know. He's the author of dozens of books — the standard texts for college physical education and fitness classes — and writes for the pulp bodybuilding trade. Tom can call up from memory any study ever made on sports, strength, nutrition or sex. It was my great honor to introduce, in the flesh, Tom and Pavel.

So, Doug walks in on Tom, Pavel and Dan discussing 5000-meter running and deadlifts, the hip flexors and squatting, the lengthening of the femurs for proper depth, steak as a supplement, and the use of percentages for each and every discus throw... literally all at once. Dozens and dozens of practical hands-on demonstrations filled the next three hours. I begged Doug to keep notes — lots of notes.

I was exhausted after our meeting. Tom passed out on his bed. (A sixty-year-old professor and discus thrower shouldn't be made the exercise dummy for splits and overhead squats, but it's fun to watch.) Pavel and I agreed to do this again soon.

The next morning, I couldn't wait to talk to Doug and hear what he learned.

"Well, Doug?"

"It was cool," he shrugged.

"That's it?" His book could've been written by recording the first half hour of the dialogue!

"Well, ya. I mean, it was cool."

There's an insight here, an important one. I couldn't get a handle on it until on the way home, when I slipped into the airport bookstore.

At the bookstore I saw a book that illuminated the whole issue for me: *Queer Eye for the Straight Guy.*

Wait, give me a moment here. You see, Doug's problem wasn't that he didn't know anything. To attempt to quote Socrates, he didn't know that he didn't know. Of course, some might respond better to this exchange from the movie *Mystery Men:*

Captain Amazing, "I knew you couldn't change."

Casanova Frankenstein, "I knew you'd know that."

Captain Amazing, "Oh, I know that. And I knew you'd know I'd know you knew."

Casanova Frankenstein, "But I didn't. I only knew you'd know I knew. Did you know that?"

Doug not only didn't know he didn't know, but he didn't know that he didn't know that he didn't know… Did you know that?

As I leafed through *Queer Eye for the Straight Guy,* my little grey cells (Poirot!) were working madly. That's it, I thought. That's what they all need! They need…

In *Queer Eye for the Straight Guy,* there are five guys who call themselves the Fab Five. Each has a specialty, from culture to cooking to dressing. Each of them offers the hapless straight man a series of hints, ideas and downright commands about what to do in each part of his life (except the bedroom, one would assume).

I decided for guys like Doug, I needed to develop my own Fab Five. These five guys could walk Doug and others through the elemental steps of training and eating and everything else he obviously missed. Doug has no idea he has no idea about his lack of know. But he's about to find out.

Let me introduce you to the Strong Eye for the Weak Guy Fab Five:

Dan'l St. Jean: Nutrition expert
DJ: Strength Guru
Coach Dan: Longevity in Training Consultant
XXX DJ: Intensity Specialist
Lord Daniel Arthur David: Culture of Body Recomposition Historian

And now, a few words for Doug from each.

Dan'l St. Jean: Nutrition Expert

Doug, you weigh 125 pounds. You need to, how shall I say this, eat. We have certain rules, if you will:

1. Eat breakfast
2. Eat at least three meals a day
3. Eat protein at every meal
4. Consume fiber at every meal
5. Take your fish oil capsules

And, yes, Doug, you need to take a protein supplement. Why? Because, you'll be changing your strength training.

DJ: Strength Guru

Doug, I see you bench and curl three days a week for your upper body. For your lower body, you noted, "I jog." Here's what I'd like you to do for a few weeks:

Day One
Back Squat: 5 sets of 5 to warm up
Front Squat: 5 sets of 2 with a light weight
Pull-ups: 1 set to max
Bench Press: 1 or 2 sets of 8
Curls: 1or 2 sets of 8
An abdominal exercise, your choice, to finish

Day Two
Back Squats: 1or 2 sets of 8
Front Squats: 1or 2 sets of 2
Pull-ups: 5 sets of as many as you can do
Bench Press: 1or 2 sets of 8
Curls: 1or 2 sets of 8
An abdominal exercise, your choice, for a nice set
(not easy, but not hard)

Day Three
Back Squats: 1or 2 sets of 8
Front Squats: 1or 2 sets of 2
Pull-ups: 1or 2 sets of half your max
Bench Press: 5 sets of 5
Curls: 5 sets of 12
An abdominal exercise to finish

Skip a day between workouts, so maybe work Monday, Wednesday, Friday or Saturday, or else Tuesday, Thursday, Saturday or Sunday. On the four days you aren't in the gym, practice your squat form with a broomstick.

I want you to learn to squat right, so let's dive in. We'll stick with your bench and curl stuff until we can move you into a better program. Each workout, do the same movements, but with focus. Obviously, Monday is legs, Wednesday is the pull-up, and you have an upper-body day on Friday.

We'll soon move into deadlifts and swings and rows and shrugs and all kinds of other things, but let's give your body about two to three weeks to learn how to squat.

Coach Dan: Longevity in Training Consultant

So, Doug, your goal is to write a book about strength training for martial arts. A few things:

1. Master a martial art.

2. Compete at a high level. You don't have to necessarily win, but show up and compete.

3. Learn all the strength sports. The Olympic lifts are the snatch and clean and jerk. At some level, you should learn them. The powerlifts are the squat, bench press and deadlift. You think you know them, but, well, you don't.

There are some kettlebell moves you should learn: the snatch, the swing, the press and a couple of the fun tricks like windmills, juggling and bent press. It wouldn't hurt to try some of the Strongman stuff, too: yoke carries, farmer bars and sled drags.

4. You need to pick up some practical information on dealing with injuries, preparation for contests, and health and longevity issues. Get some basic knowledge of nutrition, recovery and supplements (all kinds: legal, illegal, herbal, OTC, and snake oil).

Because of the Olympic cycle, I like to think in four-year blocks. If you experiment with a new idea, like a lift or a supplement, you have several options on how much time you want to take with each experiment. If you try one new idea every four years, you have expanded your quiver of arrows by one… if it works.

However, if you change something or add something or try something different every month — every four weeks — you'll literally have almost fifty times more opportunities to improve. Well, some won't help, of course, but you've only invested a month. Now, if you decide, like me, to add, subtract, change or modify something every two weeks, that gives you about a hundred chances to zip ahead of the rest of the crowd.

Moreover, you'll be keeping your brain involved — and excited — which gives you a much better chance of thriving and surviving in strength sports.

XXX DJ: Intensity Specialist

Unfortunately, dear readers, when XXX DJ heard Doug considered jogging to be a leg workout, he snapped out of his chains, ate some bark, humiliated a Silverback in a way that appeared to be a breach of etiquette in the primate world, and sprinted away screaming the words, *Go tell it to the Spartans.*

We're under the impression XXX DJ feels a wee bit frustrated at Doug's inability to figure things out for himself. We do regret sincerely any further destruction by Mr. XXX DJ or any agents working with him.

Lord Arthur David: Culture of Body Recomposition Historian

Douglas certainly missed the opportunity of a lifetime in the presence of this trio of mighty men. Much like Parsifal in his quest for the Grail, Douglas seems to have grasped the goblet too soon and, being unprepared, failed in this first journey.

Douglas, like many of his peers, seems woefully ignorant of the roots of strength sports. Certainly, we don't need to have him start with Milo, but a brief look at some of the bigger and brighter names in our field would be appropriate.

Much has been written about Bruce Lee and his lifting regimes. Douglas should investigate those readings, available at bookstores everywhere. I would insist he become comfortable with names like Arnold, Franco and Zane. It wouldn't hurt for him to understand the early strongman contests going back to the last century.

Five minutes of research into the Olympic lifts would at least give him names like Kono, Anderson and Rigert. He should understand that Kaz is not a country.

It is much easier to stand on the shoulders of greatness than it is to reinvent centuries of knowledge.

You see, it's not a bad idea, really. Guys like Doug — and guys like me — need to have some guidance along the path. My Fab Five might not make it to television, but you can bet you'll hear more from them in the future.

I know you know it.

Twenty

The Best Exercises

I'll have to admit my mind was elsewhere. We were all sitting in the lounge at the Los Angeles Strength Seminar and everyone was drinking wonderful things like beer and bourbon, often together. One lovely young woman was drinking a wine spritzer. I can allow that if you're a lovely young woman.

Where was my mind? Deep in the Velocity Diet. I spied a woman eating a wonderful chicken salad with a hint of garbanzo beans and, dare I say, *black olives*. Oh, and the way the olive oil dribbled off the edges of the leaves…

You see, during the V-Diet, you start to wander off to check out the goods during discussions. I used to check out women; now I look to see if they're really enjoying their black olives. "You know I would, wouldn't you, you little minx, you? You and your lentils… "

Sorry, back to the point. As I sat there fantasizing about a four-egg omelet and bacon, a fellow participant asked, "Do you have your kids do good mornings?" In the past twenty-four hours, I'd been asked a number of questions about great exercises… that I simply don't use. Now, to pull my mind off those lovely ebony orbs (damn, the lady had a lot of black olives in her salad), I tried to refocus.

As I started talking about teaching sixty-five high school kids the good morning, it occurred to me I actually had some strong beliefs about a lot of exercises. Listen, it's rare to find a universally good or universally bad exercise, but what makes me pull the trigger on one lift for a group and dismiss another?

Seriously, why do I think walking lunges are a disaster, but Bulgarian split squats are great? When asked if I have my athletes do dips, I can say, "Don't do dips," so fast it sounds like "doughnut drips." Hmmm, tasty.

What's my problem?

First, and this is really important, I don't think there are really any bad exercises. Oh sure, there's some guy who just got certified and we're going to hear this or that exercise is considered dangerous by the NCAASPRQ-whatever association that has over a dozen members. How dare they knock my beloved one-legged Hungarian batwing arm crushers!

The moment I write leg lifts are bad because they overwork the psoas, somebody's going to have a new study showing the psoas is under-worked and we need to overwork it. Trust me, this kind of thing happens all the time.

The young people reading this should know all the following are bad for you: squats, bench presses, deadlifts, snatches, cleans, lat pulldowns, curls, leg extensions, and basically anything Arnold did while he trained.

Of course, now they're all good for you, except for the exercises you don't want to do. "Oh, I could easily squat 700, but don't you know squats are bad for you?" You see, that's why I don't run. Running is bad for you! At least, that's what I tell everyone.

Second, when I test athletes, I only look at three things. Let's go over those.

First, I like to test the deadlift. Without straps, from the floor, the deadlift might be the single best measure of absolute strength. The learning curve is about five minutes, although I realize superlative performance requires a bit more technical rigor. If you have a bad grip or a bad core (How I loathe that term!), the deadlift will expose it and any other weaknesses immediately.

The second test is the bench press. Again, the bench is pretty easy to learn and it's fairly popular (yes, I'm serious, many people are now bench pressing in gyms across the world). As a coach I can get a sense of things quite quickly in regard to upper body strength.

A warning: I like to joke most strength coaches have huge biceps from spotting the bench. If your coach has a huge deadlift, too, you might have an awesome bench.

If someone besides the lifter touches the bar, I don't count the lift. And I don't care how many times you call me Bro, any help on the bench makes it a missed lift. Yes, I know, you didn't need your best buddy to touch the bar on your bench press; you would've gotten it by yourself, Bro. Right. Keep believing, Bro.

Finally, I use the standing long jump. The vertical jump just doesn't have enough inches to work with to measure progress, and it's often hard to gauge improvement. The SLJ is a great tool for checking to see if what you're doing really is making the athlete better.

That's it, three tests. It's funny, but when I started coaching, I had a bucket of measurements. Max snatch, max clean, five-rep-max back squat, the forty time, and on and on and on. Then I realized most of these tests had a large measure of skill involved.

As my athletes got better at snatches or cleans or whatever, the tests improved, but not necessarily the performance on the field of play. So I tossed each measurement away one by one, until I realized the three I had left told me what I needed to know: The athlete got stronger (or didn't) and the athlete could apply (or not apply) this force quickly.

How do I determine whether to include an exercise with my athletes? Well, I've actually come up with a formula. Someone can make this into a spreadsheet with algebraic notations, but I keep it a bit simple here.

1. What's the learning curve of the exercise? If it takes a year or two to master a movement, like the Olympic squat snatch, the learning curve is a long, gentle climb. The two-hand kettlebell swing? Five minutes maybe, if you have someone who really just doesn't get it.

Note: There are some excellent reasons for taking two years or more to master certain things. More on that later.

2. I coach in big groups. Can this movement be done with at least five people doing it at once, usually ten or more? If I have ten boxes, box jumps are great; I can have ten athletes moving at once. If I have one box, I can't have a class of sixty-five doing box jumps!

Walking lunges with a class is a nightmare because there's no way to house that many walking lungers. (I agree, you can. But try it.) Bulgarian split squats simply need a dumbbell or kettlebell and a place to prop up that back foot.

3. In math, there's a great term for the point here, the lowest common denominator. You decide to teach the good morning to fifty sophomores. You're going to have fifty sophomores, ages fourteen or fifteen, put loaded barbells on their necks and lean forward to work the spinal erectors. Right.

Folks, half the class will roll the bars straight over the backs of their heads before you can tell them to look up. Many will lock their knees and not let go of the bars until they face-plant. Now, use your imagination to think what the dumb kids will be doing.

Listen, the good morning is a great lift and I've had my athletes do it for years, but not in a group setting.

4. Finally, will it impact the athlete? Will it make him better? There are some great exercises that may or may not help. Which press is best? Incline, decline, flat, military or the dumbbell variations? Which? Pick one.

You see, that's the issue. Pick one press. Oh, go ahead, pick a vertical push and a horizontal push if that's on the list, but really, why do so many people do so many kinds of pushes? How can you tell which exercise is working unless you have the courage to cut down the number of exercises so you can figure out whether or not it works?

And there's the great rub. All this works, but does it work toward your goals? And, as part of this, does it hurt you or hurt your goals? Many teens complain dips hurt their sternums. I was one of them. Now I discover pull-ups kill my elbows. If your program is based on nothing but dips and pull-ups, people are going to be hurting and not training.

At the Los Angeles Strength Seminar, I presented the following info about how to teach a number of lifts over a three-week period:

A three-week approach to learning the lifts

Workout One	**Workout Two**	**Workout Three**
Buttkickers	High Knees	Strides
Snatch DL	Clean DL	Classic DL
Power Snatch Hi Position	PS from Hang	PS from Floor
Military Press	Push Press	Push Jerk
Strict Curl	Cheat Curl	Chin-up

Workout Four	**Workout Five**	**Workout Six**
Starts	Speed Traps	Long Sprint (200s)
Jefferson Lift (Straddle DL)	Goblet Squat	Back Squat
Power Clean High Position	PC from Hang	PC from Floor
Bench Press Lockouts	Chain Bench Press	Towel Bench Press
Pull-ups	Bentover Row	Renegade Row

Workout Seven	**Workout Eight**	**Workout Nine**
Bounding	Box Jumps	Depth Jumps
Front Squat	Overhead Squat	Zercher Squat
Clean-grip Snatch High	CGS from Hang	CGS from Floor
Jerk	One-arm Press	SeeSaw Press
Two-hand Swings	One-hand Swings	DARC Swings

I won't describe each, but the first exercise is a movement exercise building up to plyometrics; the second is a big lower body lift from deadlifts to squat variations; the third exercise is a way to teach the quick lifts; the fourth lift is a push, and the last lift is a pull of sorts.

You may have never heard of some of the lifts, or you may have mastered the bulk of them. The point is this: Would doing each lift for one workout ever constitute mastery? Nope, not even close.

It's funny because I love this three-week approach. I do. And, I can make it work… with one or two athletes. But with a group? No way.

Let's get back to the points concerning exercise selection. Some readers are making a living training people; not all, but some personal trainers actually make a living doing their jobs. There's a word in your title: personal. Many of your clients think personal means "Me Only!" If you can get eight people a day to pay you a hundred dollars an hour for your one-on-one coaching, quit reading now and enjoy the fruits of your labors. You're in rare air.

One-on-one training is wonderful, if the trainee can afford it and the trainer can train the trainee. I guarantee a few hours with a decent coach is pure gold for your long-term goals. But what about the real world?

Let's take a few examples and look at how I approach exercise selection:

The Two-Hand Swing

1. Easy to learn. Women love the lift, too. "Coach, I can feel it burning fat!" This is an actual quote and I wish we could transform that feeling into a pill.

2. I've had groups of sixty-five people all doing the two-hand swing at once.

3. The idiot factor is low. A kettlebell instructor friend told me about a trainee who just let the 'bell go on the way up. But that's pretty good — only one idiot story.

4. Beyond burning fat, my athletes tell me this lift helps in the jumping sports (basketball and volleyball), as you can do a lot of the jumping motion without dealing with landing. This is a big issue in sports where you jump and jump and jump. After a while, the body starts breaking down from all the landings.

The Good Morning — Standard knees-bent

1. Easy to learn, but people who watch the lift immediately ask, "Won't that hurt my back?"

2. If you have a nice setup, it can be used in large groups.

3. We have a high idiot factor with this lift. Many people despise having weight on their backs; now we're using the head to brake the bar from rolling forward.

4. If you're also teaching squats within the same workout, half the group will do good morning squats and the other half will do squatting good mornings. Carryover to sports and physique training? Probably fine, but there are dozens of other low-back exercises that work just as well… maybe. I like the Romanian deadlift better, because I think I teach it well.

Dips

Why don't I teach the dip?

1. It's easy to learn.

2. If you have dip racks, it's easy to teach in large groups.

3. Occasionally someone drops through the dip racks, but that's just funny.

4. Carryover to sports: Well, I remember an old college strength coach telling me athletes who dip don't hurt their shoulders.

So why don't I teach dips? Well, I do, except not with high school kids. Most of the class will complain, "Coach, dips hurt me right here," and point to the sternum. In the growing adolescent, the bottom position of the dip seems to rip the breastbone apart.

I learned this from my athletes: No dips. Rule number one of strength and conditioning: Don't hurt your athletes or do things that hurt (unless it has a ton of value).

Back Squats versus Front Squats

1. Front squats are hard on the wrists at first. Back squats hurt the upper back and neck in many. I find if you teach front squats (or overhead squats) first, back squats are a breeze. But for an experienced lifter who's done heavy back squats, transitioning to front squats is hell. Not only does it hurt the wrists, but it hurts the ego. I've been there.

2. If you have enough racks, either lift is fine. I do like front squats, because we rarely need more than one spotter.

3. Idiot factor is very, very high on both lifts. Don't believe me? Ask anyone at any fitness center to squat.

4. Some argue front squats somehow magically carry over to sports better than back squats. I think it might be true, but I think squatting is a really good idea and I'd rather have an athlete do some kind of squat than never squat fearing lack of magic carryover. So, squat away — somehow!

Bulgarian Split Squats

1. Balance is an issue for the first few reps or even days, but most people get it quickly. We also teach three positions to hold the weight: on the chest (goblet position), in a dangling arm (suitcase position), and arm extended overhead (waiter position). The three variations seem to reinforce everything we're trying to do.

2. Again, if you have sixty-four dumbbells or kettlebells, you can train sixty-four people. All you need are sixty-four raised places to put the back foot.

3. So far, so good. No idiot stories. I'm sure somebody has a story, but for some reason Bulgarian split squats have been story-free for me.

4. I know a lot of people who insist on one-legged work. This is the only single-leg lift I trust. Lunges, reverse lunges, leaping lunges and all the rest just don't seem to be effective with my athletes. It's probably because of the disdain I have for the word lunges. It has that whole go-for-the-burn Janefondaesque mindset of most of the fitness community. Yeah, go for the burn, and toss in her videotapes and books, too.

For someone not training large groups or simply training alone, I can bet you've used a similar process. In my home gym, I never bench press (I fear someone in my family finding me dead with a bar across my throat) and I tend to be a little more careful than at other gyms. My fear of dropping a loaded bar on my Mazda 6 is part of the issue, so I think things through a bit.

For the general fitness enthusiast, there's some wisdom here:

1. If you're really interested in a lift you see at the gym or in a magazine or book, but your attempts are clearly life-threatening, maybe a little coaching is in order.

2. After you get the coaching, ask yourself the question: Is this exercise going to carry over into my athletic goals?

3. Finally, every so often, ask if this is really helping you toward your goals. Now, before you dismiss everything difficult like squats and deadlifts, use a bit of common sense, but if something just doesn't seem to pay off like that brightly colored article in the fitness magazine said it would, consider moving on.

A little thinking can go a long way in our training.

Twenty-One

My Secret Coaching Methods

Mike sat in my front room after a six-hour drive from Las Vegas to Salt Lake City and asked a question:

"Dan, why do people ask you to coach them?"

Now, I thought to myself, "Mike, you're here for my coaching. Why do you come up from one of the most exciting places on earth to, well, Utah?"

Still, it's a good question: Why do people pay me a lot of money for coaching that almost inevitably ends up with the athlete saying, "Yeah, you're right. I already knew that."

If everybody knows everything I teach, why do I have a job? Certainly, there are people who revel in ignorance. I read a review of one of my articles on a website that had one serious error: It was obvious the reviewer hadn't read the article. Small thing, but it can lead to issues of clarity.

And I'm not the only expert out there. There are dozens of 130-pound guys who are experts on gaining mass, guys like me who put on twenty-plus pounds of fat and give advice on prudence and sacrifice, and coaches who train Olympic lifters, but can't actually lift much more than the bar.

But I'm willing to give you my secrets. I'm comfortable giving them away because few people will really apply these simple points. To quote *The Man of La Mancha*, "Come, enter into my imagination and see me as I truly am."

In truth, the great secret of coaching is the same as watching *Oprah* or any movie with a psychiatrist: Simply repeat whatever the guest or patient says. There you go, my best technique. And now everyone knows it.

Seriously, get a nice, soft couch and sit back and doodle while the athlete talks about his training. During this time, I draw fighter planes attacking dinosaurs, but that isn't the point here.

Here's the first question: So, what's the problem? What's going on?

Athlete: Well, I just don't squat right. I hate squatting, but I know I need to do more. Any advice?

Me: Here's a thought. Maybe, just maybe, we could work on your squat and get you to do it right. Then, you could do more squats. What do you think?

Athlete: Wow, it's like you know me… You and I are connected.

Me: Yeah, that's why you pay me. Oh, and by the way, could dinosaurs defend themselves with lightning bolts? I ask because I'm good at drawing them.

If you say "Polly wants a cracker" enough times, Polly speaks back to you!

Honestly, probably ninety percent of the time I work with people, they know exactly what the problem is in their training, diet or recovery. This is only true when I can actually sit down and talk with them. On internet forums where guys weigh 175, ripped, and bench over 500, there seems to be another issue or two.

It helps to say the words out loud to another person. My job is usually to ask the follow-up question: *Is this important for your goal?*

Generally, people know what's important, like eating protein and vegetables and less processed, calorie-dense foods. Hell, we all know that. We also know smoking is bad, drinking and driving is bad, drugs are bad, and the list goes on and on.

The Parrot Technique addresses that issue: The athlete knows what to do, and often he knows the solution to whatever problems have arisen, too. The issue? Let's look at the next secret technique.

Yeah, we all know the opposite axiom to this point: Physician heal thyself. Fine. Good. You win. Your cliché beat my cliché. But if I could identify the single biggest issue with most people's training, it's this:

The coach who coaches himself has an idiot for a client.

Even a good surgeon doesn't pull out his own spleen. A good coach can't coach himself. Listen, I tried it for years and here's the problem: You simply don't have enough RAM to do it yourself. Yep, that's the computer term. You simply don't have enough space in your brain to do what it takes to train yourself.

First, designing a program takes a level of honesty people can rarely match. Oh, sure, we can all see the obvious with glaring faults and issues, but the fix might blow up some happy little beliefs you're afraid to confront.

Second, anyone can design a program or plan. I see it all the time. In coaching yourself, you have to follow this program. Will you give it the time to work, or, like me, immediately begin to tweak and change it so by week two the original plan is completely lost? I know this by experience… thirty years of it! Can you follow your own plan? Some can, like Clarence Bass, but most can't. Even Bass, by the way, changes quite a bit from book to book.

Third, do you have enough will to push through your own program and not find the easy way out? I'm a master of talking myself out of tough workouts and back into my rut workouts. Like Earl Nightingale used to say, "A rut is a grave with the ends kicked out."

Fourth, can you honestly address your weaknesses at the start of a workout, in a strange gym, or when other alpha males are training near you? The moment guys who look like frat boys start training near me, I front squat. I'm not doing sets of triples in the pull-up when these guys are working their heavy triceps extensions, Bro. Sorry, my ego can't do it.

I have another idea to help you with this, but let's continue to unpack this concept. Let's just say it the opposite way. On the Velocity Diet, I drank six shakes a day. Why? Chris said so. If I follow Alwyn's workout and you ask me, why? I answer, "Alwyn said so." When Dick Notmeyer coached me, the answer was the same: Coach said so.

Said so is genius. It completely divorces you — and I mean completely — from any responsibility for your training. Why seven sets of four? Coach said so. Why fish oil? Coach said so. It's an amazing moment of clarity; you can pawn off all your responsibility on someone else. It's genius.

David Allen talks about how a neat desk, a neat car, and some basic efficiency in life can literally free up your brain to take care of what's important.

I tested this the last two weeks and cleaned my garage, my desk and my library. Allen is right. All of a sudden I was finishing things that should've been finished years ago, and began care of business. I actually think this carries over into getting someone else to take care of the program for you. I think that's the draw of all the Westside powerlifting hybrids and the popularity of many workout websites: *Hey, do this!*

I'm trying to listen to my own advice here.

These first two points usually go a long way in working with someone who comes over to try my coaching. Most of the time, the person knows exactly what's missing. My job is to come up with some ideas to incorporate these missing elements into a program.

Just giving me the right to tell them what to do seems to free up new enthusiasm for training and the stuff they need to do in training. How do we implement these ideas?

If there's a bit of advice I could probably give every fitness enthusiast in the world, it would be to train at home… sometimes.

Okay, we decide you've been cheating on your bench by bouncing the bar off your chest and raising your hips. I convince you to change your ways. Then you go back to the 24/7 fitness center and all your buddies are benching with a big bounce and hips making sweet love to the ceiling. You unload most of the weight and insist on perfect reps. Or you tell your friends, "Don't count any reps unless they're perfect!"

Sure, that's what's going to happen. Yep, that's right, we'll all strip the bar and go lighter in front of friends, buddies, and the girls on the treadmills.

I'm also going to make you go deeper in the squat, use full movements in the pull-up, and challenge you to slash rest periods. It's going to be hard in a public setting, especially when you've allowed yourself to be comfortable.

And we all know the Comfortable Workout.

Treadmill watching TV (usually *Oprah*, but *ESPN* is fine, too)

A couple of arm waves you call stretching

Several sets of benching and calling people Bro

A really long set of curls to make your 13-inch arms grow to 13.5

Sauna

Steam

Shower

To move in another direction, I suggest a few pieces of equipment.

A dumbbell. I like something around twenty-five pounds for most people, but go heavier if you like.

Those push-up handles that cost ten bucks. They allow you to really drop down deep.

A doorway pull-up bar

An ab wheel

The total investment here is maybe fifty dollars, although I've found most people have this stuff in a closet or can find them in a friend's closet. I have borrowed thousands of dollars of good equipment from my friends and neighbors that I found holding laundry or living in the back of a closet with shoes and other sports equipment never to be used again.

Here's a great home workout that allows you to train and work on the usual issues I find ailing most people:

1. Right-leg Bulgarian Split Squats with the dumbbell in the suitcase position, 10 reps

2. Left-leg Bulgarian Split Squats with the dumbbell in the suitcase position, 10 reps

3. Goblet Squats with the dumbbell cradled on the chest, 10 reps

4. Deep Push-ups, chest touching the floor, with the push-up handles, 10 reps

5. Doorway Chin-ups or Pull-ups, 10 reps

6. Ab Wheel, 10 reps

Try to do these six exercises one after another straight through without resting much between movements. Repeat this sequence, after a minute or two of rest, three to five times.

This short workout, a supplement to your regular training, will help with cardio, help with muscular development, and help with general training. But most important, it'll help you work by yourself on full movements and applying the lessons of coaching.

Training at home is the opposite, if you will, of having a coach. It demands some free will, it demands some integrity, and it asks you to monitor your own technique. Without the peer pressure of the spa or gym, or the pressure that comes from trying to not look stupid in public, you can focus on taking the time to do things right.

Your dog doesn't care if you struggle for a few weeks with twenty-five pounds in the goblet squat… nor should you.

After a few weeks of extra work, it might be time to figure out what else you are missing. Most people, it seems, miss a lot of stuff and not just in their workouts.

"Hey guys, wish you were here!" I love vacation postcards. The picture on the front usually has a blue sky and a sandy beach. Now, is it just me, or do you worry when someone sends you a "wish you were here" card on his honeymoon? Just wondering…

The idea of a good vacation postcard is to let others know you're off having fun while they're at work. It's a level of one-up-manship I appreciate. Look at what you're missing while you slave away on the worthless quarterly reports!

Most people seem to miss a few things in training. Generally, I can fix a person's training with just one or two simple "hmmms" while reviewing her or her training program. The biggest issue? The most common, usually, is ignoring half the human body. Not a big issue if you weigh around two hundred pounds; you're only missing a hundred!

What do I mean? Well, let's break down the body by movements, rather than by muscle:

- Vertical Push: militaries, overhead stuff

- Vertical Pull: pull-up, chin-up, lat pulldown

- Horizontal Push: bench press

- Horizontal Pull: row and the gang

- Posterior Chain or Deadlift

- Quad-dominant Lower Body: squat

- Abs: crunch or ab wheel

- Rotation or twist and torque movers: Russian twists

- Single arm/single leg push/pulls: This can go on forever!

Now, we can argue about this all day. For example, I don't do any twisting motions because I've done them all and I've never seen any benefit. Let me add one more point: I'm going to be doing them again in about two months because I'm trying a new variation.

What does this all mean? I'm not so sure rotational work helps rotation, but I believe there's value in doing some anyway. Not clear? Neither am I, so refer to the point above about having a coach tell you what to do. Why am I going to do them again? Coach said so.

I can help a guy who only bench presses by encouraging him to do military presses for a few weeks. The ego hit will be hard: a 400-plus bencher hates the first days of struggling with 135 to 225. But, it helps. I can often make a good athlete who squats run faster by adding the deadlift to his training. Give it eight weeks and boom, I'm a miracle-worker.

How do you get yourself to do all or most of these movements? A good coach can program these easily, but let me add one more point. I'll again repeat Dan Gable: *If it's important, do it every day.*

Do all the movements — or most of them — in the daily movement warm-up! I've stolen an idea from both Steve Javorek and Alwyn Cosgrove: Do complexes to warm up. Here's one of mine, only mildly stolen.

Power Snatch for 8 reps

Overhead Squat for 8 reps

Back Squat for 8 reps

Good Morning for 8 reps

Row for 8 reps

Deadlift for 8 reps

Do these all in a row without letting go of the bar. Rest a minute, a minute-and-a-half or two minutes, and do it again. Try three to five sets of this little complex. This particular one is ideal for a day dedicated to vertical or horizontal pushing. If you do five of these complexes, you've done 240 movements that cover practically all the other moves.

I like this approach for most people. It's certainly a volume answer to the question of covering all the moves and, generally, most of the athletes I work with would rather do more than less to fix an issue.

The other easy fix is to take a standard calendar (I use the free kind given out by the mortuary) and take the last month or the next planned month and note when every basic movement was covered. For some of us, "never" is going to be an issue sooner or later.

If you find you have a ratio of five push workouts to one pull, this could indicate trouble on the horizon. Here's the thing: Some who read this might not ever come up with these imbalance issues.

We all know guys with toothpick thighs and an upper body that's out of balance, too big. We also know this guy would be bigger with some leg work, but that just might not be a big deal for him. And, it's not wise to train for years ignoring things like vertical or horizontal pulls even if you don't get injured or, really, even bothered by it. But, for those of us who throw logs or bang into people or toss weights overhead, this is going to lead to issues.

A few minutes reviewing the calendar can really spotlight issues with your approach to training. Generally, though, most of the athletes I work with already know what they're missing in their training. The nice thing about identifying these gaps is usually it isn't that big a deal to fix. In a week of training, tossing in a few sets of pull-ups or rows or even deadlift variations just isn't that hard to address.

Now, after a few minutes of having the athlete tell me what's wrong with his training, convincing him to listen to another voice in program design, discussing some home training ideas for dealing with performance issues, and over-viewing long-term training omissions, the athlete discovers he already knows all of this anyway.

There's a range of technical issues I can cover to help the athlete with the squat, the Olympic lifts and various other moves, but honestly, usually we've found the core issues. Sure, we'll continue to tweak things as we battle the greatest challenge: To master something, you have to do it over and over and over again.

My mantra: Specificity works… but at a price. The price? Yep, doing something for a million repetitions incurs the wrath of injury and boredom. To be honest, I think the boredom is worse, as we can address injuries with proper training, rehab and, my favorite, surgery.

Dealing with this challenge will probably need another couch session, some additional coaching, further personalized work, and some review of the program… and we'll give it a few months to see how it all pans out.

Now you know what you know and you told someone else to tell you what you know, so how can I help you?

I don't know.

Twenty-Two

Nautilus, Crossfit and High/High

I began lifting in 1967 when my brother, Gary, bought a 110-pound weight set. As I sat back and realized I've been obsessed with a hobby for forty years, I thought, hmmm, maybe I should share a lesson or two.

One of my favorite books has a title that caught my eye the instant I saw it in the bookstore. It's *Great Books* by David Denby. Seriously, when you're looking around the bookstore for a new book to read and you see one called *Great Books*, how can you pass on it?

Denby spent a year doing something I wish I could do. He went back to his freshman year in college and retook the Humanities curriculum. In his mid-forties, he returned to Columbia College and sat in a room with a bunch of freshmen wearing backward baseball caps, and reread the great books.

Great books change as you age. A hung-over college freshman can't really understand the issues parents go through in great literature. Kissing the killer of your child, like Priam in *The Illiad,* or being asked to sacrifice your first born, like Abraham in *Genesis,* might not be such a big deal on a Wednesday morning in a comfortable classroom after a nice cafeteria breakfast. Now that I have teenagers, I can barely read these same passages.

The greatest gifts from Denby's book are the insights of his professors. Professor Edward Taylor constantly prods the class to think double. Another professor begs the students "DGSI," or "Don't Get Sucked In."

Sucked in? Yes, sucked into the BS. Let me pull out my bee pollen, my B-15 tablets, my sublingual L-Arginine drops... It's all BS, folks.

Think double resonates with me.

In a world of either-or and an occasional neither-nor, Professor Taylor is reminding us of both-and. In the strength community, we like to take sides of an issue. It doesn't matter the topic; just put up an internet forum post about a high-protein diet and the high-carbers will attack you. Machines are great; machines suck. Kettlebells are great; kettlebells suck.

Professor Taylor's insight is worth studying. Let's think double a little bit. I'd like to share three different times in my career when I spent at least two years trying a program, and discuss the insights from each.

It's funny to look at the advice I took (and didn't take) over my career. In 1991, a former world-class lifter told me three things I needed to do:

1. Keep my bodyweight on my heels when I lifted. (Advice I ignored until I discovered this was absolutely correct, and it changed my lifting in a second or less.)

2. Use complexes in training. (Advice I ignored until Alwyn Cosgrove made me start using them, and the body fat just fell off me like grease from bacon.)

3. I should do nothing less than tens in the squat. (Advice I ignored. Instead, I did lots and lots and lots of heavy singles, got a big gut, and lost all my snap. Now I do tens.)

Why didn't I at least listen to him? Well, I'd been training hard with a group of guys at a local gym and I'd bought into heavy isometrics, lots of plyometrics, and a serious amount of

206

heavy back squatting to improve my Olympic lifts. And I was improving. My gym lifts were going up and up. At the meets I was struggling with a lack of energy, some injuries, some burn-out, but, hey, I was looking good in the gym!

Good advice has been cast at me throughout my career. I tend to ignore it when it comes in a dull package. If you slap some color on it and fill it with bright images and make it seem exotic, rare and remote, now I'm listening.

You see, I get sucked in. But, let me think double over my experiences. As I look on my forty years in the strength game, I'm embarrassed and proud to say I've done just about every-thing. My earnestness in pursuing the secrets has led me down a lot of wrong roads, but the lessons are worth sharing. By the end of 1992, I could barely climb a flight of stairs. I was a wreck. I ignored probably the exact advice that would've kept me less injured, less fat, and a lot happier to be around.

My article, *A Religious Studies Professor's Review of HIT,* which you'll see shortly, caused quite a stir on the HIT internet forums. So much so, after dozens and dozens of posts, flames, and personal attacks upon each other in the forum, they proved my point. My point? HIT has become a religion. And although the followers used to dominate the internet (am I the only one who remembers HIT Jedis?), the bulk of the flock has van-ished with their fourteen-inch arms, and continue using the genetics argument to bemoan their parents for everything.

How did I know so much? Well, I bought into all of it.

It would be hard to find someone who trained during the 1970s who wouldn't have been swayed by the marketing of Nautilus. It only occurred to me recently, the bulk of the in-formation from Arthur Jones came in advertisements. Yes, huge ads, but ads nonetheless. The magazine, *Athletics Journal*, be-came the must-see publication during the height of the Nauti-lus hoopla.

Later, after buying everything Ellington Darden ever wrote — he was the voice of Nautilus and later of HIT for a generation — I met with him at a clinic in Las Vegas and began training on a full set of Nautilus machines in a local gym. Later, at a great discount, I owned and stored seven of the biggest and most famous of the machines. Every few weeks, I'd call Ell. He always answered my calls with intelligence and insight.

In fact, once I asked him what to do with all my spare time and he answered, "Learn to play chess."

"I already know how."

"Then teach people to play chess," he responded.

The next week, the chess coach job opened at my school (a moment of synchronicity) and I took the position. As a football coach, teaching chess was probably the single best decision I ever made for tactics and strategy.

Jones and Darden did something brilliant that was beyond marketing. They changed the definition of intensity. Rather than the classic formula based on maximums, the HIT mantra became, "Train to temporary muscular failure." By changing the definition of intensity, one could also change the perception of progress. By simply adding an additional rep or two, adding a negative, or adding another plate on the plate-loaded stack, this was progress. Soon, the results would be seen whether in body-size increase or fat loss or better sports performance.

In measured sports, track and field and strength sports such as Olympic lifting, the HIT promises failed quickly. Yes, it's still in place in some small corners of intercollegiate sports where recruiting is the key. And from time to time we'll see a host of images of bodybuilders from the era of Watergate to prove the system works, but most of us have moved on.

Did I waste two-plus years of my life doing Nautilus? No, not at all. For one thing, I learned to discern advertisements from articles, not always an easy thing. Next, I came away very impressed with Ellington Darden, who answered all my stupid questions. For those of you who remark how patient I am with your idiotic questions, thank Ellington.

One area of training on the machines I found interesting was my discovery that I did miss muscles in training the whole body my entire career. I also discovered it didn't take much to overcome this gap. The best lesson was this: *In a performance sport, you measure improvement by improving performance!*

Finally, I came away with a truth from this experience: Everything works. Well, everything works for about six weeks. The ultimate problem with the early Nautilus training is after about six weeks, improvement stopped. But, that's true with just about everything! If you went to some secret training facility and sat at the feet of the masters, you'd make great progress. Then, around six weeks later, you'd start moving to Plan B.

Plan B? Yep, you could blame your parents for giving you bad genetics; you could decide to periodize your training; you could cut back (something most people would never consider); or you could plow ahead. I've done them all.

My time training on the Nautilus system certainly didn't help with my primary goals. I should've listened to Aristotle, of course: *Both excessive and deficient exercise ruin physical strength.* I let myself get sucked into the promise of improvement by vomiting over the side of a machine that only worked my quads, triceps or abs.

Yet the lessons from these two years have certainly guided my coaching. I got sucked in, but the insights, experiences and lessons were well worth my time.

I also trained in the Crossfit style for two years. In Tyler Hass's famous interview with Crossfit's founder, Greg Glassman, I saw another interesting promise:

"If you come to us with a four-minute mile, six months into it you are going to be thirty seconds slower, but a whole hell of a lot fitter. Similarly, if you come to us with a 900-pound squat, in six months it's going to be 750 pounds, but you, too, will be much fitter. A four-minute mile and a 900-pound squat are both clear and compelling evidence of a lack of balance in your program. This doesn't reflect the limitations of our program, but the inherent nature of flesh and blood. But here's the fascinating part. We can take you from a 200-pound max deadlift to a 500-750 pound max deadlift in two years while only pulling max singles four or five times a year."

The same issue emerges here: A four-minute mile is a world-class time that would/should/could provide this athlete with a salary, or at least a free education. A 4:30-mile isn't unusual in a high school state meet. Certainly, there are lots of examples of students running these times well before their junior year. Here's the rub: We're recommending a program that literally takes one from world class to solid high school performer?

The point about the 750-pound max deadlift can only be demonstrated by the platform, but I've been around the game a long time and a 750-deadlifter is a rarity with any program, anywhere. In my only powerlifting contest, I was the last successful deadlifter that night (3:00 AM, deadlifting 628; hard on the nerves, by the way) and any program that can get me to 750 with minimal deadlifting is worth a serious study.

In this example, we see another issue. The Crossfit community took on the definition of fitness credited to Jim Crawley and Bruce Evans of Dynamax, who market an excellent medicine ball. The Crawley/Evans definition includes ten components all of us would recognize in a moment, including strength, speed and power.

However, I've always used Dr. Phil Maffetone's original definition that fitness is the ability to do a task. In his more recent works, he's changed the definition to "the ability to be physically active." I like the original.

Why do I love the original definition? Maffetone's great insight was he separated health from fitness. Health is the harmony of the organs to operate optimally. Fitness is task-based. I think fitness is throwing the discus far. I could set up an entire website using this single definition.

I recognize the limitations, but most fitness professionals don't. We tend to coach from our life experiences, a lesson that's absolutely correct. The problem is we sometimes forget my goals may not be your goals.

By doing something as simple as changing or grasping a single definition of fitness, one can completely miss the point of training. Sending a discus thrower to train with an elite bodybuilder is as mad as sending elite bodybuilders to train with me.

Recently, during a telephone discussion with Mark Reifkind, an elite coach, bodybuilder, powerlifter and author, he made a point so obvious I've nearly stopped thinking since: If you want to know about fat loss or muscle building, ask top level bodybuilders. These guys know it.

In other words, quit buying fat-loss devices off the late-night TV ads from former sitcom actors, quit buying fat-loss stuff Grandma tried after her cribbage partner heard about it, and quit trying fad diets. Instead, listen to the best of the best.

This is my advice to you. I doubt I'll follow it myself, though. The advice is this: If you follow Maffetone's definition of fitness — the ability to do a task — run it past your goals, find people who are doing your task and follow them.

If your goal is a big deadlift or squat, read the Westside articles. If your goal is to look good nekkid, read the articles explaining nutrition and training for that exact goal. If your goal is to be good at pull-ups, do pull-ups. Just make sure your fitness approach matches your fitness goals.

The problem is yes, everything works. Doing everything at once makes you marginal at everything... at best. Yet there are great insights to steal from my Crossfit experience. Yep, I'm horrid at pull-ups. I gas out quickly when doing anything over thirty seconds, but I warn you, those first thirty seconds are a dangerous thing. Crossfit exposed issues for me, much like my Nautilus experience.

Somewhere during your training year, you need to unpack a few challenges and measure yourself against your goals. I've always had great respect for Clarence Bass' idea of an annual photo shoot. I believe he uses September, but it doesn't matter. As a track and strength athlete, it's relatively easy for me as I just go to a meet and find out whether or not some training idea is working. The week after the Velocity Diet, I broke a state record in the snatch. In my narrow view of thinking, this works!

Alwyn Cosgrove said an interesting thing to me at a recent seminar, "Well, now you can talk about the Velocity Diet."

"Huh?"

"Yeah, you did it; you can critique it," he said.

You know, I've been around for a while and it's the first time such an obvious point has crossed my mind. We should begin a list of Things I Tried and share the information. We could call it the internet.

Seriously though, I thrived on the Atkins Diet… and stopped doing it because it worked so well for me. The Velocity Diet? Yep, I loved it. Turns out I need more fluids than I realized, and it takes a lot of work to be disciplined in diet.

Here's the key for me: I enjoy getting sucked in. I enjoy trying new training ideas and new equipment. Some things, like kettlebells and chains, work even better for me than advertised. Other things are rusting in my backyard, but I must've learned a lesson or two from the failures as well.

The lesson of my training career has been the ultimate Think Double. There are two factors, really, in training: volume and intensity. For your own purposes, define those as you wish, but try not to kid yourself too much.

> Low Volume/Low Intensity
> Low Volume/High Intensity
> High Volume/Low Intensity
> High Volume/High Intensity

Although there are probably a billion gradations between, let's focus on what I've learned in my career. You see, I've done them all. And they all work.

Low Volume/Low Intensity

There's a time to take off and a time to take it easy. Now, for me, I just don't do anything. There was a time where I found those light, easy workouts refreshing and fun, but now I just take the dog for a walk rather than a light tonic workout, as we used to call them.

However, don't ignore the value of light and short workouts. These can be stimulating and can even remind you of what you're supposed to be doing.

Low Volume/High Intensity

If I may, let's just pretend this is High Intensity Training, shall we? I know this: There's probably no better time spent than a focused six-week attack on the body with this approach. Yes, it's Frankenstein training. True, it's machine-based training.

I know, I know, it isn't going to do this or that or this… but for a short experiment, I'm not sure much else can work better. The learning curve on the leg curl machine is quite low and you can have your buddies help you with negatives, rest-pauses, partials, or whatever, almost from day one. Don't try any of that with snatches!

High Volume/Low Intensity

Most of us live here. Forever. When I go to most gyms and watch people train, I'm not sure why they don't just do push-ups and pull-ups at home. Most gymrats bench press weights that surely aren't much more effort than push-ups.

This is why 5K runs are so popular on weekends: Waddle around for half an hour, pick up your T-shirt, and eat your bagels on the way home while you convince yourself you trained hard. Oh, I love it, too. I spend the bulk of my time doing garbage workouts that only keep me in the game. But, that's good! We need to spend a lot of time here.

High Volume/High Intensity

Here's where thinking double comes in. Not long ago, I wrote about a workout I did in 1979:

Back Squats
315 for 30
Rest
275 for 30
Rest
225 for 30

Usually, when I write an article I get a dozen emails that say, "Dan, I did this workout and got nothing out of it." Not one email has reported doing *this* exact workout produced nothing.

High volume and high intensity, or as we used to say, heavy weights and high reps, is probably the lost art of weight training. Most of my workouts are designed to push the athlete to that world. Take this:

The Litvinov Workout
Front Squat
405 for 8 reps
Run 400 meters immediately after
Repeat three times

Having problems with your quad development? How about just front squatting 405 for three sets of eight?

I don't care how you train. The key is to find a way, as often as you can, to get yourself to train with high volume and high intensity. In addition, and probably more important, you need to have the skill or insight or coaching to know when to stop doing High/High to spend time in the other quadrants.

Like Denby, I wish I could go back and relive my first lifting experiences and try to explain to myself the long, long road ahead. I can't. I couldn't possibly explain to that twelve-year-old Danny John the challenges ahead. He needed, like the rest of us, the journey.

And, to be honest, I envy him a bit.

Twenty-Three

Blood on the Barbell

The whole incident must've taken close to an hour, but it seemed like just five minutes.

I'd taken our track and field team through Sardine Canyon on Highway 6 down to Emery High School for a qualifying track meet. The timing system had been based on the starting gun's flash, but problems with that system in the afternoon lightning caused the meet to drag on and on.

We got back on the bus late and I fell asleep. Descending into just one more of those massive curving canyons, I woke up when I heard the athletes yelling.

Off to the side of the road was a still-smoking car that had passed us on another twisting turn not long before. It had gone out of control into oncoming traffic and spun back across our lane and off into a canyon. A semi had jackknifed over the edge, too, just above the car.

As we slowed, our bus driver called 911 and I grabbed my first aid kit. The car was empty, all the airbags deployed. I looked around, and found the driver lying on the hill.

I'd brought a knife to a gunfight. Popping open my first aid kit, I realized there were just enough medical supplies to pull out a splinter, cover a blister, and clean a paper cut. This guy needed a helluva lot more than aspirin.

I pulled out some gauze, pushed back the flap of skin coming off his skull and just held on. As more people arrived, one guy noted a big gash on his leg. "Do you want to take a look at that?" he asked me. I did the kind of triage Hawkeye Pierce would envy, "No, I think I'll try to stop the bleeding from his head."

Someone behind me noted there was a fire starting under the car. I looked up and saw the semi pitched down the canyon toward us, but not moving. Fortunately, a trucker dealt with the fire and the real help showed up soon to relieve me.

As I climbed back up the embankment, I saw two buses filled with teenagers looking down at all of this madness. Laid out flat next to the buses was a dead elk the size of a car, most likely the cause of the accident. And then it occurred to me both of my daughters were in the buses, as well as the children of my best friends.

That's when I realized the awesome responsibility we put on teachers and coaches on a typical day. On a school night in a dark canyon, miles from the nearest restroom, I organized calls to home, food issues, homework situations, and a bathroom break.

Nobody prepares you for this stuff. Marriage, kids, bills, life. I can quote Gilgamesh at length, but I don't know crap about life. So, a couple of times a week, I hide in my gym and let it go.

I used to work with a woman named Maxine. Maxine lives to follow rules. She doesn't put up Christmas stuff until Christmas Day because it's still Advent until the day of Christmas. Then, she puts up her stuff.

We all work with Maxines. If break starts at 10:15, they'll tell everyone you left at 10:14 and, "Well, I'm not going to say anything to anyone, but Dan John leaves at 10:14 and still returns to his desk with the rest of us."

There are times in our lives where we live like Maxine. If you're in school, your life is like Maxine's. The bell rings, the clock ticks, you move into one desk and back into another.

You eat breakfast in the morning (hell, someone might even make it for you), lunch at noon, and dinner in the early evening. You watch must-see TV and you know the characters on *Heroes* and *Lost*. Why? Because you watch those damn shows.

For people living in the world of regular hours, regular meals, and regular bowel movements, I have only one bit of advice: *planned spontaneity*.

The last thing you need in your training is more Maxine. How can you tell if you need a bit more randomness in your training? Look around the gym. If everybody there is part of the same group you see Monday, Wednesday and Friday from 4:00 to 5:30 and you're all doing the same workout, you need some spark.

You need some fun, some play. I know Monday, Wednesday and Friday are International Bench Press, Curl and Lat Pulldown Days, but let's juggle things up a bit, shall we?

Learn some new skills. Learn the snatch and clean and jerk. Sign up and compete in a Highland Games or Strongman contest. Learn some new lifts. Hey, there's an idea!

Now, someone always asks, "Dan, how do you train during track season?"

You see, I don't train. Not during track season. Instead, I storm into my home gym and "work out."

Please don't read this as workout. It's work out. I work out my anger. I work out my rage. I work out my fears.

One of the things I do involves my workout-randomizer trick. I take a single die (singular of dice) and I roll it three times. The die instantly changes my workout approach.

This is how I do it.

The Three Rolls

- Roll One: Lift of the Day
- Roll Two: The Program
- Roll Three: The Finisher

The First Roll: Lift of the day

Roll a one: Press
Roll a two: Squat
Roll a three: Snatch
Roll a four: Clean (or power curl)
Roll a five: Deadlift (any variation)
Roll a six: Clean and Jerk

The Second Roll: The Program

Roll a one: Litvinov Workout. Do eight reps with the lift, then sprint.

Roll a two: 5-3-2

Roll a three: 3 sets of 8 with a one-minute rest. Do two exercises with this workout. Front squat and overhead squat; bench press and incline… that kind of thing.

Roll a four: 3-3-2-1-1-1-1-1

Roll a five: Tabatas. Go light, light, light here! Twenty seconds of lifting, followed by ten seconds of rest for a total of eight circuits.

Roll a six: The Big Fifty-five. That's fifty-five reps of the lift you rolled. Fifty-five singles or three sets of ten plus five sets of five, whatever. Just make sure it adds up to fifty-five.

The Third Roll: The Finisher

    Roll a one: Sled sprints
    Roll a two: Sleds carrying a rock
    Roll a three: Rock runs
    Roll a four: Sleds with a heavy pack
    Roll a five: Sleds with a heavy pack carrying a rock
    Roll a six: Farmer walks to death!

Note: Feel free to do anything you like here. A lot of this depends on your available equipment.

If my math skills are right, you have 216 workouts here. If you want to do this three days a week, you might not repeat a workout for years! It's just the thing for people who live in a situation where there's a lot of structure.

But there are others who can benefit from this, too, like me during track season. Recently, my teams competed in six track meets in twelve days. That's six long bus rides — to the venue and back home — and six long track meets. That's enough chaos for anybody. The last thing I need in my life is more insanity.

During track season, I train three days a week. I do two exercises each workout. I rest one minute per set. I do three sets of eight. Yes, it's the most boring program the world has ever seen. Here's exactly what I do:

Day One: Monday

Power Clean and Press: 1 power clean and 8 presses

Three sets of eight with a one-minute rest between sets. If there's a single key to the program, it's the one-minute rest period. By strictly monitoring the rest period, and obviously keeping track of the weight, one can track progress.

Power Curls: 3 sets of 8, one-minute rest

Using a curl grip, slide the weight to just above the knees and curl-clean the bar. Let it come down under control. Again, get all eight reps in, don't change the weights, and monitor the rest period.

Finish with some kind of ab work.

Day Two: Wednesday

Power Clean and Front Squats: 1 power clean and 8 front squats

Once again, 3 sets of 8 with a one-minute rest. Stay tall in the front squats and keep your elbows high.

Overhead Squats: 3 sets of 8, one-minute rest

Using the wide snatch-grip, lock the elbows with the weight overhead, and squat down. Athletes who do this exercise will not only develop flexibility, balance and leg strength, but also an incredibly strong lower back.

Again, finish with some kind of ab work.

Day Three: Friday

Whip Snatches: 3 sets of 8 with a one-minute rest

With a wide snatch-grip, stand up and hold the bar at crotch level. Dip and snatch the bar overhead. Continue for eight reps. You'll be surprised how quickly this exercise can get into your blood. If you want big traps, this is the king.

Clean-grip Snatches: 3 sets of 8, one-minute rest

With a clean-grip, stand up and dip the bar to your knees. Then explode up, driving the bar in one basic movement overhead. It's like a clean and press, well, without the clean.

Ab work if you wish.

I get bored looking at it, but, it's exactly what I need during my crazy times. If life is crazy, you can't have a crazy workout, too. That's my knock against most perfect training programs; rarely do they consider the life circumstances — social, nutritional support, just plain reality — of the trainee.

That's the genius of one-set-to-failure machine training. It's a perfect do-this answer to a crazy life. Nautilus and Curves really seem to resonate with people who want to work out, but can't afford one more drop of free will.

Sadly, I can't use machines. Um, let me say this nicely: I have testicles… I can't use machines. Sorry.

None of that really answers the question of how I use weights to work out life's issues. It involves a bar, a kettlebell, or a sled. I have three workout ideas that will serve you well when you need to vent with weights.

The 100-rep Challenge

I once entered a friendly 100-reps competition. Nothing to the rules: 100 singles with an exercise. Not ten sets of ten, mind you… 100 singles.

The first time I tried it, I did squat snatches with 165 pounds. That was insane. I lost about six pounds the few days after the attempt. I think most of it was skin off my hands.

Another time, I power cleaned 205 for a hundred. Another, I clean and jerked 185 pounds. I also front squatted 255 for a hundred singles. Unrack, squat, rack, rinse and repeat.

It will take you a few hours. You will be changed.

Ten Minutes of…

The next workout is based on the sport of kettlebell lifting. As I type this, I'm reminded of a recent Saturday when the North American Kettlebell Federation held its national championships here in Utah. Without knowing what I was in for physically, I entered the event.

It's a model of simplicity. Grab a kettlebell. Snatch it as many times as you can with one hand and, without putting the 'bell on the shoulder, ground, or any other support, switch hands and continue… for ten minutes.

The agony of time is apparent very quickly. I'd catch an occasional peek at the timer and wonder how right Einstein was about relativity. Every so often, my chest would heave out a sigh that came right from my soul. Yet, upon finishing, my mind was clear; the clutter had fled.

You can model this by taking a dumbbell or barbell, picking a big move, and doing it for as long as you can. How about ten minutes of jumping jacks? Oh, the next day… those are your calves. Enjoy walking.

I'm thinking an empty Olympic bar and ten minutes of clean and press just might be the answer to all questions.

Fat Loss in Four Minutes, Revisited

My most misunderstood article of all time is my Tabata front squat workout. It involved time. It involved hard work. After 4,000 emails asking, "Dan, if this is so good, why not do it every day?" I began headbutting my computer screen. I did it until I saw pixels flying around my head.

The answer, of course, is this: Did you ever front squat for four minutes with ninety-five pounds with twenty seconds work and ten seconds of rest? No? Right, because then you'd know why you don't do this every day! You might be able to do it if the fate of the world was in your hands, but short of that, once every two weeks is plenty.

I decided to simplify it a bit. Now I recommend this.

> Front Squat for 8 reps *(quality, deep reps, please)*
> Rest exactly ten seconds
> Front Squat for 8 reps
> Rest exactly ten seconds
> Front Squat for 8 reps
> Rest exactly ten seconds
> Front Squat for 8 reps
> Rest exactly ten seconds
> Front Squat for 8 reps
> Rest exactly ten seconds
> Front Squat for 8 reps
> Rest exactly ten seconds
> Front Squat for 8 reps
> Rest exactly ten seconds
> Front Squat for 8 reps

Now, keel over.

The floor will feel cool. The ground is your friend. Love the ground. Recover long enough to send me an email saying, "I think I should do this every day."

Goals? How about 135 on the bar and deep reps? I'd like to see the video evidence of doing 225 with this variation. I've seen sixty-five pounds nearly kill a man.

That's the sad thing about these workouts. They don't take long. You don't see tempo mentioned. You don't worry about whether or not the rhomboids are working through the full range of motion. You just try to survive.

And that's the lesson here, I guess; you try to survive. *The Big Book of Life* doesn't cover dead elk next to school buses.

Sometimes, you have to wing it. As I held that man's skull flap, I didn't worry about my torn calluses anymore.

Oh, I had to deal with all of this. I had to work out some issues with a barbell and a quiet gym. For the record, I did front squats.

Twenty-Four

A Religious Studies Professor's Review of HIT

I'd only been in college a few days when I met her. She was a young lady who had "entertained" the bulk of our university's football team. Six months later we bumped into each other after she had gone to the Middle East — on her parents' orders — to a "retreat" that involved long hours of work, little sleep, and a lot of childhood songs. We call that brainwashing, but regardless, she informed me I was going to hell because I drank beer. A year or so later, at a party, she had a semester's worth of tuition stuffed up her nose in the form of cocaine.

After I graduated from college, we bumped into each other at a friend of a friend of a friend's wedding. She again told me, because of her new religion, I was going to hell because I drank beer.

Does it sound familiar? Do you know anybody like that? For those of us in the iron game, if you last long enough, you're going to meet people like her at every gym, spa and fitness center where you train for more than a few days. (Maybe that's why I train in my garage.) You know the kind, people who leap from one religion of lifting to another, back and forth, to and fro, who never really make any true progress. They quote research, studies, facts, graphs and testimony from the new church of lifting, and fill internet forums with reams (bytes?)

of inflamed monologues on the ills of all other training paradigms, and the need for one set of squats every three weeks to achieve full muscular development. A few months later, in the same gym, they can be found doing sets of thirty quarter-squats because of a book they found at Barnes and Noble.

The world of lifting, strength training, and sports conditioning has come a long way since the early years when lifting was considered one step from pedophilia… or, at least, an example of rampant narcissism and a sure road to bestiality.

When I first started lifting weights during the Nixon Administration, most of the girls in my school asked if it would make me musclely. I certainly had hoped it would, but back in the day we had little guidance beyond monthly magazines featuring pictures of Mr. Someplace. Few athletes ventured into the weightroom save the throwers from track and field and a few football players like Green Bay Packer Jim Taylor and Billy Cannon, the Louisiana State University Heisman Trophy winner. Basketball players always worried it would, and I quote, "ruin my shot." It's hard to believe the change in just a few decades.

Most people who train with weights will never have to deal with questions like, "Won't that make you muscle-bound?" With grannies wearing spandex waiting their turns to use the adductor machines, gyms now cater to nearly everyone. Yet a couple of things you can usually bet on are the area near the squat rack will be dusty and the Olympic bars will be used for curls. We can only be thankful for a roomful of aerobicizied kickboxing nymphettes in clear view so it's easier to keep our eyes off of Granny doing innies and outties.

And, like all institutions, we're now experiencing the schisms. A few minutes of studying the internet forums dedicated to lifting will let you in on a level of hatred and name-calling not seen since the middle of the Reformation.

To really experience the battle lines, write something negative — anywhere — about HIT. Your intelligence, your courage and your real relationship with your father will all be put into question if you make one or two comments on High Intensity Training.

Now, we have to be specific here. We are talking not about training with intensity at a high level, like sprinting, the Olympic lifts, the power lifts, full-contact football or gymnastics; we're talking about the religion called High Intensity Training (HIT). It can appear under many guises and forms, but like many cults, its definition is impossible to pin down.

Many in the HIT world are not unlike those who have recently experienced a life-changing relationship with their Creator. With my full-time careers as both an administrator and professor in Religious Studies and Religious Education, I consistently engage people who are converts. It's a rare person who's recently converted to another faith tradition or who's recently re-embraced the faith of our fathers who can avoid acting in one or two predictable patterns:

"I'm right. I used to think I was right, but I was wrong then. Now, I am right — and you are wrong to think I am not right now. Even if I argued earlier about being right, now you must understand I was wrong then, but now I am right."

"No, I can't define it. But, you must understand I understand it completely."

In religious studies, I understand the issue perfectly. To move from one way of life to another, to learn the dietary habits, the manners, the movements, the dress, and acquiesce to demands that the believer abandon much of the past and travel along a very different path is similar to the story HIT converts follow.

Let's summarize the usual story.

"For years, I have been pushing the squats, learning the cleans, hitting the iron and generally blaming my parents (genetics), my supplier (the local nutrition center versus a guy named Tony with a supply line to some third-world steroid dealership), and my gym (not enough equipment, the wrong line of machines, not allowed to use chalk). Then, I came across this article/forum/book that talked to me: It's not your fault… everything you know is wrong."

Why do I know this? I've been there. I'd finished my first decade as a lifter and thrower competing at the national level as an Olympic lifter and a Division One discus thrower. My joints hurt, my body ached, and my tummy hung over my belly. I'd recently started coaching high school football and I'd been invited to my first coaches' clinic. The Saturday morning speaker, a noted name in what was then known as Nautilus Training, took one of the attending coaches through a quick weight workout of leg curls, leg extensions and squats. The coach was unable to stand up with the forty-five-pound bar to finish his sets. His heart rate was off the charts and he was still limping the next morning.

Obviously, I did everything wrong. Here was the answer: Rather than expending my time and energy adding more and more plates to the bar, I needed to train briefer, but harder. I became a convert instantly.

For two years, I paid an extra fee at a local fitness center to use the Nautilus machines. I followed the advice of every book I could find on the topic. I ended up with two people standing on the stack of plates on the leg press machine; I mastered one-arm-down and two-arms-up lifting, and spent the exact same amount of time on calf flexion as I did hip extension.

At the same time, I continued my career as a discus thrower. As the weeks turned into months and into years, I noticed I'd become a good golfer rather than a better thrower: My scores were going down… fast. I called the experts on a regular basis and received two basic answers; I was training too hard and/or my discus throwing was not biomechanically correct.

I'm proud to say I'm one of the few people who've been studied in the discus on two separate occasions by a three-dimensional video study where I became a series of dots on a computer screen in X, Y and Z coordinates. (One researcher told me to start on a cycle of steroids to see if that would help, not great advice considering where he worked.) I took the first expert's advice: I trained less. I threw less, but with the best technical style I could accomplish, yet the distance still suffered.

Like many converts who feel they've been lied to, I left the church of machine training. I gave away a stack of glossy books all promising "Titanic Trapeziuses (Trapezii?) in Ten Days," and I went back to my roots. I started Olympic lifting again… oh, the soreness… and relatively soon, my discus was flying back over fifty-five meters.

I've shared this story with many HIT trainees, and the most common response is simply this:

"That wasn't HIT."

"What?"

"No, that isn't HIT."

"One set to momentary muscular failure isn't HIT?"

"Right. It is one set to momentary muscular failure, but it can be several sets, too, or not."

What?

Exactly. One of the things that leads most High Intensity Training forums to constantly eat their young is no one can define (H)it.

I've followed the long and distinguished career of Dr. Ken Leistner (including his late 1960s' writings in *Strength and Health*) and fully agree with his approach to HIT, with his deadly heavy high-repetition squats, straight-leg deadlifts, dips and farmer walks. But when he posted his famous twenty-three reps with 407, he was attacked by the high intensity world. "That isn't right, you go too fast… you go too heavy… you…"

There's a wonderful scene in the Burt Reynolds movie, *Semi-Tough*, where the characters argue about the latest psychobabble. It goes something like this:

"If you understand it, then you don't understand it, but if you don't understand it, you understand it."

"Understand what?"

"It."

Welcome to the world of High Intensity Training. When I got a nasty email from a HITter complaining I didn't understand "it," I wrote him back to say one of the world's most famous HITters guided me through it. He responded — and I'm not kidding — "Well, he doesn't understand it, either!"

Listen carefully here: HIT works… for about six weeks. In fact, everything works for about six weeks, but that's not the point. My good friend, Charles Staley, was recently dared by a writing-challenged individual to put the Staley Method up against the "System"… for six weeks. If you have a career that's only going to last the next six weeks, go ahead and do anything you like.

The subtle, secret truth few in the world of strength training want to admit is this: For six weeks or so, everything works. All the strength-training books and articles on the dusty shelves of Portland State University, Arizona State University, Utah State University, Dennison College and several other schools I wasted so much of my life flipping through; all the prime movers of the isometric craze of the early 1960s, as well as the key figures in the Nautilus movement with whom I talked… they're *all* right! They're right for about six weeks.

Again, if your career is only going to last the next six weeks, do anything you like!

The bottom line is this: I'm going to receive death threats over writing this, but it all comes down to competition. One of the HIT mantras is "We build strength; we don't demonstrate it." Unfortunately, demonstrating strength and skill may be the only true measure of training programs!

I've competed in countless Highland Games where young men in the crowd wearing muscle shirts have asked me, "What muscles does the caber build?" They just don't get it. Serratus muscles don't live in isolation when you pick a 130-pound piece of wood off the ground at the vertical. To toss a caber, tackle a runner, or jam the ball, you have to demonstrate some serious levels of strength. All the glossy before-and-after shots in the world aren't going to get the shot past sixty feet.

Athletic competition also has standards. A sixty-foot throw in the shot, at any level, is an excellent mark. Snatching bodyweight is a standard that demonstrates the lifter is no longer a novice. The HIT reliance on machines misses the whole point: Save for the small confines of your gym, nobody in the world gives a damn that you moved from "P" to "Q" on the leg press stack. Honestly, nobody cares. A 400-bench press is a quality lift for anyone, anywhere, at anytime.

Competitive athletes, in my estimation, understand strength training better than anyone else who lifts in the gym. It's a simple formula: Did X or Y help me compete? If the answer is yes, we keep doing it. If it doesn't, it's dropped… discarded. This process is not exact and many of the things tossed aside may have value, but competition rarely allows the athlete to experiment too long in a blind search down the wrong training program.

Everything works, no matter how crazy, for about three to six weeks. Even those miracle strength devices on television that guarantee the loss of several dress sizes work, but your results may not be the same as a Los Angeles model's results.

Even though everything works, research is sometimes valuable. However, because everything works, research findings will always come to certain basic conclusions: Less food and more exercise is good for people who want to lose fat and training with resistance tends to make people stronger. As such, beware of the studies with untrained people getting stronger; anything helps the untrained.

Measure your training with something outside of the gym. I know several women who use old clothes as a gauge. Hey, if you can fit in your wedding dress after six months of training, you're doing something right! If you can finally dunk, maybe you're on the right track, too.

Finally, and the most important: Look at your goals and lifting career outside a quick fix. It's fun, I agree, to buy into the concepts of "Tighter Tushies in Two Days," "Terrible Pythons of Power in Three Weeks," and "Totally Tremendous Thunder Thighs in Four Weeks." There's no question short-term fixes work and provide a nice shot of enthusiasm into a training year. But keep your eye on the long-term.

There are no Great Mysteries to strength training and body recomposition. That's the realm of religion and theology.

Twenty-Five

New Associations, New Muscle

I've been lifting weights since my Aunt Florence died back in the early 1960s. She left my brothers and me a little bit of money, so we invested in a Sears Ted Williams Bar and started lifting weights. Our technique was poor and our programs were worse, but we were lifting weights.

The bar came with an instruction manual and it outlined a variety of exercises that included three bentover-row variations and about a dozen different ways to press. There was little in the way of safety instruction because when I was growing up, when you got hurt it was always your fault.

Now, forty years or so later, I think I'm starting to get the hang of some of this stuff, although I still press and I still blame myself when I get hurt.

There were some truths when I first started training. First, you only lifted three days a week. Something mysterious would happen to you if you did more. I believe the term was overwork. According to my father, of course that was impossible.

Second, the key in training was simply how much you could put over your head. There was one number and one number only: Waddya press? That changed, too, you might know.

Finally, a high-protein diet was the answer to any and all problems. Carbs were bad and fats were the juicy parts of steaks. So, three days a week we'd all convene in the garage and press,

press, and press, then drink a bunch of glasses of milk. Things have changed. Some of it is for the better, but not all of it.

A few years ago, I went to a workshop about something or other and I learned something that really opened my eyes concerning the strength and fitness game: associations. In other words, when I'm talking about something as basic as strength, you literally might be reading something vastly different than what I'm thinking.

Okay, what does that mean? If I say sugar and you answer spice, we have a simple association. Go ahead, try it: black and white, night and day, rich and poor, and on and on. Which is why when I say leg work, I think squats while some think innie-and-outie machine.

In this workshop, we learned a trick advertisers use to come up with ideas to break those simple associations. I tried it with two willing victims — my daughter, Lindsay, and my neighbor, Vance.

I asked them to come up with as many associations as they could between French fry and airplane. Now, I had my own thoughts, but I wasn't at all ready for their answers. Lindsay noted you need oil for both the fries and the plane. Vance mentioned you salt a runway in a snowstorm and you add salt to your fries.

From two words, we began the process of bringing in new associations: oil and salt. I sat back and tried to think of links between these two. My mind leaped to the Olive Garden here in Murray. When we were seated last time to celebrate our trip to the state championship, the young waiter poured olive oil in a bowl, lightly salted and peppered the oil, then added balsamic vinegar. My neighbor thought you use salt to get the engine oil off of the driveway, so we were stuck in the food-and-machine mode around my house.

I have a real world example of this. My brother-in-law, Geoff Hemingway, brought home an idea that sounds awful at first, but is a pure delight. We all like peanut butter. We all like hamburgers. Geoff's solution was to swipe some peanut butter on the hamburger patty. Yep, it sounds awful, but it tastes great.

That's the key to using associations: We need to take two good ideas and combine them in a way to make a great idea. For the record, T-bone steaks and peanut butter are not as good as we hoped.

The value in this process may or may not be evident, but if we take a look at most people's training, we may find they're literally stuck in a box. Certainly, there's a value to doing an exercise over and over again and perhaps even using the same weights, but most people do the exact same weight workout over and over and over again.

In college, when everyone was doing Arnold's program, you could set your watch by the way some guys lifted. At 3:01, back squat 135 times ten, screaming, "It's all you." At 3:09, after a vigorous leg stretching and checking out the biceps in the mirror, a back-off set with 115 pounds for ten. From 3:15 to 5:00, as many sets of EZ-bar curls as possible. That was leg day.

Associations are literally what run the fitness industry. Just flip through a women's magazine at the store. Preteen girls or anorexia patients are often the models for the perfect body. This association leads some to think thin is popular, thin is sexy, thin is the only way to be in America.

Covert Baily wrote a book called *Fit or Fat*. Not long after the book came out, articles were written called *Fit and Fat*, arguing it's possible to have a healthy cardiovascular system and a high level of adipose tissue. The association for many people regarding fitness is thin first.

In strength training, it's usually just big. I can't tell you how many times I've been told the following, "Dan, it's funny you throw far because those other guys are bigger than you." Yeah, funny.

We can use associations to really up the level of our training intensity. In some ways all of my little ideas have only been an attempt of combining two common training practices and smashing them into a new idea. The lessons of a wrist injury became the basis of one of my favorite training methods, one arm at a time.

I've later used this as an in-season training method for a number of athletes, including baseball pitchers. Simply train one arm one day, train the other arm two days later, and finish the week with a whole-body workout. I mixed the lessons of an injury into a worthwhile in-season training program.

When I first heard about the Tabata protocol from Clarence Bass, my first thought was, I'm not jumping on an exercycle. The original program was based on cycling. I mean, exercycles are like lunges; it's okay if your girlfriend or your mom does them, but… you know.

So, I attempted to do military presses with them. The first three minutes were awful and the last minute I discovered I could barely finish a single in each twenty-second cluster. A week later, I tried the Tabata front-squat workout and discovered the single best quick workout I've ever tried.

These are just two examples of taking a common idea — one-armed training or the Tabata protocol — and tweaking it just enough to discover something that radically changes my athletes. The two single-limb sessions allow the athletes to maintain strength and continue to provide the protection weightlifting brings a thrower without beating up his nervous system or further depleting recovery. The Tabata front squat workout hits the cardiovascular system harder than any traditional workout (jogging or whatever) and is probably the second hardest thing I know behind the 400-meter sprint.

With my busy schedule, I found myself in the past year floundering around without enough time to train. What I'm about to say is odd, but some will agree: I spend all day in a weightroom, follow it with several hours at track practice, then help a few people at my home gym. In other words, I'm around weights and fitness and training tools literally all day long, but don't have time to train.

Some of you know what I mean. Of course, some of you poor bastards are sitting at a computer screen at work hoping your boss won't look over your shoulder while you scroll through workout forum threads. I spend my day in shorts and a T-shirt worrying about whether we should do front squats with one set of chains or two. Although not nearly as fun as using an Excel spreadsheet to determine whether or not the Henderson account will have enough widgets for the big project in Salinas, I make myself enjoy it.

One thing I can't do is coach myself. The problem is this: First, I don't need to do my athletes' workouts. They need more repetitions and more volume to learn the movements. Second, at fifty, I have needs slightly different than those of a teenage football player.

I need to train and train hard, but I need to mix things up to keep my enthusiasm high. To do this, I need to listen to others, then adapt these great ideas into something I can do and keep fired up about doing it again in a day or so. This is the key to changing one's associations.

Let's make it simple. There are basically ten different movements you should do as a human:

- Vertical Push

- Vertical Pull

- Horizontal Push

- Horizontal Pull

- The Squatting Motion

- The Posterior Chain (I call these deadlifts)

- The Anterior Chain (sit-ups, leg raises)

- The Twist or Torque Moves

- The Total-body Explosion Exercises (If you're limited by time, these are the ones to do.)

I lump all the single-limb movements into one group. Certainly, these are important, but don't equate a lunge to a 600-pound squat, thank you very much.

Next, we have a variety of tools you can use to do any of these ten movements within a workout. From bodyweight to machines to kettlebells, dumbbells and barbells, the options available to you are unlimited. This is the problem for most people. Push-ups are relegated to high school P.E. or boot camp; Olympic lifting is for that thing every four years, and dumbbells are for biceps.

What I've discovered recently is I'm the biggest offender of this method of thinking. So, I've consciously decided to radically attack my associations. Let's go through a couple of ideas first, then look at a program I'm working on now.

The One-arm Bench Press

I first tried this exercise after I broke my wrist. Later, I discovered Ethan Reeve over at Wake Forest had come up with a standard. He asks his athletes to bench press 125 pounds with one arm for five, then match it with the other arm. I laughed (silently) and thought, "Hey, I bench over this or that, so this'll be cake."

I tried it. I failed. The next morning my abs felt like I'd been in an auto accident. What was going on here? By shifting all the balance to one arm, my body had to literally take up the slack… and I wasn't ready for it.

Kettlebell Snatch

The same problem hit me when I took on the kettlebell challenge. As a guy who's snatched close to a hundred-fifty-percent of bodyweight, how could a little seventy-pound 'bell hurt me? At rep seventy-four, my hand ripped and a piece of my skin landed ten feet in front of me. My hands were purple and my heart, lungs and back were trashed.

Barbell Rollouts

I love those damn five-dollar ab wheels.

I loved them when they came out in the '60s, I loved them when they returned with the advent of the internet, and I love them as my favorite anterior-chain exercise.

Someone told me I should try them with a barbell. I figured, it's a damn wheel, right? The weight shouldn't matter. Well, I was wrong. Rolling 135 back is nothing like rolling back the cute little ab wheel I bought for five bucks. It feels like exercise, for God's sake!

Now, with thanks to Alwyn and Pavel, let's look at a recent workout of mine that honestly attempts to add new associations:

Warm-up
(an Alywn Cosgrove complex)
With 95 pounds on the bar:
Power Snatch for 5
Overhead Squat for 5
Back Squat for 5
Good Morning for 5
Behind the Neck Push Jerk for 5
Bentover Row for 5
Rest 60 seconds and repeat for a total of four sets

Although I work the squat motion, horizontal pulling, the total-body-explosion motion, the posterior chain, and the vertical press, you'll note I still need more of the pulling or pushing. However, my heart rate goes through the roof doing this and I feel like I've lubed the joints pretty well.

The workout itself is a variation of Pavel's *Enter the Kettlebell* workout. To build up my lousy shoulders after years of throwing, I recently decided to take his advice and work the one-arm clean and press along with the pull-up. It's the rungs-and-ladders workout, and it looks easy on paper.

Rungs and Ladders Workout
With the seventy-pound kettlebell, I do the following:

With the left arm: One clean and press
With the right arm: One clean and press
One pull-up

With the left arm: A clean and press followed by another clean and press
With the right arm: A clean and press followed by another clean and press
Two pull-ups
With the left arm: A clean and press followed by another clean and press followed by another clean and press
With the right arm: A clean and press followed by another clean and press followed by another clean and press
Three pull-ups

After a short rest, I repeat this for a total of five sets — correctly these are called ladders.

After years of competing in strength sports, the tonic effect of this workout seems to allow me to keep on keeping on. But again, although this takes of vertical pulls, I still need a little more.

I've been experimenting with a very interesting little double lately. I'm mixing the barbell ab rollout with the one-arm bench press. As a thrower, I need abs and I need some rotational work, and this little combo might be just the thing I need to keep in the game.

Abdominal and Rotational Assistance
135-pound barbell rollout for 8 *(and no, I don't think going heavier is the key here)*
Left-arm kettlebell bench press for 8
Right-arm kettlebell bench press for 8

I do this circuit for a total of three sets. Okay, three sets of eight… that isn't exactly a new paradigm for associations, but it's just fine for my needs.

Finisher: Timed Kettlebell Snatches

Finally, I finish off with a timed set of kettlebell snatches. How long? Good question. I can either roll a pair of dice and use the total as the number of minutes I go, or simply try to go max-left followed by max-right, and call it a day.

What's the point to all of this?

1. There are literally hundreds of lifts and variations, but most of us normally use just a handful. By simply experimenting with any new idea and program, you can break out of a training rut. You start each day with a hundred sit-ups? Great, now start each day with a hundred pull-ups.

2. We all know we need to change our grips in pushes and presses and maybe even our methods of squatting, but I'd like to ask you to consider changing your equipment choices, too. Try switching out barbells for dumbbells, machines for kettlebells, exercise balls for some damn weights.

3. As a coach, I have to ask you to make sure you cover the basic moves in most of your workouts. If today is a push day, play around with some variations of squats or pushes and just see what happens. Do everything one-handed or one-legged. Just see what happens. It's okay to experiment!

4. Over the long run, the more you experiment, try new things and master movements, the better off your

physique will be. Moreover, this will lead to better joint health and more enthusiasm for coming back to play for more of this game.

Sure, this stuff is serious, but it's fun serious stuff!

Twenty-Six

Coach Pain's Slosh Pipe

The day after I came home from my annual two-week vacation at Discus Camp in Ohio, I helped my young friend, Sarah, move into her new apartment.

I was still gassed from training four sessions a day for two weeks, but I have those important skills necessary for being a mover: I'm Mongo, Blazing Saddles strong and I can walk backwards up a flight of stairs while holding just about anything. Sarah is only in her mid-twenties, and hasn't amassed a fortune in furniture, so it was an easy move. The only hard part was continually asking people to get out of the way. You see, Sarah had about thirty-five friends and family members show up to help.

I don't know how much she makes as a teacher, but it is hard to ignore the amount of social capital she has in her life account. The term social capital might not be familiar, but I'm sure you know the concept. When your water line breaks and a bunch of people show up to help you dig it out at three in the morning — none from the city water services — you have a lot of social capital.

It's those social strings and social ties that go deep through the people you know. So much so, in fact, you may at times ignore what a great resource you have at your grasp. If your dad is a plumber, your brother is an electrician, your sister runs a hair salon and they all live within a few miles of you, your life is probably much easier than most others.

And now you know my secret: I have great social capital in the fitness and lifting business. When I was struggling hourly on the Velocity Diet, I called the man who invented the diet, Chris Shugart. If I have a problem with stretching or general physical preparedness (GPP), I call Pavel Tsatsouline. My post-Velocity Diet fat-loss program was a gift from Alwyn Cosgrove.

Yeah, okay, I guess you could say I'm bragging here, but what most people don't know is some of my best ideas come from a group of guys who come out to Ohio with me every summer. We share insights, train together, and occasionally come up with something brilliant. This year, Greg Henger brought the slosh pipe. It's relatively cheap, under twenty dollars, and easy to make, even with someone from Utah on hand to help.

Many of my long-time readers will recognize the names of those who show up at camp. Among them is Mike Rosenberg, the inventor of the Rosenberg Bars. These are the thick-pipe farmer bars that rehabilitated my grip after my two wrist surgeries. I'll never forget what the surgeon told me in 2001, "You will probably never be able to lift weights again."

Three months later, I competed in an Olympic lifting meet. Why? Well, the fact that I'm stupid played a big part, but the thick-bar farmer walks allowed me to work my grip without any stress on my recovering pieces of bone. When you slip the Joe Garcia handles on the Rosenberg Bars, you have a standard farmer bar.

That's the essence of social capital right there, folks. Friends helping friends sweat blood. It's a beautiful thing.

Also visiting us in Ohio was young Lonnie Wade from Vermont. He comes from the land of Tree Tappers, but we allow him in our group anyway. When my dad retired and moved back to Vermont, Lonnie was the little boy across the street. Today, three decades later, Lonnie is an excellent throws and lifting coach and still brings his heart and soul to every training session.

Which brings us back to Greg. Greg is from West Virginia, and really, what more need be said? I have a theory all men in the universe can be classified into two groups depending on which of the following questions they answer yes to:

1. *Have you ever partied with cheerleaders?*
2. *Have you ever been bitten by a snake?*

Asked both of these questions, Greg's famous answer was, "Venomous or non-venomous?"

For the record, no snake has ever bitten me.

I have reported our exploits of idiocy in other places, for example, the famous contest where we held a 175-pound steel pipe in the Zercher position, dragging an eighty-five-pound sled uphill to see who could go the highest.

This year, however, Greg brought the Slosh Pipe.

It's a four- or six-inch diameter PVC pipe with the ends capped, filled with water about two-thirds full. Filling it all the way up defeats the purpose, trust me.

Our pipe stands nine feet, four inches, and weighs about thirty-eight pounds. I'm begging you not to ask me about PVC pipe cleaners or glues or cutting or anything like that. If you can't figure out how to put this together yourself, ask your friendly neighbor guy and he'll take care of you. That's what I did for my pipe here at home. I can give you one piece of advice, though: Cap one end first, then fill it with water, then cap the other end. Any other method won't work too well.

The darnedest thing about the slosh pipe is this: The water doesn't stay still and behave. It sloshes. Back and forth. Uncontrollably. Just picking up the pipe and holding it quickly becomes the Core Workout from Hell.

Now, as you probably know, I despise the word core because it has become such a grab bag term for the fitness industry, like functional and fit and weight loss. These terms get tossed around by the nice ladies at the spa like NFL strength coaches and, really, with apologies to Wittgenstein, nobody knows what we mean when we say these words.

The first day after trying the slosh pipe, my cobra muscles were killing me. Basically, those are all the upper body muscles you flex when you imitate a cobra. My serratus muscles felt like someone had ripped them off my ribs. What did I do the first day to get this sore? One exercise with a thirty-eight-pound pipe, a Zercher carry for distance.

I've been around for a while, and I have a fair amount of experience with dragging and carrying stuff for general training. I was stunned by the soreness the next day. Remember, this is only thirty-eight pounds! We had a number of athletes who couldn't (wouldn't?) pick it up the next day.

The Zercher carry alone might be a great complement to the training of anybody who fights, hits, tackles, throws, shoves or bangs around with other humans during a game. Greg Henger, whose nickname, by the way, is Coach Pain, said walking with the slosh pipe is like wrestling a python. I've never actually wrestled a python, so I'll just have to take Greg's word for it, he being from West Virginia and all.

For those interested in fat loss, walking a slosh pipe for a specified distance is like being in a wrestling match. Your heart and lungs will be pumping as hard as possible while practically every muscle in your body will be straining to lumber ahead. The slosh pipe could become a fat-loss sensation. Jump on the wagon now, folks! Somebody will be hawking these on late-night television before the month is out.

Trying to do curls or deadlifts with this sadistic nine-foot beastie is a great way to get kicked in the face by the laws of physics. I can't think of a better way to train for a change of pace than a fun workout of just picking up and moving the slosh pipe.

A quick hint if you choose to put the slosh pipe overhead: Start with the pipe caber-style. This way, all the water will be, for a few seconds, on one end of the pipe. The pipe feels amazingly light with all the water at one end. This will soon change.

We found doing military presses with the slosh pipe as taxing as doing near-maxes in the exercise. Walking with the pipe overhead was a full-body workout and a ruthless gut-buster.

You might say it's a hardcore core workout.

The slosh pipe will take about an hour to make, including the run to the hardware store. You will need to cut the flanges off the ends, if you have them, clean and glue the ends and cap them. Don't be too heroic and try to use a longer piece, and be careful of using the slosh pipe in a confined area. You may think you can keep it under control, but you can't.

The slosh pipe. The nine-foot pillar of pain. Walk with it. Carry it. Lift it. Enjoy the agony.

Social capital is one of the least appreciated aspects of economics. In education circles, social capital is considered the key to a great institution… all those hidden benefits of knowing this person or that person and what they can do for the school.

Begin the process of mining your social capital in the fitness and lifting game. The crazy guy at the gym might just be me or one of my friends. And those lunatics running up a hill with a large piece of PVC pipe just might be on to something.

Twenty-Seven

Lessons from Southwood

About a week ago, the loudspeaker came on towards the end of my all-female weightlifting class, "Teachers, go into lockdown immediately. This is *not* a drill." If you've lived on another planet for the last twenty years, you might not know what this means. But every student and teacher knew what was going on — we had an armed intruder.

For an hour, we sat in total silence, hiding from windows and doors. In my mind, I thought of my children, my God-children, and the friends and family who were also hiding throughout the building. It turned out the gun was only a life-like Airsoft pellet gun. The parents of the kid later argued to the media the school had "over-reacted." A few days later, in Finland, the story was tragically different and many students were killed. Over-reaction? I think not.

My daughter, Kelly, later told me the kids had been discussing in which room it would've been best to wait it all out. It turns out students were sobbing throughout the hour and many kids melted down, almost in turns. Well, nobody cried in the weightroom. Certainly my physical size helped, but I have to argue there was something else: I train warriors in the weightroom.

The girls had just finished one of the best workouts I know, and these girls have been transformed by this training program. Let me share with you the Southwood workout and its cousin, the Big Five: Five by Five.

Every so often, I'll get an email from a high school coach struggling to teach a group of kids to lift weights. The emails often sound like the task of getting kids to lift is insurmountable. Some of the coaches sound like they need a miracle-worker to come in and exorcize the student body before they begin to exercise.

I always argue back to these fine men and women that it can be done… easily and inexpensively. I can't claim any credit for the following program; I'm indebted to Mr. Dave Freeman, my ninth grade physical education coach for making us do this.

After eight years at St. Veronica's School, I transferred to Southwood to begin junior high. It was a helluva transition. From Irish nuns to public school is big enough, but I was also going to play football. At 118 pounds of pure nothing, it was obvious to everyone I needed to lift weights.

It was at this time I was introduced to Southwood's lifting program. In a portable building, the school had outlaid about fifteen of those cement-filled weightlifting sets everyone from my generation remembers as their first weights.

Mr. Freeman spent little time explaining the rep-and-set system of eight, six, four, because everybody except me knew what to do. That's part of the brilliance of the program. You learn it once, and then you lift. Not exactly rocket science, but who needs rocket science on the football field?

The program was very simple. First, groups of four boys were given a bar. The bars ranged from very light — maybe twenty-five pounds — up to nearly a hundred pounds. Each cohort of boys would lift one at a time, put the bar down, and then the next boy would lift. The four would constantly move from lifter to watcher — the bar never stopped. The three sets, explained in just a moment, wouldn't take very long. In fact, it was hard to catch our breath in time for the next set.

First set: 8 reps
Second set: 6 reps
Third set: 4 reps

The goal was also clear-cut: When you got all eighteen reps, you added weight. If you started with a bar that was too light, you'd be bumped up to the next weight and a stronger group in the next workout. Of course, actual variations could include making an entirely new group with more weight, too — whatever was necessary to make the group work together.

The program involved four lifts.

Power Clean
Military Press
Front Squat
Bench Press

Each lift was done in the eight, six, four rep format. The bar was cleaned (once) for the set of military presses, and the bar was also cleaned (once) for the front squats. So, each workout the athlete cleaned the bar from ground to chest twenty-two times. If, as some people believe, the power clean is the king of the exercises, that's a lot of reps with the king!

To hurry up the training (as if necessary) there were times when Mr. Freeman had us combine the power clean and military presses. One clean and one press, repeated for a total of eight reps. This was done with a lighter weight. One could also do the front squats after the clean and presses, too. I've only done this once, and it was an amazing cardiovascular workout.

Each day to warm up, we ran two laps and an obstacle course. The two laps were about 600 meters. The obstacle course had a wall, various upper-body challenges, and some balance-walking. All in all, this wasn't a bad program.

The Southwood Program

To be performed three days a week in the weightroom

Power Clean, 8-6-4 reps
Military Press, 8-6-4 reps
Front Squat, 8-6-4 reps
Bench Press, 8-6-4 reps

As I began coaching, I adapted this workout several times. One thing I've returned to with training groups is we no longer use the racks on the bench press. Instead, I have two spotters deadlift the weight and bring it over the head of the athlete.

I discovered young athletes don't set their shoulders right when they get a lift off, but naturally grab the barbell correctly when two spotters raise the bar over their eyes. Also, this method insures proper spotting, because you simply don't have time to start doing something stupid.

There are three basic methods for doing the Southwood workout. The first, or the Classic, as we called it, is to use one bar with one weight for all four exercises. What holds the athlete back on this variation is the military press.

The upside of this variation, and this is something to think about, is the athletes aren't afraid to go deep with the lighter weight in the front squat. Since depth is more important than weight in the early learning process, this classic variation might be the best.

However, the kids really know they can do much more in the bench press. I usually find them doing lots of extra sets on their own after the formal workout is over. I don't see the issue of athletes doing extra work on their own as a real problem.

The second variation is to change the weights for each exercise. The front squat will still be held back by the power clean, but I think an athlete who's early in the learning curve can get by with less weight on the front squat.

I'm still a believer in movement over muscles, and I believe even more in correct movement over weight. In other words, I don't think a 600-pound front squat is a quad exercise, since you better have your whole body ready for the hit. And if you barely bend your knees, don't brag about your big squat, either.

In a large group setting, this requires a lot of plate changing and juggling of athletes here and there. But this second variation is great for a group of up to about twenty, as well as being ideal for individuals.

The final variation is the Southwood workout used as a warm-up. I know everybody in the world is advanced now, but there's something about doing four big movements to get the body going. There's going to be some fat burning in all of this whole-body lifting.

For fun, try doing the eight power cleans, military presses and front squats back to back to back. Then continue with the six reps and finish by tackling the four-rep sets. I tried doing the bench presses in this cluster, but I was wrestling with the bar too much getting up and down. Certainly safety is a concern, but I just found it too taxing for a warm-up.

From the Southwood Program, we progress to the Big Five workout. It's a simple linear progression workout using five sets of five reps of the same four lifts, with deadlifts added to the mix. You read about the Five by Five earlier in the book.

Athletes add weight each set, and finish the fifth set as heavy as they can go. With young male and female athletes at any level, you might find they can lift within ten pounds of their max single for five reps. This doesn't happen to lifters with more than two or three years in the gym, but for a young lifter this isn't uncommon.

So, the next workout looks like this:

Power Clean, 5 x 5
Military Press, 5 x 5
Front Squat, 5 x 5
Bench Press, 5 x 5
Deadlift (any variation), 5 x 5

This Big Five workout is one anyone would recognize from the annals of bodybuilding history. The late Reg Park used this with great success and his devotee, an Austrian bodybuilder with political ambitions, followed a similar program.

The Five-Three-Two Workout

Every fifth workout, we change one small thing by playing with the reps and sets. We shift to just three sets. A set of five, add weight, a set of three, add weight, and then a heavy double. This is the Five-Three-Two Workout. The goal is to go as heavy as possible on the double.

The problem with going heavy on singles with the young athletes is we run into an old thought called fuzzy logic. It's one of those phrases that got beat to death a decade ago, and seems to have fallen into the same bin as, "Have a cow, man," and, "I didn't inhale."

When most people go heavy with singles, the spotters help "a little," and the depth gets suspect on squats. The legs work harder on military presses, and well, the list just goes on. With a double, I can always be assured at least one repetition was really a rep. We don't want fuzzy maxes in the weightroom.

I moved to the every-fifth-session Five-Three-Two Workout when I started to see the athletes really improve as the volume of the five by fives built up. An easier test day every two weeks seems to keep the athletes' enthusiasm high and keeps them coming back for more. There's nothing worse than a program that's both boring and non-progressive, and sadly, boring and non-progressive defines most training programs. I don't worry about boring my athletes when they're making progress.

After three, or at most, four weeks of the Southwood program, I shift to the Big Five. After two months of work on the Big Five with the chance of maxing four times during the two months, and with a final max day at the very end, the athletes can now move on to other programs.

There's a level of mastery in the five major lifts that's evident to the eye of any viewer. There's also a lot of weight on some of the bars, as I've had sophomores sneak into the 200s on power cleans for a set of five. That's some good lifting for an adult and amazing from a fifteen-year-old.

The Southwood and the Big Five are just two of the many things I do to indoctrinate students into the world of lifting, fitness and health. I've had many students who really bought into the program. They've supplemented their diets with fish oil capsules multiple times a day, and tossed back a protein shake before, halfway through, and at the end of their workouts. The gains in hypertrophy and strength are impressive.

After a few weeks of doing battle with the weights, my students are warriors, ready for anything.

Twenty-Eight

Recovery Methods 101

Whenever somebody tells me about something new in the world of physical conditioning, the first thing I do is check to make sure my wallet is secure. Next, I reference John Jesse's book, *Wrestling Physical Conditioning Encyclopedia*, published in 1974. I picked up a copy as a young lad and promptly ignored all the excellent advice because... well, the technical term is, I am an idiot.

No matter what new and exciting thing has emerged in the last three decades, Jesse already wrote about it: isometrics, sandbag training, ligament strengthening, Olympic lifts, grip work, swingbells (a.k.a. kettlebells), combining sprinting with calisthenics (I thought I invented that), get-ups, and flexibility training that still outpaces what most of us do today.

In his recommendations for starting out a new year, he has a basic weekly approach. It's simple and has the hallmarks of a great program. I think this advice stands the test of time:

1. Three sessions of strength development and injury prevention, with near-maximum loads

2. Three sessions of flexibility exercises

3. Three sessions of endurance training

4. The strength development, injury prevention work and flexibility exercises should be done one day, and the endurance training on another.

5. The strength development, injury prevention work and flexibility exercises slowly increase to an hour-and-a-half a day, and the endurance work to one hour. This will total seven-and-a-half hours of training time each week.

Years ago, I realized my calendar and my daily schedule didn't have enough days and hours. As a father, a college instructor, a husband, a school teacher, a coach and as an athlete, it was difficult to fit in my usual three hours of training each day. During junior college, I often trained close to five hours a day between throwing the discus and Olympic lifting. Even at three hours a day, I felt like I was coasting.

I decided to do something singularly unusual: Use my brainpower. I sat down with pen and pad, and looked at the waste in my training programs. I noticed I did hours of junk work, including assistance exercises that assisted nothing and long, worthless aerobic sessions. I also noted certain things worked well and took very little time.

I've been free with my insights from this long process. The One Lift a Day program — where the athlete trains just one lift a day — spawned one of the largest discussions in weight training forum history.

And as a reminder, if you do two lifts a day, that's not the program. I will say this one final time: If you honestly squat for forty-five minutes, please let me know if this is easy work.

For fat loss and sports performance prep, I still argue Four Minutes to Fat Loss is the best I can say on the subject. From my experience with other athletes, I would no longer consider the thruster a viable option — I now only recommend the front squat.

In other articles, I've included my transformation program. It's a nice training program to keep an athlete in shape through the difficult period of transitioning from off-season to competition. I still consider the Litvinov Workout — mixing heavy front squats with sprints or sled drags — to be the single greatest workout of all time.

You'll note I always argue for workouts that have clear boundaries. The focus is on whole-body movements done with measured intensity (reps, rest time and weights need to be intelligently focused), and the particular goals of the athlete or fitness trainee stay clearly in vision at all times.

Usually, we discover less is more when it comes to training. Again, I have noted with glee I have yet to receive an email saying the following workout is too easy:

Back Squat
315 for 30 reps
Rest
275 for 30 reps
Rest
225 for 30 reps
Go home and rest

It's only three sets and I did this workout in June of 1979. I will be repeating it as soon as I recover.

With the insight that one can improve capabilities in less time, I found the rest of my life also improving. Hey, the four-minute Tabata front squat workout leaves you plenty of time to do things with your career and family. You'll find yourself sitting a lot, but that seems to be okay, too.

Recently, I also began to realize I've been slowly coming to grips with the other side of training… recovery. As odd as it sounds, as one moves past fifty years of age, one doesn't recover like a teenager. My school-age athletes can do an exhausting hour-and-a-half workout, take a gulp of water, and then play full-court basketball until I kick them out of the gym.

I have to actually work on and think about recovery. It used to be so easy. My post-workout electrolyte beverage had a flip-top and came in a six-pack. I put my feet up and tossed down all six or more. And I could lose bodyfat by walking to the refrigerator.

Before I spiral down into my lost youth, let's look at several options for optimizing the recovery side of hard training and intelligent nutrition. If there's a single key to the discernment process concerning recovery it's this: You must balance the cost-to-benefit ratio, also known as getting the biggest bang for the buck.

A one-time investment of a 310-pound Olympic weight set, a single kettlebell and a doorway pull-up bar can honestly last you a lifetime and provide endless hours of training for about five hundred bucks if you shop around. Or you can spend that much in one day at the spa, or the emergency room undoing a bad training decision.

I'm certainly no expert on rehab, injury recovery or surgery, but like most people, I've spent many hours and dollars on rehab, recovery *and* surgery.

On the first day of my collegiate athletic career, our team trainer told us the key to dealing with hurts, pains and injury was RICE.

Rest
Ice
Compression
Elevation

And, as most know, there's no better formula for the first twenty-four to forty-eight hours after an injury than just lying down with a tight bandage and a bag of ice with the limb elevated. Ice is a miracle worker… for the first day or so.

Intuitively, after that first forty-eight-hour period, we head for heat. I am convinced heat therapy in any form, from creams to tubs to hot rooms, is the road to healing. When I think about restoratives, I turn to warmth.

I also turn to stretching. This is important. I've made a career telling people warming up and pre-training stretching are not only a waste of time, but probably impede progress.

Of course, you don't want to go out stone cold, but do we really need a half-hour of treadmill, seventy-five twists and contortions, plus a boot camp of calisthenics just to walk over and do a set of pull-ups? With athletes who insist on long warm-ups, I have them do the workout and say, "This is the warm-up."

In light of these intuitive truths concerning formal recovery, over the past few years I tried to figure out what's worked best. Here are the best and brightest.

Bikram Yoga

Yes, I said that. Hot Yoga. There are several reasons I recommend Bikram Yoga for my athletes, and none of them relate to the hype. I know the founder has been on *60 Minutes* and he drives expensive cars, but there's much to be said about the actual classes.

First, the classes are ninety minutes long. If you decide to go twice a week, that's three hours of stretching, pulling, twisting and relaxing. For most, that's two hours and fifty-nine minutes more than we typically stretch and relax in a week.

Next, I must say the intense heat — nearly always above 103 degrees and often around 110 — and the humidity does "something" for the body. For me, I sweat. A lot. Seriously folks, I'm talking about sweating that confounds the law of thermodynamics.

During the session, I can tell you exactly how many pieces of salami I ate at the snack counter during the day's meeting, because I swear the damn things are coming out of my forehead. And there's no question the heat allows me to stretch out that injury I swore I would take care of in 1977. During Bikram Yoga classes, I find the time to deal with four decades of misuse.

But neither the time nor the heat is the real reason I recommend Bikram Yoga. It's the dialogue. Throughout the entire ninety-minute session, the instructor talks to the class and walks us through the stretches and movements. Or, lack of movements, I guess you could say.

For many of us, that's the most coaching we might ever receive.

In my youth, I had people like Dick Notmeyer, whose great patience allowed me to learn the snatch and the clean and jerk. "Pull it high and back to you," is the phrase Dick repeated to me countless times until I figured out it was easier to pull it high and back to me.

My coach, Ralph Maughan, had the great skill of being able to watch throw after throw after throw and continue to find faults and corrections no matter how far (or not far) I was throwing.

Where do you get this coaching today? Sure, you might hire Ricky, the personal trainer at the gym who was certified after a whole few hours the previous weekend. But what do you get for that? Someone to walk with you over to the next machine, look at the card for you, and tell you the curl machine works your biceps? Here, send me the money and I'll tell you squats work your legs. Thank you very much.

A walk-in session for Bikram Yoga around here is fifteen bucks. That works out to ten dollars an hour for someone to make you stretch for ninety minutes. That alone makes it worth considering. Whether you believe whichever stretch builds up the ascending colon or clears out the thyroid is beyond this discussion, but for recovery purposes it's well-worth considering Bikram.

Massage

Let's now consider this most popular and, occasionally, suspect recovery method. I remember years ago being told by a European athlete the problem with the American system of training was the lack of restoratives in our general training plan, especially the lack of massage therapy. At the time, I was far too polite to note there was absolutely no American system for anything in any sport.

Tommy Kono, arguably the greatest Olympic lifter ever to wear USA on his chest, notes in his wonderful book, *Weightlifting, Olympic Style*, the American system is to get to the goal as simply and as quickly as one possibly can.

Kono, also a Mr. Universe winner, discussed this issue years ago:

"The US lifters have to go back to the American system of training and not follow what the Europeans are doing. The lifters must return to basics and not have tonnage or intensity govern their training.

"Believe it or not, it is the old system of light, medium and heavy; training three to four times a week, with each workout lasting no more than ninety minutes. It is a matter of taxing your muscles and giving ample time to recover. Too many of our current lifters are overtrained and getting injuries because they lack the recovery time."

Whether we get hurt from lack of recovery time or lack of active recovery is still a debate.

Most people at some level agree with the basics of massage therapy. It just seems right. Like many athletes, I've tried massage therapy and there are few things in life as good as a good massage.

But like we say about Scotch, there is nothing as a good as a good Scotch and nothing as bad as a bad Scotch. I've had bad Scotch and bad massages.

The standard rate for a massage seems to be around eighty-five dollars an hour, and that number slides up quickly depending on the economics of your area.

And this is may be the primary problem with massage. First, you have to develop a relationship with a good masseuse. Getting the masseuse to go deep enough while still addressing the problems of overtraining issues is a task for both you and the practitioner.

It seems to take several visits to get it right. And let's be honest, several massages is not exactly the most difficult prescription you've ever been given. But at the cost of several hundred dollars and several weeks of dialing it in, I have to ask the question again: What about the cost-to-benefit ratio?

A monthly massage tab of up to a thousand dollars is something I just can't do. I certainly believe in massages; I enjoy the benefits, but beyond an occasional splurge, I can't justify them as a major restorative tool in my arsenal.

Hot Tub

On the top end of long-term recovery tools is the hot tub. My hot tub was a fortieth birthday present to myself, and we've since gone through two motors and a lot of chemicals in those ten-plus years. The initial cost is high; I was amazed to see one the other day for $10,000.

The upside? Maybe it's my '70s experiences echoing around my head, but hey... it's a hot tub! Few things in life are as good as soaking in a hot tub on a snowy night in Utah. It's good for conversation and companionship, too, but that might be outside the bounds of this discussion.

The downside is simple. Did you see that little bit about $10,000?

I also have an outdoor shower hooked up to my garden hose and during the hot summer months, I soak, then cool off in the cold shower. One can do this with a normal shower, but I can extend a hot tub with stretching and a cold-water shower for up to thirty minutes. Again, that's twenty-nine minutes and thirty seconds longer than I stretch in a typical week.

For pure limbic satisfaction, I'm convinced there's no better choice than a soak. It's more than rehab, it's a party!

Z-Health and flexibility

I'd be remiss if I didn't offer two cheaper options I use with my athletes and myself. First, after seeing the work of Dr. Eric Cobb firsthand, I'm amazed with Z-Health, although in full disclosure, I have no idea why it works.

Recently, Dr. Cobb came out with *The Quick Start Guide to Z-Health*, a thirty-five-dollar DVD that demonstrates the biggest-bang Z-Health exercises. After watching the DVD once through, you can follow along doing one side, then the other. The explanations give much of the same benefits as the Hot Yoga dialogue. It isn't perfect, since the DVD won't stop and correct your errors, but it isn't bad either.

Finally, a few years ago I read a book that opened my eyes about how one really gets strong. Oddly, the book was *Relax into Stretch: Instant Flexibility Through Mastering Muscle Tension* by Pavel Tsatsouline.

Not only are the stretches like yoga on amphetamines, there are also several short chapters providing insight into the big questions about performance. The section on the reminiscence effect, that wonderful gift from the Cosmos that makes us better when we quit or take time off, is worth the price of the book alone.

I use the tricks from this book daily in my work with athletes, and the techniques work faster than all of the rest of the voodoo I do for injury recovery.

The real point of isn't to encourage you to sign up for a yoga class or to buy anything. The point is we need to practice the process of discernment to meet our physical goals. As we're bombarded daily with new ads for pills, diets and ab-doers, we have to protect our wallets and our time.

To sum:

> **1.** Although food and housing might be the most expensive part of keeping your body in shape, if you choose wisely, training equipment can be the cheapest. Maximizing that training equipment can really make you tired and sore, and maybe injured, too.

> **2.** Recovery aids, beyond nutrition and supplementation, can be very expensive and should be considered in light of your pocketbook.

> **3.** Just because you spend a lot of money doesn't mean you are going to get a lot of return in your restoration investment. Try to do a basic cost-to-benefit analysis of your training, your lifestyle and your needs, then see what you can manage. A ten-dollar foam roller can do more good than a bad massage that costs ten times as much.

> **4.** Finally, if your four-hour training sessions are killing you, think through your training, too.

Twenty-Nine

That Guy

It all comes down to this: I want to be *that guy.* Let me explain by using something that dominates the American landscape during periods of spring — the high school prom.

The other day, I heard a story about voting for prom royalty at a local high school. It seems in one homeroom there were too many ballots delivered, and two desperate-for-attention cheerleaders put their names on the extras.

I can only imagine the scene if they would've won: You like me, you really like me! Where's Sally Field when the world actually needs her? For the record, this little accounting error was discovered, so I'm left shaking my head and laughing at these clichéd high school cheerleaders. And a bit like our four friends from *Sex and the City*, I pity the nice, young man who says "I do" to either of them in a few years. Meow.

I have another prom story that took place when I was about nine years old. The day before my brother, Gary, left for Vietnam to fight in a war (I don't really remember why we fought that war), we hosted a nice going away party for him. Halfway through the evening, a neighbor girl came over in tears. She'd been stood up for her prom. Gary looked over and said, "I'll take you." He ran upstairs, got into a suit, and took this young lady to prom.

As he left, I thought to myself, "I want to be *that guy.*"

You know, I've had some amazing workouts and competed at a pretty high level. But the ability to have those amazing workouts and compete at the top end requires months and years of prep. And to be honest, during the middle of track season, my daughter's graduation and prom, and my wife's busy road schedule, just getting in a workout is worthy of dinner and dancing.

Let me continue my goal of becoming *that guy* and be completely frank. First and foremost, let's always remember I started lifting in 1967, roughly when Gary left for Vietnam. I've competed at an organized level in Olympic lifting, powerlifting, kettlebell lifting, track and field, football, soccer, basketball, baseball, softball and Highland Games. I've also coached formally since 1979. I've produced national champions and have been thanked by Olympians for helping out. In other words, I've been around and can keep my ego in check.

With that said, a few warnings are in order. One, nobody has a typical week. I've yet to find someone who can honestly follow a program for two weeks without tweaking it. Second, I train at home even though I have the finest gym in America to play in every day. Like many who coach, I can't train where I work. I know others do, but when you work with teens, well, it just doesn't work. I usually describe coaching as being pecked to death by a hundred ducks. Third, I can't help myself, I love changing things constantly. Sorry, but I do.

Sunday

Often, Sunday is the only day of the week my wife, Tiffini, and I have time together. That's the day we do the Costco shopping. It might be the single best health choice I make the entire week. If we eat something healthy and filling before we shop, write up a list before we go, and plan our meals all week, well, we eat smart all week.

We've also discovered the 4:30 Bikram yoga class is a perfect start to the week. We spend an hour-and-a-half sweating in 110-degree heat, while I rediscover every injury I've ever enjoyed.

The best part is driving home after and having a glass of wine that works like ten. We both laugh about the Bikram sleep after the workout where we just zone out as if on a warm beach on a beautiful day.

Monday

I always have Monday and Thursday evenings free, so I have a chance to train with my buddy, Nick. He comes over to the house and we move some weight around.

We usually start with the Great Eight sprints. In the back of my house, there's a long parkway and we do eight build-up sprints. (The idea is to start slow, then ease off.) Actually, we do try to accelerate through each set, but the goal is to get the sprint work in without hurting anything.

The eight sprints are between forty and sixty meters. We try to accelerate in the middle of each set, increasing the intensity with each sprint.

Nick is weaker in his upper body, so he does pushing and pulling every workout. One of our favorites for Nick is this:

Back Squat for 5 reps

Pull-up for 5reps

Push-up for 5 reps

Power Curl for 5 reps

Military Press for 5 reps

Nick will do these one after another, performing up to five total sets.

While he's doing that, I'm doing ladders on the kettlebell clean and press, along with some pull-ups. This is my track season workout. Carefully note: This is the workout I do while I coach. I go up to twelve or fifteen hours on some days with work, meets and road trips, so the load I can handle in training is reduced.

The ladders are almost always one, two, three, so it looks like this:

1 Left-arm Kettlebell Clean and Press

1 Right-arm kettlebell Clean and Press

1 Pull-up

2 Left-arm Kettlebell Clean and Presses

2 Right-arm Kettlebell Clean and Presses

2 Pull-ups

3 Left-arm Kettlebell Clean and Presses

3 Right-arm Kettlebell Clean and Presses

3 Pull-ups

I do this three times most of the year, but I extend it to five during the summer months.

I finish Monday with one of two things. We either do a long farmer walk, which complements the sprints, or I just do kettlebell snatches if the weather is rough.

The snatches look like this:

Left-arm Kettlebell Snatch for 10 reps

Right-arm Kettlebell Snatch for 10 reps

Rest and repeat for whatever number of sets feels good.

Tuesday

The plan for Tuesday seems easy enough: a snatch-grip deadlift, topped off with an explosive shrug. This is done for either two sets of five, five, three, two, going heavy, or six heavy singles. It changes weekly.

But things rarely go as planned. Tuesdays are usually very busy, so sometimes I do thick-bar deadlifts or pull-ups during the day. I don't think I can do enough pull-ups. Tuesday is a fun, take-care-of-business day.

When my wife is in town, I tend to go to an evening Bikram yoga class with her, as my goal is to go to two sessions a week during the season. It does matter that I don't get home until after midnight on the nights we have track meets in some of the more remote parts of Utah.

Wednesday

Forget it. It ain't happening. I have no time on Wednesdays, as we always have a meet.

Thursday

Nick comes by again on Thursdays, and we pretty much repeat our Monday workouts with just one or two little changes.

I change Nick's workouts all the time, but I stick to my Monday workouts with two changes. I do kettlebell swings instead of snatches, and I usually front squat.

I try to just get reps in, like five sets of five, and I put no ego into the weight selection. I let my spirit guide what I put on the bar; I don't worry if it's 205, 255, or 135. Those readers who have lives probably know what I mean by this.

Friday

I gain a bit of joy coming home Friday, even though I know Saturday will be spent at some Godforsaken corner of

Utah at a twelve-hour track meet. I find myself doing a work-out of snatches, presses, or something without any real rhyme or reason nearly every Friday. I'm just a guy playing with weights.

We walk the dog a couple of days a week, and Friday afternoons are a great time to just wander with the dog after a few sets of whatever.

Saturday

I look forward to training Saturday, every Saturday. I just have to wait a few months, that's all.

A handful of supplements

I have a theory supplements work best when you aren't in a perfect training situation. I take a ton, but these five top the list.

1. I start and end all supplement discussions with fish oil. Take it. A lot of it.

2. The best supplement from a cost-to-benefit ratio is sugar-free Metamucil. Talk to any athlete about the issues of elimination and you'll understand the benefits. It also seems to do wonders for blood profiles.

3. ZMA before bed. Yes, I know the history, but this stuff seems to work. I've always thought magnesium is under-hyped, anyway.

4. I sure like this stuff called AlphaMale. I don't know what It is or why it works, but it works as advertised. If I even notice a supplement working, I'm amazed, so this is saying something.

5. The bowl of oatmeal with protein powder and cinnamon is still the best snack for a strength athlete. I've

heard it does marvels for you, but I like the fact it hits whatever spot needs hitting when in a heavy training mode.

There you go. I make sure I eat a breakfast of eggs and meat every day. I gorge on a huge salad at lunch and do my best at dinner. I eat a lot of fiber and even more protein. And I take my supplements. I try to sleep, but I wake up worrying about bus drivers, the weather, and a thousand other details.

But, I keep going. I have a goal. I want to be *that guy*.

Thirty

Are You Making Progress?

Recently, a buddy of mine gave me some bad news. According to one of the gurus in the fitness industry, I have no squat. It's funny to think about that really, as I look back on the four decades I've spent in the lifting world.

I thought back to March 30, 1974, when I ripped my knee apart and was told by the doctor, "Well, you're done for the year."

Six weeks later, I won the league title in the discus throw with a new personal record. When my coach asked me why I kept my sweat pants on when I threw, I told him they made me feel lucky. The truth was the second set of stitches ripped a little, and my sweats stuck to my leg.

When you sit back and look over a training career, you have to add it all up. It? Well, it's the good — the good coaching, quality supplements, restful sleep and positive experiences — and the bad. For some, we can include the ugly, but I'm sure they're beautiful on the inside.

The bad? Oh, yes, the bad. The bad literally cripples us. From the injuries suffered, to the bad tips and lousy advice. I bet you wish you could forget the book that caused you to train one day every six months, or the site you visited that told you to pound your head against a wall for time. And the entire block is still shaky after the supplement you tried that sent the hazardous material team to your house.

What's the single greatest issue facing each and every one of us? It's the same for the guys in kilts who throw rocks in snowstorms and those who email me because, and I quote, "I want to look good nekkid."

For the record, I'd like to ask people, unless they're beautiful women, to stop asking me about looking good nekkid. And, for my health and the wellbeing of my marriage, stop sending pictures. Thank you.

And now it's time to ask that all-important question: *Are you making progress?*

It sounds so simple. It looks so simple. Turn to your neighbor and ask, "Are you making progress?" The man turning beet-red and screaming as he behind-the-neck presses sixty-five pounds while dreaming of winning the Arnold Classic is waiting for you to whisper in his ear, "Are you making progress?"

You see, few of us are really making progress. I'd like to change that. In a recent workshop, I summed up three ways to measure progress for the typical trainee. Of course, no one is typical today — each of us has been told we have a special skill set, and you may even have a list of initials explaining why you're so damn unique — but you can at least ask the person next to you whether he's making progress.

Step One: Drop a pound

In the next 365 days, I'd like you to lose one pound of fat. That's right. In fact, I'll give you a program.

If a pound of fat is 3,500 calories and the bathtub model is correct — if you bring in the same amount of calories you burn, your body will be the exact same forever — then I'm going to ask you to cut nine-point-five calories a day for the next 365 days.

So, if there's actually a one-calorie drink like we see on the television, you merely need to cut back on nine-point-five of them a day.

Oh, one pound of fat a year isn't good enough for you? Well, then, what'll it be? A pound a week? A month? Listen, this in itself is the number-one reason why most people don't make any progress. They have no reference to anything past, present or future, so trying to judge where to improve is impossible.

Before you go hog wild on the *Dan John Lose One Pound of Fat a Year Program,* do me a few favors:

> 1. Start keeping a training journal. Your numbers should go up. After gritting out more reps with the same weight, the weights should increase. If they don't, that's a problem.

> 2. I learned a really valuable lesson from the Velocity Diet: Before and after pictures are worth the weight in gold. Take an annual photo shoot — the pressure of this event leads to sticking with the details.

> 3. I started keeping a food log after some advice from Josh Hillis. I have to admit writing down the fact I ate two old-fashioned doughnuts stopped me from wondering why I've been putting on weight.

With these three ideas, at least you'll know where you are when you begin. Then, cut those nine-point-five calories and call me in a year with the amazing results!

For the truly dense, if you don't know where you're going, any road will get you there.

Step Two: Mark your lifting territory

Measure your progress in the weightroom one of three ways:

1. Your deadlift max increased.

2. You did more real pull-ups.

3. Your three-jump increased.

Why the deadlift? Well, I have yet to see any aids — besides straps; don't use them — that make deadlifts easier. In fact, I don't even know a trick that really works besides just getting stronger. Your buddies can help you bounce a bench off your chest, help you through the sticking point, and assist the top part "just a little," but I don't know anything to aid a deadlift. When in doubt about your program, try a new max in the deadlift.

Caveat: Don't tell me you did 405 for twenty reps with the trap-bar deadlift, so that equates to a 700-pound deadlift. My good friend, Lane Cannon, followed the advice (no, not from me) to do high-rep deadlifts and discovered a 405-trap-bar deadlift equals a max of 455. It broke his heart, and nearly his back, to discover ripped hands don't equal a big deadlift. Sorry.

The pull-up also fits this bill. A pull-up is done on a horizontal bar without the feet touching the earth. Start with absolutely straight arms and pull until your chin can rest on the top of the bar. Be as strict as possible. Why? Because no one gives a damn about how many pull-ups you can do. There's no professional league, no Olympic gold medal nor any celebrity endorsements. It's a measurement. Don't cheat and turn this into some kind of dance move; just use your arms and back.

An odd thing: In the past few years I've noted, as have many others, the kids who do the highest number of strict pull-ups tend to also have the best forty-yard sprint times. I'm thinking improving pull-up numbers will improve speed. Why? I don't know, but those of you who test on the forty should join this mad experiment and let me know what happens.

The final test I use is the three-jump. It's three continuous standing long jumps without a pause after the first and second jumps, so it looks like *boing, boing, boing.* I used vertical jumps, but I found something interesting. A 118-pound freshman might jump twenty-six inches. As a senior weighing 188, the same kid will again jump twenty-six inches. Did we fail the athlete over these four years? No, the vertical jump has two faults: There aren't enough increments, and it takes little into account besides one pop.

The three-jump has over thirty feet of increments. Going from twenty-two to twenty-six feet makes it obvious to both me and the athlete something good has happened, whereas going from twenty-six inches to twenty-six-and-a-quarter is really hard to see. Moreover, if the athlete does the first long jump over eight feet and then rebounds with two straight four-foot jumps, I can make some guesses about what we need to work on next in the weightroom. If you don't know, try upping the raw deadlift and back squat numbers for a couple of weeks and retest. If that doesn't bring up jumps two and three, I suggest chess.

The bottom-line on these three tests is this: These are the *least fuzzy tests.* It's hard to cheat on any of them, and any progress tells you the program is at least somewhat on the right track.

It's like the football coach who went from a zero-and-thirteen winning record to thirteen and zero in one year. He suggested it was the new strength program. He honestly thought it was the addition of more sets of something. I thought it had to do with the five excellent athletes he pulled in from out of state who were simply better than anybody else on the field. Call me crazy.

The impact of strength training on football and other team sports is as fuzzy as one can find in this game of strength and conditioning. However, show me a program that increases my deadlift, pull-ups or three-jump in a month and I'm listening.

Step Three: Give your CNS a call

Have you checked in with your central nervous system (CNS) lately? Years ago, the late Stefan Fernholm showed me an interesting test: Take a pencil every morning and put as many dots on a page as you can in ten seconds. Let's say you knock out forty to forty-five every day for two weeks. Then, one morning you struggle to hit thirty. Making dots on a paper is pretty simple, but now you're down twenty-five percent. As Stefan noted, "This is bad."

Later, my friend, Mike Rosenberg, made a little computer program for me where he used the space bar as the "pencil" and added a built-in timer. For two years, I started my day with this ten-second test. And, after charting all of this, it was certainly true: When my numbers dropped, I ended up getting sick or hurt.

Clearly, the reduced performance on my finger tap-test was indicative of CNS fatigue.

After that, when I saw my numbers drop, I eased my training, increased my protein, and took care of the little things like sleep, hot tubs and resting. It was a miracle.

Not long ago, I bought the *Younger Next Year Journal,* and began noting my morning heart rate. It isn't as fun as the tap-test, but I noted some interesting things. First, my typical morning heart rate is fifty-four. When I give blood, it shoots up to sixty-eight. I'm fifty and change, and haven't done cardio since Jimmy Carter was president, so I have to be careful when

I read those charts on the machines in most gyms. It might be okay to ramp this ancient heart up over 120.

Second, I'm not sure what my small, daily fluctuations in heart rate tell me. While at the Olympic training center, I was told a ten-percent rise in morning heart rate indicates over-training. Usually, ten percent higher than normal means I have gas. It's a good thing to monitor, but please let me be clear about this, I'm not sure yet what that heart rate bump might mean.

Most of us miss the importance of the entire body's relationship to fatigue. I call all of this CNS fatigue, but that's about as correct as listening to my morning gas. Yet when I discuss it in groups, many people seem to know what I mean.

"Out of nowhere, my typing skills just fall apart."

It's not surprising, because our fingers are filled with nerve connections. Some of our most complex movements are the simple ones we take for granted, like typing or picking our noses.

"I get edgy, achy, bitchy, [*fill in the blank*] when I start to overtrain."

Yep. We all do. You can only ask the body to do so much before it starts banging its way into your emotional and social life. Trust me, don't be the jerk at the party.

"I just can't go heavy."

You can always get medium sets of medium reps with medium weights. It's like what Socrates tells Dan Millman: This is like lukewarm tea, the Devil's brew! Medium is the death song for training. You can train medium (also known as crappy) for years and years while making no progress. Go find average in everything. Buy the damn pale-green, four-door Ford Escort of your dreams and wave at hot babes. Get all Cs and ask your counselor, "What's my skill-set?"

In other words, training a lot at lousy is still lousy. If you can't go heavy, back off until you can!

I'm out of my league on this CNS stuff, but most people who've been in the game long enough understand the point. Don't keep training when taking a workout off might be better in the long run. If you've been through disastrous training weeks because you insisted on going and going 'til you're gone, you'll see the wisdom in this approach.

Sometimes an illness or a blown knee leads to break-throughs that few people expect because it drives them from their more-is-better training zone.

Misplacing a pound of fat a year is far better than what ninety-nine percent of most trainers are currently doing.

Remember, it's about progress.

Thirty-One

Distain Medium

A couple of days ago, my friend and occasional workout partner, Dan Fouts, said something interesting, "Danny, you just hate medium, don't you?"

I answered, "Why do you say that?"

"Because, you always say, 'I just hate medium.'"

It's funny and it's true. Talk to any police officer and ask if the force likes this description: medium height, medium build, with medium hair. Imagine your daughter coming home from college announcing she's found the love of her life and describing him as mediocre in every way, but poor or excellent in nothing.

A quote of mine has been running around the internet for a while:

"Fat loss is an all-out war. Give it twenty-eight days — only twenty-eight days. Attack it with all you have. It's not a lifestyle choice; it's a battle. Lose fat and then get back into moderation. There's another one for you: moderation. *Revelation* says it best: 'You are lukewarm and I shall spit you out.' Moderation is for sissies."

Now, gentle reader, I have to warn you: I acknowledge I'm probably wrong about my issues with medium workouts, medium training, and moderation in all things.

Actually, I know I'm wrong.

But, there are dozens of fine authors, coaches and trainers urging you to keep a balance in your diet, your training and your life, and, well, most of us don't listen to them, either.

Hesiod, the Greek historian, noted, "Observe due measure, moderation is best in all things." Yeah, but what could Hesiod bench press? Plato, noted for underperforming in the squat, said, "We should pursue and practice moderation."

Here's my issue: Every four years or so, I start getting emails. Not long ago, I even received this thing called a letter with something called a stamp on it.

The messages are dire.

Hard-working, intelligent, genetically gifted athletes who've just competed at the Olympic trials write to tell me after four years of hard work, on the day it mattered most, "I just didn't have it."

"Have what?" is the best question to follow up with at this point, but I know exactly what they mean.

When I ask about their training programs, they often send back literally dozens of pages of charts, graphs, diaries, programs, projects and spreadsheets. It's easy to deal with all the paper, as I ask just one question:

Picking a random month or time period, "What was the goal of October 2007?"

I always get an intelligent follow-up: Ah, yes, that month, we were trying to focus on:

> Fat loss
> Power
> Strength
> Coordination
> General conditioning
> The Olympic lifts
> Technical preparation
> Learning new drills
> Increasing muscle mass

And, we see why these athletes fail.

Let's review the two great principles of strength and conditioning.

1. Everything works.
2. Everything works, but for only so long.

Don't ignore number one: *Everything works.* Yep, everything. That's why we sometimes find radically changing our workouts leads to remarkable body composition changes in a short time.

Say, for example, you're like me and think long, slow running is really a method of getting information out of terrorists, but after reading John McCallum's *The Complete Keys to Progress*, you decide to add a little running to your training. Just going from one lap without stopping to a mile without stopping will drop fat off your body over a few weeks as quickly as those deadly cocktails of rat poison some underground fat-loss experts touted.

A few weeks later, at a party, someone will note you look leaner or, worse… better. This will get you to run until your knees ache, you lose muscle and your body comp is actually worse than when you started.

You see, remember number two: *Everything works, but for only so long.*

So yeah, it all works. Nautilus training really developed my pecs and biceps. Jogging can really help with fat loss. Joining a gymnastics team will increase strength and flexibility. Doing ultimate fighting will help with all kinds of things.

But, doing everything all at once will destroy you.

You see, to do everything at once, you have to be lousy at everything. To be great, you have to focus on very few things — most of us can barely handle more than one.

Don't believe me? Ask an elite sprinter to try another event. There are hundred-meter runners who won't run the 200 because they don't want to be embarrassed. They'll run a time faster than anyone you've ever met, but it'll be an embarrassment for the athlete not to post an elite time.

We all fall into this trap.

The best summary of training I've ever heard was from Charlie Francis at a clinic I attended one spring. He described most people's problem as this: *Their highs are too low and their lows are too high.*

I've been as guilty as anyone in taking potshots at the High Intensity Training crowd, but the original work of Arthur Jones still demands respect.

Years ago, I had an interesting conversation with an eyewitness at the original training facility, who told me Jones nearly had to use firearms to get people to train with him the second time. Screaming, threatening, cajoling and inspiring didn't seem to work in getting people to attempt to go to that level of pain again.

Here are two leg workouts done by Casey Viator, as reported by Steve Wedan.

The first workout observed
Leg Press — 460 pounds x 25 reps
Leg Extension — 200 pounds x 22 reps
Squat — 400 pounds x 17 reps

On June 10, he did the following
Leg Press — 750 pounds x 20 reps
Leg Extension — 225 pounds x 20 reps
Squat — 502 pounds x 13 reps

These were done back to back to back without rest between sets. This isn't a medium day. These highs are high.

Dr. Arthur De Vany has more insights based on early human activities. A while back, he did a great interview; my favorite part of the interview were his few words on cardio work:

"My cardio is the fast-pace of my workout. And it's sprinting in a field or on a stationary bike. I alter the pace intermittently. I never put in the miles or time on a treadmill. It's boring and worthless.

"Look at joggers and distance runners. They aren't slender; they simply have no muscle mass. They're weak, they can't generate power, and in spite of their slender appearance, joggers aren't lean. The average body fat content of jogging club members was twenty-two percent in one study. Anything above thirteen percent is deleterious.

"I wouldn't jog for health, but playful runs are wonderful. Vary the speed and terrain and you have a really great activity that's fun and healthful. Routinized jogging is factory work, not natural activity. If you log long miles on a track, I believe you're compromising your health."

De Vany's points lead us directly to the second part of Charlie Francis' insight: *Their lows are too high.*

Call them off days, easy days, recovery days, or whatever you like, but the bulk of the people I work with miss the point entirely on these light days.

I used to allow my athletes easy days, but an interesting thing started to happen. I won't name the guilty, but I had an elite athlete, in some ways the single best athlete I've ever worked with, who once came to me the afternoon of a major championship and told me, "You won't believe my workout yesterday."

Yesterday? Yesterday was the last of three easy days.

He went on, "The weights felt so light, I did a 425 bench press for five. Unbelievable. It felt effortless."

The goal for the day was a single with 335, but, like he said, "the weights felt so light."

He then went out and had the single worst track and field performance I've ever witnessed. He left it all in the gym the afternoon before the meet. His low was too high.

Most of us have a form of addiction to training, so off-days are nearly impossible.

I've lost athletes to off-days of playing pick-up basketball games and twisted ankles, broken arms in backyard football games, and frostbite to an off-day of cross country skiing (a strength athlete in a long-distance snow activity… please help me here).

Josh Hillis, in his brilliant blog, had an insight that hits the mark for those of us with training addiction. Two days a week, he recommends our "workout" be preparing all the meals for the week. He notes Sundays and Wednesdays work very well for this. I agree.

These days serve two purposes:

- You'll eat the way you say you'll eat. I don't care what diet you're on, sticking to it is the key. If you do Atkins, don't eat chips. If you store everything you need for each meal, you're going to reach for the meal rather than the chips.

- This might be more important: The time it takes to shop, prepare, cook and store will take the place of your usual training period. Besides locking your nutrition down, you'll also insure that your off-day is — how does one describe this? — off!

Josh then goes on to recommend two strength days a week and two killer workouts along the lines of my plan of Fat Loss in Four Minutes.

You know, for someone contemplating losing fat, I can't imagine a more perfect week. Two days of locking down nutrition, two days of lifting, and a total of eight minutes getting the system to burn fat. Oh, and the other day? Have some fun. Life is more than all of this nonsense.

The idea of lifting twice a week is actually quite sound. A few years ago, because of my life taking the lead over my training, I dropped down to two training days a week.

The original plan was this:

Tuesday
Snatch and Bench Press

Saturday
Squat and Clean

Soon, it became evident I should bench on Saturdays, too, and we dropped the cleans.

Tuesday
Snatch, 8 x 5
Bench press
10 x 135
10 x 225
10 x 315
Max reps with 335

Saturday
Clean, 8 x 2
Bench press
10 x 135
10 x 225
10 x 315
Max reps with 365

In a six-week period, my lifts went through the roof (a nice 405 bench wearing a polo shirt and khaki pants) and I threw the discus very far.

It was such a good program I continue to wonder why I didn't keep doing it!

To recap, so far:

- I dislike medium training.

- I like really hard training, but you can't do it every day.

- I'd like to recommend easy days and off-days, but few people really take them easy or off.

Which leads us where? This is why medium training is so popular. Five sets of ten or five sets of five can be done year-in and year-out, especially if you don't squat, clean or deadlift.

These workouts have great value; there are virtues of medium lifting.

We use a word in lifting called tonic. It means a workout tends to refresh you, inspire you, and keep you in the game. After doing a few months of vomit-inducing training with Arthur Jones, you'll find joy in doing curls for five sets of ten.

Medium workouts hold on to strength and fitness, or whatever we call it this week. You'll "stay in shape" like your P.E. coach used to say. You won't drop too far down having these tonic fun workouts.

The best part of medium training is it's repeatable. That's also its curse. But, it's nice to have a workout you know you could do for weeks, if the situation should arise. The curse is most people do the same lousy workouts for years at a time.

A few years ago, I did Pavel's Forty-Day Workout, where I did the basic movements, sets and reps every workout for forty workouts. I'd go as heavy or light as I felt. The key is there was no emotional buy-in to do the workouts. I just went into my home gym, did the movements, and walked out. I often didn't even take the plates off the bars. Sometimes, it's nice to just go train and not have to spend an hour psyching yourself to get ready.

Notice all the boons of medium training are also fraught with its problems. Medium workouts, also known as submaximal training, can lead to long periods of flat-lined training, which may or may not be a bad thing. Just remember what your primary goals are at the end of all of this work.

Finally, what did I tell our elite Olympic athlete? I told him the same things I tell everyone:

Instead of taking four years to drop fat, take twenty-eight days and do the Velocity Diet. Can't do it? Then why do you think you have the discipline to train for four years?

Instead of taking four years to tweak your flexibility, go to a Bikram yoga studio and sign up for the thirty-day challenge. Let the coaching, the heat, and the yoga get you more flexible. Can't do it? Then why do you think you have the discipline to train for four years?

Master the Olympic lifts. Take some time with a good coach and compete in a few meets. Get as strong as you can the year before an Olympic year, then coast through the big year with that as your foundation. Can't do it? Then why do you think you have the discipline to train for four years?

You know, I could go on, but you see the point.

In the end, the message is this:

Everything works, but, it's well worth your time getting good at something.

Everything works, but for only so long. When you add something new to your program, it'll improve you. Be sure to double-check a few weeks or months later to see if it's still working or, as often happens, is actually hurting you.

Instead of off-days or easy days, consider prep days when you take care of the other side of good training: your good nutrition.

There's a place for those punch-the-clock workouts where you do everything in the middle ranges. Just be sure to plan on punching it up often, too.

Thirty-Two

The Big Five

Everybody knows certain things are good for you. In fact, I am usually amazed at the lists people can spout off in just a moment or two without really thinking about it.

Like my quick list:

> Don't smoke
> Wear a seatbelt
> Floss daily
> Eat vegetables
> Get eight hours of sleep

This is not a bad list. Follow that short set of five and you will do well to insure a healthy life. Those of us who lift weights usually have a short list of movements that are good for us. Yet, whenever I enter FastFitness 24/7 Spa and Supplement Superstore, most of the guys are doing bench presses, curls and lat pulldowns. Yet, if I sit around with strength coaches, fitness professionals or people who bring fear to the heart of mere mortals, they rarely do those three movements.

What are the Big Five most people recommend? You won't like the list:

Squat	Deadlift
Good Morning	Bentover Row
Plank	

Why am I sure you won't like this list? Because I never see the average gym rat doing any of these movements! Or — and this can simply be sad — if I do see people "squatting" in most gyms, frankly, my dear, those aren't squats!

These movements require a bit of introduction for the body and usually need a few days of orientation to get right.

But, wait, what's that last one? Planks? Yes, planks. Recently, at a workshop, a guy kept asking me about lunges. "Do your athletes do lunges?" No. "Do you do lunges?" No. Finally, he asked the real question, "Why do you guys (meaning strength coaches) hate lunges?" Okay, he had me. Like planks, lunges are one of *those* exercises. You know, the kind that Jane Fonda does. The kind of exercise you see the manic aerobics instructors screaming, "Go for the burn!" and, "Feels good, alright!" doing in a roomful of mirrors and a disco ball. Then, in the quiet of the night, you try them and fail. And the last things we want to do in a gym is to, one, look like an idiot, and, two, perform poorly looking like an idiot. Planks are the worst kind of exercise… they are miserable and they just don't look that hard!

So, let's make a goal: One, let's not look like idiots, and, two, let's perform these lifts well.

Squats

We'll start with the bane of most lifters life in the gym, squats. Years ago at a clinic, a young man told me, "Squats hurt my knees." I asked him to demonstrate for me, and after he did said bluntly, "Squats don't hurt your knees; what *you* are doing hurts your knees." Squats do more for total mass and body strength than probably all other lifts combined. Doing them wrong can do more damage than probably all the other moves, too.

We'll go basic. Find a place where no one is watching and squat down. At the bottom, the deepest you can go, push your knees out with your elbows. Relax… and go a bit deeper. Your feet should be flat on the floor. For the bulk of the population, this small movement — driving your knees out with your elbows — will clarify squatting forever.

Next, try this little drill: Stand arm's length from a doorknob. Grab the knob with both hands and get your chest up. Up? When I'm coaching, I have the athlete imagine being on a California beach when a swimsuit model walks by. Immediately, the athlete puffs up the chest, which tightens the lower back and locks the whole upper body. The lats naturally spread a bit and the shoulders come back a little. Now, lower yourself down. What people discover at this moment is a basic physiological fact: The legs are not stuck like stilts under the torso. Rather, the torso is slung between the legs. As you go down, leaning back with arms straight, you will discover one of the true keys of lifting: You squat between your legs. You do not fold and unfold like an accordion; you sink between your legs. Don't just sit and read this — *Do it!*

Now you are ready to learn the single best lifting movement of all time: the goblet squat. Grab a dumbbell or kettlebell and hold it against your chest. With a kettlebell, hold the horns, or with a dumbbell just hold it vertical by one end, like you are holding a goblet against your chest. You see… goblet squats. The weight is cradled against your chest; now squat down with the goal of having your elbows — pointed down because you are cradling the 'bell — slide past the inside of your knees. It's okay to have the elbows push the knees out as you descend.

There is the million-dollar key to learning movements in the gym: Let the *body* teach the body what to do. Listen to this: *Try to stay out of it!* Thinking through a movement often leads to problems. Let the elbows glide down by touching the inner knees and good things will happen. The more an athlete thinks, the more the athlete can find ways to screw things up. Don't believe me? Shoot a one-and-one with three seconds to go, down by two points… get back to me later if you decided "thinking" was a good idea.

I'm not sure I should tell you this, but I think goblet squats are all the squatting most people need. If the bar hurts in back squats (I won't comment), your wrists hurt in front squat (swallowing my tongue here) and the aerobics instructor has banned you from using the step boxes for your one-legged variations, try the goblet squat. Seriously, once you grab a bell over a hundred pounds and do a few sets of ten goblets, you might wonder how the toilet got so low the next morning.

Let's just keep that dumbbell at hand for just a minute. The biggest problem I see with most people's deadlift is they've forgotten how to pick things up off the floor. I have been told to not use my back when picking things up. That's like saying don't use your tongue when talking. You know… you can do it, but it is just not very efficient.

Stand tall and hold the one end of the dumbbell again. This time, though, hold it at arm's length, pointing straight down to the ground. The 'bell should be slung between your legs. These are called potato-sack squats and are a great reminder of how to deadlift. Imagine picking up a potato sack from the floor; you want to get down and get your arms around it. Let the 'bell descend to a point between your feet. Keep your head up, chest proud, lower the bell, touch and return.

Easy.

Now, why don't you deadlift like that? It's the deadlift… the world's simplest lift! Well, Grandma's voice is probably in your head nagging, "Don't use your back."

300

To move on, step on two boxes or two thick forty-five-pound plates. Descend down again and touch the ground between the two boxes. That is as far as you will probably ever need to go.

Always when deadlifting, use forty-five-pound plates... or plates that position the bar at the same height as a forty-five. I have my young athletes do a set of ten potato-sack squats, then step over to the bar and try to get the same feel of descending to the bar. After that, it's a done deal. A couple of key hints:

Keep the weight on the heels. To test this, slide ten-pound plates under your toes until the balls of your feet are on the plates. It is going to stress your hammies and gastrocs (hey, free stretch), but push the ground away through your heels. I insist on teaching my athletes, "Push your heels to China." It seems the Chinese National Coach is now teaching his athletes to push their heels back to me. I am worried about deforming the earth.

Use the standard opposite-hands grip from day one in the deadlift. I do suggest, though, switching your grip often until you find which way allows the most weight.

Your arms are steel rods in the deadlift. Lock 'em out and leave 'em.

Keep your head up. Many of my athletes upped their deadlift in one workout by having the chin lead to the ceiling. When ten people tell me something worked in one day, I believe them.

Good Mornings

Most people who do the good morning doom themselves to a lifetime of bad mornings. A few months ago at the after-party of a strength clinic — imagine something like the after-party of a big movie opening, but eliminate free food, free booze, and good-looking guys — a buddy asked me about good mornings. According to the story, I said: "I can do good mornings; you can do good mornings, but that fat dude over there in his overflowing sweatshirt and fanny pack, he can't do good mornings."

What's the big deal? Toss a barbell on your back and lean forward. Besides the chiropractor industry applauding, what's so wrong with this picture? First, know what we are trying to do here: I teach good mornings as a hamstring move, not a lower-back builder. Why? It's nothing, really; I want my athletes to walk next week. So, before you begin, two things:

First, stand up and place your hands in the V formed where your torso meets your legs. You know what I am talking about.

Push your hands into the V and push your butt back as your hands disappear into the folds. That is the movement of a good morning. Yes, keep your head up, shoulder blades pinched back, and hold a big chest, but the movement is simply increasing the V. If you do it right — even with no weight — you will feel the hamstrings stretching. This is good.

I strongly suggest learning the movement with a broomstick first. A nice little adjustment is to stand with your back against the wall and push your butt *back* into the wall. Then, scoot out a few inches and push back again. Keep moving away until you literally can't touch the wall any more. That is the position I'm looking for in the good morning.

Do not make this a yoga exercise. There is no need, beyond my need to laugh at you, for you to fall on your face. Don't make this a stretching contest and don't try to go as far forward as possible. Make it a lift. Surprise me with your ability to do it right.

Bentover Rows

Stop right there. Yes, I know. I know some guy named Arnold once said pull-ups are the greatest exercise for the lats, but you need rows for thickness. I know. I know.

Here's an idea: Let's do them right.

Before you go any further with rows, I want you to do a few sets of "bat wings." Yes, I invented them… just after I invented the internet. Lie face down on a standard bench with two dumbbells on the floor. Now, here is where it gets confusing; I don't care at all about your range of movement. I only want you to pull the last four inches of flexion. If you were doing push-ups, it would be from the floor to about four inches off the ground. All I want you to do is squeeze those 'bells as high as you can and cram your shoulder blades together. You can't jump, bounce, swing, hop or do any of that crazy stuff most guys do when rowing. Do a bunch of sets of five.

The next day, that really cramped-feeling muscle in your upper back is called the rhomboid. Oh, and you're welcome. You see, the development of the rhomboids will save your shoulders, make you stand taller and lead you to a life of wisdom and wealth. Maybe.

Why bat wings? It sorta kinda looks like bat wings at the top of the squeeze. If you look carefully… from the side. Sorta.

Now, back to bentover rows: One of the things missing from those guys with twelve plates on each side doing wide-grip bouncing leap shrugs they call "bentover rows" is any work for the rhomboids. They will also soon be missing discs, but that is another story.

When you row, get into that good morning V position and strive to touch the chest. Ignore the part where you have long arms and focus on the last four inches at the top. A great rowing exercise is two-part rows. Rep one comes up to the belly button and rep two comes up to the nipples. Really strive to feel how much more your elbows have to come up to make the lift.

I suggest doing bat wings at least every time you do a horizontal push like bench presses or incline bench presses. And when you row, row. Finish the stroke!

Planks

Like most people, I hate planks. It was Josh Hillis who got me to start doing them and I discovered a funny thing. I hate planks.

Why? Well, there you are shaking from stem to stern doing nothing but holding a position. It is very hard to look calm and collected while shaking. Let's make it harder!

I have one drill to assess all kinds of issues with my athletes. It is a one-minute plank done as follows:

The first twenty seconds, the right leg is raised as high as it can be raised towards the ceiling… an Arabesque right leg, if you will. Without leaving the plank position, do the next twenty seconds with the left leg Arabesque position. Finally, do twenty seconds of the plank. This is how to increase your life: That minute will feel like forever.

How do we assess what happened? Many of my athletes who have done far too many bench presses and hard baseball throws complain the planks hurt their armpits. For these athletes, we need bentover rows and bat wings. Lots of bat wings.

If the athlete flops to the ground and maniacally begins stretching the hamstrings or complains about hamstring cramping, I know the goblet squat and maybe the deadlift are needed for repairing the posterior chain, especially a thing called Sleepy Butt Syndrome — wake up your glutes! These athletes probably should be doing light good mornings every day, as well as a daily dose of light goblet squats.

If we just have a shaking torso and screaming in the last ten seconds, well, that's easy: Include planks as part of your workouts, usually after you do anything heavy.

The last issue with planks is simply an observation from my experience, but it is worth considering. I had athletes complain about cramping calves on planks and I just couldn't get my mind around it. In our discussions, it always seemed like the cramping calves were also the same athletes who were missing little things like meals, sensible diet practices, supplements, recovery aids and an understanding that nutrition may have some value for the athlete. Hence, the conclusion: My athletes who get calf cramps are missing something in their diets. Wonder of wonder, miracle of miracles, one or two smart meal choices and a multi-mineral supplement and the problem vanishes. This isn't science, but experience has some value.

These five lifts — the squat, the deadlift, the good morning, the bentover row and the plank — develop the parts of the body that will instantly impact your game on the court, pitch or field. These five lifts will transform your body. These five lifts are hard and take a few weeks to master.

Which is why you rarely see people do these five lifts.

Thirty-Three

Secrets to Long-Term Fitness

First Commandment

There is one truth to long-term fitness: *There is no perfect program.* Yes, I said that: *There is no perfect program.* If I could give one piece of fitness advice to most trainees it would be to stop doing what you are doing and try something else. Everyone knows Monday is National Bench Press and Curl Day. Every single guy in the gym does upper body on Monday. And, after three years of it, your body might just possibly adapt to it! In truth, *any* change will trigger progress. That is why shifting to just one set of each exercise or substituting dumbbells for barbells works so well: *It is a change.*

Most people should at the very least adopt four different seasonal plans. I encourage a disciplined set-and-rep scheme for autumn when many of us go back to school and when football rules the television screens. Autumn seems to be a time to organize our lives. In winter, I recommend going heavy and hard. I also tell my athletes to use their slow cookers and enjoy hearty stews and soups that time of year, so they can warm the belly after training. In spring, start getting outside again and add some fun to your workouts. And as summer comes around, make your fitness lifestyle as active and fun as your budget allows. Following the four-seasons approach can add years to your life as well as benefiting your body composition goals.

Second Commandment

Attack fat separate from any other goal. I fought this for years, but I have to come to this simple conclusion: If you are doing this and this and that and this… you can't also have the energy to lose fat. I recommend two-week to four-week periods of commitment. Doing something as simple as the Atkins two-week induction, literally a feast of fish, meat, eggs and cheese for two weeks, will allow you to focus on the single goal of losing fat. One or two concentrated two-week fat attacks a year seems to do better than the fifty-two-week-a-year diet failures most people endure.

Third Commandment

People tease me about one of my key training principles: I recommend flossing twice a day. Yes, floss. If you ask any dentist or dental hygienist, he or she will tell you not only does flossing save your teeth, but new research tells us it might be the best thing you can do for heart health. It seems keeping small dental infections at bay is a great thing to do for the rest of your system, too.

There is a point beyond the issue of cardiovascular health. If someone asks me to design a multi-year training program that peaks with an Olympic championship or a Mr. Universe victory, but can't set aside two minutes a day to floss, well, why are we wasting our time? And that is the issue here: What are the secrets to long-term fitness? Sadly, most of us know this already, but let's decide right now to rededicate ourselves to running with these concepts.

Fourth Commandment

Cultivate the free resources that can keep you in the game for a long time. Here is one thing: sleep. I can often improve an athlete's career merely by insisting on going to bed earlier.

Sleep is free and it does wonders for the hormone profiles, recovery process and fat burning. Fat burning? Sure, do you eat while you sleep? For most of us, the answer is no. Another free, or nearly free, resource includes drinking water as your chief beverage. Don't swallow liquid calories, or at least limit them to special days like the Super Bowl or College Game Day. Finally, don't sit in the car waiting for the parking spot next to the gym. Park a little farther away and get some extra work for the whole body. Take the stairs, too. Over a decade or so, the extra flights of stairs and the extra paces across the parking lot are going to add up.

Fifth Commandment

Your P.E. teacher and the drill sergeant were both right: Push-ups do wonders. Not only does the standard push-up work the upper body's pushing muscles, it is also a great exercise for that loathesome term, the core. I'm amazed as I work with adults and adolescents who simply cannot hold the plank as they do push-ups. Not convinced about the value? Plop down on the ground with a dictionary lined up with your sternum. Crank out as many push-ups as you can in one minute. If you can't do forty, I don't allow you to lift weights until you can! And, tomorrow, that odd sorencss in your muscles is reminding you maybe the simplest exercise of all is still one of the best.

Sixth Commandment

Always choose intensity over volume. When in doubt, do fewer sets or fewer reps, but go heavier. Still unsure, go faster, not longer. If you are truly interested in being ripped, join the track team and run the 400 meters. I see skinny-fat joggers every single day at the park where I train, but you can't find a person who runs a sub-fifty-second 400-meter who is anything but cut. When in doubt, go to the track and run one lap as fast as you can. Enjoy the last hundred meters of the fat-burning zone. That thing on your back is called the bear, by the way.

In the gym, don't waste your time with lots of sets and reps of not much more than baton-twirling. Pack the plates on and go heavy!

Seventh Commandment

When you rest, rest. I used to believe in light days and easy weeks, but as the years in the gym add up, I notice an interesting thing. When I stayed away from the gym for a week or two on a vacation or work trip, I began to miss the sights and smells and fun of training. I looked forward to my workouts. I took the advice from my mentors; on workout days, I work out. Rest days, I rest. I no longer have those easy days that do little more than cut into my time with friends, family and football games on television.

Eight Commandment

Eat more protein. Eat more fiber. I know you think you do, but you don't. Not long ago, I experimented with adding two additional daily low-carb protein shakes to my diet and, besides the fact my belt got too loose in a week, my energy and general level of happiness soared. I then started adding an orange-flavored no-sugar psyllium supplement to the protein and my blood profile improved at my next check-up.

Here is the deal: I have athletes who are struggling keep a two-week food journal, and overwhelmingly the biggest lapse is protein. "But, I ate chicken with dinner," they'll argue. Right... a 200-pound guy eats forty grams of protein and thinks that is enough? Try to eat a palmful of protein at every meal and a palmful of veggies or beans, too. Eat breakfast. Eat!

Ninth Commandment

Cultivate community. Whether at the gym or the park or a rec league team, make training a part of your social world, too. I have buddies in lifting and Highland Games here and there who I genuinely look forward to seeing in competition. I also have fitness buddies who are always happy to try something new in the world of training. Walk your dog, at least. Many have noticed fat dogs have fat owners and, for the love of the dog, walk your puppy back into condition. Finally, try my favorite training idea: Invite friends over for a workout and a BBQ afterwards. You will get the workout of your life and a great protein-rich meal, too.

Tenth Commandment

Avoid things that hurt. You know, every so often I will read somewhere about a puke-inducing workout or a program that guarantees sore joints or whatever. It is hard to work out for more than a decade throwing up three days a week. In fact, there is probably a disease named for this! Certainly, soreness and fatigue are part of the deal, but learn, and learn quickly, the difference between good soreness and fatigue, and agony and injury. You can't always avoid these, but use a dose of common sense occasionally and look to the next decade of training… and the decades after that.

Writing for magazines guarantees one thing: Your email inbox is going to fill up. I get dozens of emails a week from really hardworking people who make very little progress.

I get emails from people who weigh the portions of each meal, count their daily carbs, proteins and fats, and train with stopwatches, calculators and as many charts, journals and print-outs as they can fit in a gym bag. When I train, I try to remember to wear some kind of pants and shoes on the correct foot.

If there is an overriding point to my advice to my email correspondence it is this: Trust your experiences, but also trust the rest of us who made the same mistakes as you and have learned to move on.

Thirty-Four

One Hard Thing

I live for moments like this. If you say that to yourself often enough, you might actually believe it. I was halfway up a hill in Ohio, holding a 175-pound steel log in the Zercher position and dragging an eighty-five-pound sled behind me. Remember, uphill.

I couldn't breathe. Squeezing the steel log cuts off breathing and, as I've discovered, breathing is underrated for athletes dragging sleds up a hill while lugging a steel log. The heat and the humidity were making the contact points between me and the bar more and more slick with every step, although I think the word step is an exaggeration here.

My friends were beginning the process known as heckling by pointing out I was only halfway up the hill. I wanted to comment on their parentage, but I couldn't speak. I wouldn't speak for a while, either.

A few days later, still nursing huge hickey marks from the bar (well, that's what I told the wife), I reflected on the secret to long-term success in sports and body composition. Ah, what is this elusive secret?

Of all the articles I've ever written, I continue to receive the most feedback on a piece I wrote called *The One Lift a Day Program*, which you read a bit earlier.

Here you go, a reminder:

1. Pick one lift a day and do it.

2. Um, there is no number two. I can't think of anything else.

Yes, that's it. I received tons of email and forum posts with some interesting questions, such as:

"Dan, if I do benches and curls on Mondays, curls and benches on Wednesdays, and benches and curls on Friday, will that be like your One Lift a Day Program?"

Gentle reader, you may think I'm exaggerating (again) but, unfortunately, no.

Climbing up a hill in Ohio with a sled and a steel bar reminded me of one of the keys to the success of the program. No, it's not stupidity. It's synergy. Yes, that overworked word ranks right up there with "outside the box" and "paradigm" as the most beaten-to-death phrase. Indeed, synergy is the magic that makes programs work.

In this case, my good friend, Greg Henger, brought the steel bars. My other good friend, Mike Rosenberg, brought the sled. A young friend of my father, Lonnie Wade, brought youth and vigor. I brought the idea of doing just one hard thing that day. So, within minutes, we had a challenge.

The value of going to workshops and conferences and scanning internet forums is the exposure to literally dozens of new ideas a day. Which is great. Which is also awful. In other words, you get all these new ideas — lifts you've never heard of, programs, and rep variations beyond anything you've imagined, pictures of women in outfits that make you wonder how to find that beach — but how do you put those into your personal workout program? From that Ohio hill, I offer you a glimpse of how I approach this issue.

Simple. Hard. Work.

A few housekeeping points before we begin:

1. When I talk about synergy, I'm using the idea that sometimes one and one make three. You can get more bang for the buck by focusing on those hard or difficult things in lifting (and life).

I'm always amused by Art De Vany's response to the question, "How do I lose fat?" He answers, "Don't get fat in the first place." Harsh, perhaps, but if you spend the bulk of your training time working off keggers from college, it's going to be hard to do a lot of the productive new ideas you pick up in this book.

2. Honest, hard work trumps volume every time for long-term success. Please don't bore me with how heroic some low-carb eating, stretchaholic distance runner is when he starts wobbling on the straightaway at the end of a marathon. I don't want to hear it. Put 405 on the bar. Put it overhead any way you can. Put the weight down. That's hard work.

3. Finally, it's always simple. What's always simple, Dan? Everything! Life. Love. Money. Success. It's all simple.

Simple, though, like buy low and sell high, isn't easy. Saving ten percent of what you earn is simple, but not easy. My training programs are simple. Not easy.

Since writing the one-life article, people hound me about the idea of taking every fourth week off, the rep-and-set system I recommend, or wonder if they can do two exercises on a one-lift program. Simply, the answers come from my experiences of running myself and others through the options.

We discovered, like the Soviet coaches did years ago, taking a planned week off is miles better than being forced to do it because of injury or illness or the end of the season. With a week off each month, there's no season end; you strive to continue to build up over the years.

Assume each fourth week is off. A Highland Gamer, wouldn't lift, but could certainly do some light drills. Same for the track athlete and most power athletes. For the body composition folks, maybe you need that week to focus on something you tend to enjoy ignoring. Do I hear calves?

Strongman Training: One lift a day

Let's look at a few ideas. My friend, Bernie, recently trained for a Strongman contest using these principles. He asked around and figured the contest would have a surprise or two (Strongmen events often enjoy having variations on the variations of the variation), but he knew certain things would be there. Here's how he trained:

Day One

Farmer walks… to death. It works every muscle in your body when you do a loaded farmer walk, and you might as well do it fresh. If you don't have Strongman equipment, use the heaviest dumbbells in your gym.

Day Two

Clean and press. Bernie added an interesting idea. He worked a number of speeds into his workout by starting with the classic pyramid (see Milo and his bull), then lightening the load and going fast, fast, fast, in a number of variations. He tried to get as much volume in forty-five minutes as he could.

Day Three

An interesting squat variation a few of us have been kicking around might help the Strongman. Start off with a light squat exercise. Begin with overhead squats. As the weight gets hard to manage, do front squats. Too heavy? Move to back squats.

Finally, finish with some quarter-squats or even a heavy-loaded squat support. Try it. Think about fifteen to twenty sets with the weight on the bar going up each set. You're done. Go home.

Day Four

Do the day-three squat workout, but with deadlift variations. For example:

> Frog-stance Snatch-grip Deadlifts
> Snatch-grip Deadlifts
> Clean-grip Deadlifts on a plate
> Clean-grip Deadlifts
> Sumo Deadlifts
> Normal Deadlifts
> Lockouts on a rack

Pre-press the nine and the one on your phone so you only need to press the final one for this workout.

Day Five

Rest day. You can figure this out.

Day Six

Ah, the point of all this rambling: *The synergy workout.* Take a short tour of what you own or have available to train with. Maybe ask a friend (especially someone who you don't necessarily need to keep as a friend for long) to come over with their toys, too. Line everything up. Now, with a stopwatch: *Go!*

Huh? Yeah, try to do a workout of back-to-back-to-back exercises. A favorite of mine: Hook into a sled. Now, snatch two kettlebells (while still hooked to the sled) for as many as you can do in one or two minutes (your friend records the number). Drop the 'bells and sprint away to the next station.

Dump the sled and perform as many pull-ups as you can do. Grab the farmer bars and walk back to the start. Pick up a stone and run to the last bar loaded to 225 and get ten perfect deadlifts. Stop! Time? Just once, try that one. Your friend has to beat your time.

The funny thing about synergy is this: When your friend finishes with just a slightly better time, you find yourself changing the workout and racing away again. I find we tend to do three sets or groups or reps or whatever you want to call these medleys. Then, we stop.

Funny. No one has ever asked for more.

Since the One Lift a Day program first surfaced, I've seen variations with kettlebells, gymnastics, Highland Games, and even machine training. If you go the machine route, promise me you won't do leg adductors on one day. Well, let me re-phrase that: Don't tell me, please. You can tell your OB/GYN, though. That would be important information.

One Exercise a Day, One Hand a Day

One interesting idea is doing one-hand-only work and combining the idea with the One Lift a Day program. As I'm noted for leading from the front, I tried the following:

Day One

Left-handed swings, snatches and press. Five swings, three snatches, and two presses for as many work sets as I could do.

Day Two

Front squats. I decided an exhausted side of the body might not be worth pushing too hard. Eight sets of three was my choice.

Day Three
Right-handed swings, snatches and press. Five swings, three snatches, and two presses for as many sets as possible.

Day Four
Rest day

Day Five
Deadlift (I did some easy walking, too.)

Day Six
Travel

Day Seven
Pull-ups to death

One could, I imagine, really push this idea. One of the lost bits of wisdom is you're actually able to handle sixty-to-seventy percent of your two-handed max with one hand. (You still use both legs, your back, and stabilize like crazy with the "off" arm.) And, you're still only using what you think of as light weights. I can't help it, but there's no way I can think of a kettlebell as heavy, even if I struggle to lift it. The number tells me light!

In other words, you could do two right-arm days, two left-arm days, a full-body day, and I'd still recommend a squat-movement day. Something like this:

Week One

Day One
Right-arm clean and press

Day Two
Front squat

Day Three
Left-arm clean and press

Day Four
Rest

Day Five
Right-arm swing and snatch

Day Six
Deadlift

Day Seven
Left-arm swing and snatch
I wouldn't repeat this the following week. Rather I'd move
to a second week with only four days of training:

Week Two

Day One
Rest

Day Two
Front squat

Day Three
Rest

Day Four
Right-arm day

Day Five
Deadlift

Day Six
Left-arm day

Day Seven
Rest

Repeat for a total of four weeks. Then, test yourself somehow and see if this is working.

I like the idea, but what's missing (and some readers will have caught this) is the program looks more like the plans for putting together a car on an assembly-line than the synergy stuff I promised from the beginning. Yet, it is there.

You see, this program came from a reader who emailed me the idea of doing the One Lift a Day variation. Always dumb enough for a challenge, I tried it. I wrote an article; a buddy added another layer of insanity; I used the lessons from kettlebellers and various crazies to put together a program, and jumped in. That is synergy.

The biggest problem most people have when they first start lifting is looking at others as having all the answers, especially those at the gym who wear golf shirts with their names embroidered on the chest pockets.

"He must know what he's talking about; he has a golf shirt with his name on it, for gosh sakes!"

In truth, the answers — the secrets — are just not that hard to find. Every reader has at his fingertips (literally) a vast warehouse of information, but you need to add one little bit extra: you… your experiences, your resources, and your sense of adventure.

When I discuss the One Lift a Day program, there's no question it's the simplest program ever devised. Simple, but not easy.

Now, you have to take it to the next level.

Thirty-Five

Principle Lessons

Principle One

Advanced training methods are for advanced trainers. Yes, I know, we all know that, don't we? Well, I often note my years with the world famous Pacifica Barbell Club where Dick Notmeyer took me under his wing and had me do the following workouts:

Three days a week
Snatch and Clean and Jerk (two hours' worth)

Two days a week
Front Squat and Jerks off the rack (two hours' worth)

Yes, I was working my legs five days a week and my body responded by packing on forty pounds in four months. What most people miss is I had workouts like this:

Front Squat
135 for 3
155 for 3
175 for 3
185 for 3
195 for 3
205 for 3
215 for 3
225 for 3
235 for 2
245 for 1

You see, I was learning the lifts! I was training my body to be more flexible, to learn the positions and to prepare for the loads I would lift months and years later. A few years later, I would do maybe six or eight total reps in a front squat workout with the reps all hovering around 400. I'm not doing ten-pound jumps for triples very often after getting over 300. But, at around 200 — early in the learning period — volume is appropriate.

Much of a beginner's training is with weights not beyond much more than bodyweight. Yet I will get emails from delightful young people with intense periodization schemes and dozens of curl variations. Here is a little workout I recommended recently for a man my age (just past old) who hadn't lifted in three decades.

> Goblet Squats
> Half-Turkish Get-ups
> Lawn Mowers *(one-arm rows)*
> Push-ups
> Suitcase Carries *(walk with one dumbbell for fifty yards, turn around and come back using the other hand)*

When I explained the reps and sets, and I quote myself, "Do a couple of reps with the exercise and get a feel for it. Do it again, but make sure you are doing each rep right. Try to do a little more each time… either more sets or more reps. In two weeks, try to do this workout six or seven times."

He emails me back to tell me, "This isn't what they are doing in the magazines."

Right. And the magazines don't recommend taking off thirty years first.

Principle Two

Strong guys forget hypertrophy, and bodybuilders and lookgoodnekkid guys forget strength.

I only know this because I am the greatest sinner about forgetting this principle. Yearly, I come to the end of Highland Games season and try to find the license plate of the bus that hit me. You see, as the season goes on I rarely get over doubles and triples in the weightroom. I rarely do a lift to keep a balanced physique. My focus is on throwing farther, higher and better. And, every year I do two or three workouts of three sets of eight or five sets of twelve and my body sings, "*Yes, that is it!*"

It is a lesson I have relearned a dozen or more times. The problem with specificity is it leads to the highest marks possible, with the small issue of crashing almost immediately after the competition. As difficult as it is to plan and recover from both hypertrophy and strength training, I recommend this to anyone who will listen: You need to do both. Now, if only I would listen.

For many bodybuilders, the issue of being too strong isn't an issue. In earlier years, many of the best bodybuilders also competed as powerlifters and Olympic lifters. Franco Columbu deadlifted weights for reps that are still beyond belief, and the governor of California snatched 242, clean and jerked over 300 and famously won a stone-lifting contest. But, many of my email correspondents seem to think muscle growth is simply a factor of moving about quite a bit. I like that, the Moving Around Quite a Bit Protocol (MAQABP). I have opened emailed Excel spreadsheet workouts that would destroy a marathoner, a drill sergeant and an Olympic champion. The workouts are for one guy! I see running (from what?), cycling, some variety of marital art, the powerlifts, the O lifts and lots of calisthenics. Okay, I get the push-ups, sit-ups and pull-ups, but shouldn't there come a time when someone who wants to put on muscle should try lifting weights?

To get more muscle mass, the body needs to be put under some stress. Recently, I worked with a young man who couldn't gain weight, but when I quizzed him about his workouts, he didn't do a single movement with over 200 pounds. You have got to move the big iron to get big muscles.

Principle Three

Fat loss is not a long-term process. Sorry, I used to believe one cut fat by long, involved, brilliant calorie-cutting and cardio, but the evidence from the Velocity Diet can't be ignored. Fat loss demands total focus. It can't be done in conjunction with your county basketball tournament and a Strongman contest. You have to be single-focused. And, please, don't email to claim the Velocity Diet is hard. I know that. My single clearest memory is calling my brother and asking him how to survive one more night. He told me to quit the diet the next day, but tonight I would hang in there. I went to bed obsessing over roast chicken, but I woke up the next day back on track.

Fat loss is a war. There are no little steps. Oh sure, I support a group here on campus that does baby steps toward the goal. I appreciate the idea. I appreciate the small life changes they are making. But, if you want fat loss, you must take the scorched earth philosophy. When you take the baby step from Twinkies to low-carb bagels, your body still acts fat.

Give fat loss its twenty-eight days. Then move on to the rest of your goals.

The next time you need a question answered, think through these three principles and see if these help answer your questions.

Remember:

- Make sure your program fits your experience level.

- While you might have specific, focused goals, be sure to also check to see what you might be missing. Most people need to get stronger!

- Separate fat loss from the rest of your yearly goals and try to find twenty-eight days to dedicate your life to it. It works better this way.

Thirty-Six

Three Basic Concepts

Training programs are great. I love to read new ones and I enjoy tinkering with old ones. I'm like one of those old guys who hangs around junkyards looking for spare parts for the hot rod his wife despises. Exercise selection is fun to consider, and learning a new lift can be fun, stimulating and treacherous. Watching someone trying to learn the squat snatch from a fitness magazine with a fitness model demonstrating something the model has obviously never done before is not unlike watching a locomotive approaching a car stalled on the tracks in a movie. It's not laugh-out loud funny, but funny like "what the hell are you doing?" funny. Shopping for a new supplement or trying out a new herb can be like the early moments of dating: the first days of waiting for a reaction, the exciting new smells as you urinate, and then, usually, dumping the exciting new herb or supplement for something new.

And, that is the problem with most of us. Training programs and exercise selection and nutritional tweaks bombard us nearly every time we open an internet browser or a new fitness magazine. We get deluged with "try this" and "do that." How do we filter what works for us? How do we discern what will or won't work?

I have a bit of advice that goes back to the Greeks: What is your philosophy of training? I'm serious, too. What are the basic suppositions that drive your vision of training, health and fitness? In this short piece, I will overview my training philosophy as it has developed over the years. Before I take too much credit for genius, please understand nearly every concept I hold near and dear has been stolen from others much brighter and better than me.

In fact, as a football coach I once heard Jimmy Johnson speak, and he literally turned around my approach to coaching. Johnson, one of the rare people to win a National Championship in football (Miami Hurricanes) and the Superbowl (Dallas Cowboys), keynoted the annual coaches' gathering in Las Vegas. Now, to be honest, I expected little. Generally, the big names come unprepared, talk to the high school coaches like we're newspaper guys, scratch a few marks on a board, and leave to go golf.

I was wrong. Johnson changed my vision of coaching.

He summarized his approach to coaching with three basic concepts:

1. **Simplicity.** During the talk, he stressed he didn't like lots of "this and that," which confuses people. One point he made still strikes me, "When in doubt, play the guy who makes the fewest mistakes." Not a bad way to think about a lot of things in life.

2. **Conditioning.** Johnson didn't want a player who could only play in certain situations. He stressed he didn't like people coming and going on and off the field. To keep things simple, the athletes needed to be in condition

3. **Win the Sudden Change.** Now, this is a technical football issue, but he simply wanted to beat the percentages when an interception or fumble happened for or against his team. His thinking was if his team could handle instant adversity or an instant gift better than his opponents, he would win. He did.

From this talk, I began asking other coaches. In baseball, I talked to Coach of the Year, Steve Cramblitt. I wasn't surprised when Steve had a list of three keys to success. On an airplane, I sat next to a Division One basketball coach and asked him his secret. Again, three keys.

As a track coach, I took this advice and developed my keys to success in track and field. You shouldn't be surprised there are three points.

1. Simplicity. We need to break down each event into basics and have a word, a key phrase, for every movement. I knew I had mastered this when I had a Japanese foreign exchange student place in the Region… barely understanding English, she nailed our discus technique with only the key words, "Stretch 1-2-3."

2. Repetition. Nobody is going to do the full movements more than my team.

3. Etching. Etching is a mental technique where the athlete not only has a clear image of what he or she needs to do, but has a single-focus term or concept to hang on during the highest levels of competition. For most of us, simply having a ritual is enough. I beat rituals into the head of every athlete I coach so they are on automatic pilot under pressure. I've had state champs tell me all they could think of was "*Stomp*," a term to simply get one foot on the ground in an event. Nerves can override years of training, so I teach the athlete from day one to practice a single-focus concept.

How can all this help the general strength trainer or the fitness enthusiast? We need to have a philosophy of how to train to filter out all the noise we get from television, books, magazines and the 'net. Seriously, click on the TV and watch the infomercials talk about fitness and training and diet. You will be assailed with dozens of conflicting messages about how to shrink your body with spot-conditioning, pills and machines, and the next segment will argue the opposite!

My philosophy for strength training — and no surprise here — is based on three concepts:

- Movements, not muscle

- *If it is important, do it every day. If it isn't, don't do it at all.* This is a quote attributed to wrestling Olympic gold medalist, Dan Gable.

- Repetitions... lots of repetitions

Let's look at each separately.

Movements, not muscle

I believe in coaching movements, not muscles. I am almost to the point as a coach that we never talk about anatomy in the weightroom, and I insist we run screaming from the pseudoscience that dominates the industry today. Honestly, I have been told we still don't know what causes a muscle to grow — and it is obvious from the plethora of crap available on weight loss we know even less about fat. The moment one of my lifters mentions a muscle group, I know he has been at the magazine rack at the supermarket reading the muscle mags.

Blitz the Serraseruaputus into Submission! What I have never understood is this: Are these muscles in a war or is this a group of dinosaurs threatening to take over the world? What did the muscle do to deserve this? Certainly, we should find a peaceful solution to this crisis.

What begins to happen when you coach muscle groups is you end up with what Pavel Tsatsouline calls Frankenstein Training. Rather than being body, soul and spirit, you end up with biceps, triceps, quads and pecs. Well, most people don't work their quads, but you get the point. I argue a different strategy: *Work movements.*

The Big List

1. Horizontal Push (Bench Press, Push-up)
2. Horizontal Pull (Rows and variations)
3. Vertical Push (Military Press and variations)
4. Vertical Pull (Pull-up, Pulldown)
5. Explosive Full Body (Swings/snatches/cleans/jerks)
6. Quad-dominant Lower Body (Squat)
7. Posterior Chain (Deadlift)
8. Anterior Chain (Medicine Ball Ab Throw)
9. Rotational/Torque

It's funny about number nine. For years, I thought these exercises just didn't work and I didn't use them. Then, I had a young intern follow me around for a week, and he noted our athletes did half-Turkish get-ups, windmills (three variations), suitcase carries, tumbling and dozens of variations of medicine ball throws. Hmmm… right. Besides those 200 reps a day… we don't do any.

It can be that simple, really. Strive to cover the nine major movements in your training and you'll be fine. More than fine, really. Now, the big question: How often?

Dan Gable: If it is important, do it every day.

Great, now we know the moves. How do we decide when to do them? I argue every damn day! Half the fitness professionals in the world suddenly just had heart attacks! How do we do it? We use the warm-ups to attempt to do every one of the big moves.

Currently, I have my athletes do this:

Crush Press Walk/Horn Walks/Waiter Walks/ Suitcase Walks/Crosswalk/Farmer Walk/SeeSaw Press Walk

Light Goblet Squats, 2 sets of 8 *with Hip Flexor Stretch*

Bootstrapper Squats

Alligator Push-ups

RDL Stretch and Deck Squats

Hurdle Stepovers (right, then left)

Pull-ups, 3 sets of 8

Ab Ball Throws, 1 set of 25

Half-Turkish Get-ups, 1 set of 50

Rolling Abs/Windmills

Goblet Squats, ten seconds with a "123" bottom pause

Swings

Don't worry about the specific exercises or names here. The general idea is to do every move, lightly, in the warm-ups. Lightly, is, of course, a relative term. I have junior football players using a 110-pound kettlebell on the goblet squats. Here is the point: I think all nine movements are important, so we do them every single day.

With most athletes, the movements need repeating… far more than most people think. At the elite levels of track and field and Olympic lifting, the total number of full movements is staggering. Many young people today are out of touch with movements like squatting because they've used chairs their entire lives, and have been kept from deadlifting and rotating by the Safety Lifting Police.

Now, maybe you don't agree with me on this idea; it really is contrarian. Most people don't train this way. I just know this: People on the cutting edge of fat-loss programs and others at the top of the food chain in sports performance are doing methods like this every single day.

There are a million ways to do all the movements, but I have found it works best in the warm-up. In other words, do all the movements — or most of them — in the daily movement warm-up. I've stolen an idea from both Steve Javorek and Alwyn Cosgrove: *Do complexes to warm up.*

Here's one of mine, only mildly stolen:

> Power Snatch for 8 reps
> Overhead Squat for 8 reps
> Back Squat for 8 reps
> Good Morning for 8 reps
> Row for 8 reps
> Deadlift for 8 reps

Do these all in a row without letting go of the bar. Rest a minute, a minute-and-a-half, or two minutes, and do it again. Try three to five sets of this little complex. This particular one is ideal for a day dedicated to vertical or horizontal pushing. If you do five of these complexes, you've done 240 movements that cover practically all the other moves.

Oh, what about the movements that aren't important? *Don't do them at all.*

Now, will this get you strong or buff? Well, it will rip the fat off you, but the rest of the workout is the key to strength, fitness and health goals. How do you get strong, the base of all performance improvement?

The Formula
Maximum Effort
Speed Work (dynamic)
Isometrics (dead-stop)
Repetitions... lots of repetitions

Getting strong is probably more art than science. Exercise science generally tells us what we figured out in the gym a century or more ago. Several things seem to work:

1. Maximum Effort. Pushing the limit on a lift seems to make you better at pushing the limit on the lift. Merely holding a heavy weight helps you lift more. There is no question in my mind going heavy trumps all the other toys we have in the gym for getting stronger. Of course, if you go heavy all the time, parts of your body begin to break off.

2. Speed Work or the Dynamic Method. Why do guys who snatch a lot seem to be able to deadlift a lot, too? Speed works in the weightroom. Going fast with weights makes you able to handle more weight. Yep, you can take this too far. I don't want to hear about how doing 500 fast push-ups is the same as benching 500.

3. Isometrics, the Dead stop Method. Overhyped, but it works. Pushing as hard as you can without movement makes you really strong when you move. I prefer the "dead-stop" method of putting a bar exactly at a sticking point and lifting from the dead-stop. I even hang off the bar for a second to further limit the stretch-reflex, then try to blast the bar up.

The key is repetitions

The most obvious and most ignored of the methods is just getting the reps in.

And, I get it. Nobody is a beginner anymore. Two weeks at the spa with a personal trainer and "I'm an advanced guy." I recommend three sets of eight for a lifter, and the world condemns me for faulty thinking. But, here is the deal: The fastest road I know to strength and body composition changes is increasing the reps. My athletes do hundreds... thousands of reps a week in the important moves.

A typical press workout for our athletes on a typical day is up to fifty-five reps using the ten, nine, eight, seven, six, five, four, three, two, one method. Sure, it's for beginners. Remember, though, if you don't bench at least bodyweight, I consider you a raw beginner, no matter how many T-shirts you own that say *No Pain, No Gain,* or whatever idiotic phrase of the day dominates the strength industry.

With maximum effort, I have a little thing called the Rule of Ten. I think you have about ten heavy, quality reps in a workout. It can be three sets of three, five sets of two, six singles, or two times five, but around ten reps seems to be the maximum an athlete can roll out in the big lifts like the deadlift, snatch, clean, squat and bench. Sure, you can do more lighter movements, but in maximum effort, you only get so much.

Speed work, on the other extreme, seems a natural for more repetitions. I am not arguing for more reps in a set, rather more total repetitions. Instead of four sets of ten, my athletes often use eight sets of five. Speed work doesn't seem to work with singles, doubles or triples for the younger athlete, but one little sign of growing competence is the ability of my athletes to get faster on fewer reps. It is hard to explain, but you know it when you see it.

For the dead-stop or isometric method, the rule is simple: one rep. Now, let me phrase that in reality. It might take up to five reps to figure out the weight for the one truly heavy isometric. The weight has to be so heavy the bar doesn't move! With the dead-stop variety — isometrics' crazy cousin — there might be a need for one or two (or more) lighter attempts just to be sure everything, including the equipment, is ready.

A coach has to embrace something I learned from a fabulous high school football coach years ago. When I asked him how he got so successful, he told me, "You can't get bored watching the basics."

"You?"

"Yeah. The coach all too often has seen the same thing over and over and wants to move on, but the team and the individuals are just learning it."

In other words, if you want to teach someone to squat, you have to watch them squat a lot.

For the individual fitness trainee, this means you are going to have to learn and do lots and lots and lots of movements. I can't say it any better than what I learned from a deaf discus thrower with whom I worked a few years ago. He had become very good and I asked him his secret. He took his right middle finger and twisted it over his right index finger, and then slapped it into his left palm. In sign language, that means repetition.

Get used to it.

Two typical workouts using my system:

Example One

Warm-up Complex (five total sets)

Power Snatch for 8 reps
Overhead Squat for 8 reps
Back Squat for 8 reps
Good Morning for 8 reps
Row for 8 reps
Deadlift for 8 reps

Workout

Bench Press with Chains, 10 sets of 2
(*try to increase weight as you go… within reason*)
Lawnmowers, 8 right/8 left (one-arm kettlebell rows)
Snatch, 5 sets of 3 (technical work)
Power Curls, 5 sets of 3 (increase weight each set)
Hanging Leg Raises

Example Two

Warm-up

Crush Press Walk/Horn Walks/Waiter Walks/Suitcase Walks/
Crosswalk/Farmer Walk/SeeSaw Press Walk
Light Goblet Squats, 2 sets of 8
with Hip Flexor Stretch
Bootstrapper Squats
Alligator Push-ups
RDL Stretch and Deck Squats
Hurdle Stepovers (right, then left)
Pull-ups, 3 sets of 8
Ab Ball Throws, 1 set of 25
Half-Turkish Get-ups, 50
Rolling Abs/Windmills
Goblet Squats, ten seconds with a "123" bottom pause
Swings

Workout

Double-chain Max Bench Press
Single-chain Max Bench Press
Drumline: 5-4-3-2-1 (In the group of exercises, do the first
lift for five, the second lift for five. Then, the first lift for
four, the second lift for four, adding weight each lift)
Front Squat with two chains
Pull-ups
Power Snatch and Overhead Squat
Thick-bar Deadlifts

Thirty-Seven

Goals and Toilet Seats, A Men's Room Epiphany

On our way to Montana for the National Weight Pentathlon, my wife, Tiffini, and I pulled over for a break. It's a beautiful drive, but I drink a lot of coffee and I'm middle-aged, so we have to pull over for a lot of breaks.

As I went into the men's room, I noticed a funny thing: Some time in the past few weeks, a young gangster decided the men's room toilet seat was the place to write his name. This is called tagging and I guess, *"You're it."*

Since that day, this young man's name has had a variety of sweaty, car-seat-wrinkled, flabby old-man buttcheeks stretched over the second gift his parents gave him after the gift of life. As a bonus, his name proudly sits inches from drying fecal material and a stench that gagged even me — and I've used dry toilets in the Middle East... dry as in 120 degrees, no water, and mummified poop.

I began wondering about all this.

And what is all this? You know, all this: the names, the mottos, and the posturing that makes up so much of the internet and general society today. I've been wondering if we should take a step back and rethink our goals through the lens of what we actually believe.

What?

I know that's the question going through your mind. I've written about goal-setting before and I tend to ask the question, "What are your goals?" more than any person giving ad-

341

vice on the internet. That is, of course, if my writing *What are your goals?* counts as actual advice.

No matter what I write about or talk about in a workshop, people always ask me questions that can be answered only through the lens of the goal. Yet there's always one important element missing in goal-setting, and this is what I want to discuss here.

First, we have to rehash some moth-eaten concepts about goals. I like to encourage my charges to assess things through a thought I repeat over and over and over again: Look for your answers through the lens of your goals.

"Dear Dan, should I do the snatch, the Litvinov Workout, the Velocity Diet, the Tabata front squat workout, and the One Lift a Day program to win this year's Mr. Olympia? I am a sixteen-year-old from Assdrop, Iowa, and I can't decide whether to lean out or bulk up. Please help me!"

What? Okay, if you want to be Mr. Olympia, you don't need to listen to my discussion on the Olympic lifts. Sure, Arnold and Franco and Zane did them, but you don't need to anymore. The sport has moved on. Oh, and don't be very tall either. And if you want to be in the NBA, don't ask me about sled-pulling. Oh, and don't be very short either.

In fact, if you want to be Mr. Olympia, I'm probably not the best person to ask for advice. I don't know how to help you. Sorry. But, I can help you discern your goals.

The One Minute Manager said it best:

Look at your goals
Look at your behavior.
Does your behavior match your goals?

It's the million-dollar question for those of us in the strength world: *Does your behavior match your goals?* As I write this, I'm deep in the protein-shake Velocity Diet. My friends, both here in Utah and the internet, continually ask me, "How does this help you?" Craving both Scotch and steak, let me think about this.

Hmm, one of my long-term goals is to live long-term. I looked down at my belt recently and noticed I'd pushed it down to fit under my belly. Under-belly belts are a sure sign one is starting down the road to the morbid kind of fat that lives under the abdomen and that, statistically, kills you. In other words, belly fat kills.

My mom wasn't much older than me when she died, and she never had a chance to see me as a normal human. I'd like to see my two daughters as mature adults, mainly so I can move in with them and walk around the house complaining, "it's too cold," "now it's too hot," "there's no food," and, "who stole my underwear?"

I have other goals, too. One of my goals is to continue to throw farther and farther, and still remain healthy. Healthy, in my definition, is the optimal functioning of the organs. If I can't climb a flight of stairs without a rest, or my pancreas doesn't do whatever a pancreas does, it isn't worth the tradeoff of throwing farther. Carrying a bunch of body fat not only decreases performance, but as I move, I have to toss my lard off the ground in addition to what I'm throwing. That has to impact my health.

But the real reason I went on the diet? When you become famous for your Scotch drinking, one day you have to honestly ask, "How did I become so good at drinking?" (Well, it's training.) Can I take off twenty-eight days and not drink? If I become even more of a lunatic and stare at pictures of single-malt Scotch the way my officemates stare at… whatever they star ate… well, I need to really stop drinking, and soon.

Does dieting fit my goals? Yes. Do all my behaviors fit my goals? Nope. So, either I change my goals or change my behaviors. Either one will do.

It's like the advice Ben Franklin gave about becoming rich: Either increase the amount of money you take in or decrease the amount of money you spend. Either one will do, but both are better.

Here we are at the great crossroads of success: What are your goals and what are your behaviors? Old Ben Franklin had it right. In fact, you can achieve your goals by setting them at a very low level.

- I want to sit around and play on the internet all day and look at women's pictures in various stages of undress.

- I wish to gain a lot of weight around my midsection... mostly fat, if possible.

- I want to go to the gym with my buddies sometimes and talk about stuff not related to the gym.

- I'm willing to change my diet to only things that are really easy to eat and taste good to me.

See? Thank you, nobody else has the courage to state this but me: To reach your goals, really lower your expectations and standards! Why the networks don't have me on television is a mystery to me, too.

You may be one of those people who choose slightly higher goals. My first question is always this: Can you tell me exactly what they are? As I review the list of goals I've achieved in my life, one of the great insights (truly a moment of absolute clarity) is I can tell you precisely the goal.

A quick example: After my freshman year of high school, my brother, Richard, drove me down to the old *Track and Field News* headquarters. I was a burly 118-pound freshman football player and discus thrower and I wanted to learn more. I bought a book, *J. K. Doherty's Track and Field Omnibook*, and the discus section covered Coach Ralph Maughan at Utah State University.

On the ride home from Los Gatos, California, in the backseat of my brother's car, I decided to get a full-ride scholarship to Utah State University and throw the discus there. A few years later, Coach Maughan was on the telephone offering me a full-ride scholarship to throw the discus for Utah State University.

Don't you love these oh-how-wonderful-I-am stories? Here's the thing: I changed my behaviors, too. I spent the better part of a year doing odd jobs around the neighborhood and community, earning money for an adjustable bench press. (I'd stolen all my neighbor's weights already.)

I started reading *Strength and Health* magazine like it had all the answers; I trained every day on weights; I didn't go to dances, parties, or the prom; I drank those horrific soy shakes from the 1970s; and I sought out the best coaches I could find. You see, it's one thing to have a goal. It's quite another to line up your behaviors with your goals.

Having said all of this, the most important thing I can teach is this: You need to solve an important dilemma… probably by yourself, too, but I can give you a few hints. What is this dilemma? It's this (and don't ignore the importance here): *What are your perceived rewards for getting your goals?*

We have to be very careful here. There's a trap. Your mother and father and your grandfathers and grandmothers had some level of impact on your life's goals. "Get a good job with a good company and they'll take care of you" was once good advice. A good life to some is a good job with a good company.

We have to come to grips with something (at least I do). We probably have three, perhaps four, generations of people reading this book, and we might all share goals, but we probably don't share the perceived rewards that accompany these goals.

Five years ago, the government realized much of its workforce was on the verge of retirement. It soon became apparent in many agencies the new hires had a radically different outlook on, well, everything. For our purposes, let's summarize some of the studies.

My generation, the Baby Boomers, the post-WWII generation born from 1945 to 1965, really has some interesting issues. Generally, there's a mistrust of bureaucracies, save to get what you can from them. (I'm a master of working systems.) How do you make a Boomer happy? Give him a title. I'm sure the day I'm made *Chief Senior Writer in Charge of Weightlifting Philosophy*, my life will be perfect.

My wife's generation, the Xers, seems to be a little different. (Consider yourself an Xer if you were born 1965ish to 1980-85ish.) For one thing, they grew up watching their parents lose those cushy lifelong jobs, lose their pensions, and lose some of the freebies everyone used to expect.

Xers are an interesting group, and the bulk of them, according to the research, began retirement savings before the age of 25-30. I have friends in their late forties who don't have money set aside for retirement! Xers understand money, even if they don't have any at the moment.

The next generation, known as Nexters, are a group that probably used a computer about the same time they learned to write with a pen. It might be the most asynchronic generation ever, literally. Time means something quite radically different to someone who carries on long internet discussions with people around the world while text messaging on one phone and talking on another. My daughters do this multitasking with ease, while I can't figure out how to answer my damn cell phone.

How does this relate to goals, goal-setting and rewards? You can see it in the weightlifting forums online. Baby Boomers will want to do specific challenges on a specific day. My goal to win the Greater Mr. Murray Open Novice Masters Class B Over 225 Born in August Contest will be a specific event on a specific day with a clear title. I want to do this, on this day, and win this or that or whatever.

Xers will ask a good question: How much do I get? What's the payoff? It can go beyond money, of course, but the follow-up question with these good people usually involves the why of things: Why do you want to throw a big telephone pole end over end? If I tell them I want to be the Loch Aidle Highland Games Champ, they shrug. If I tell them I get $100,000 per turn, they get it.

Nexters are even more fun. When I read a guy wants to look good nekkid, the first thing that runs through my Baby Boomer brain is "When? What day?" Yet to this generation, time is flexible.

This isn't a knock, but someone of my years has to acknowledge that someone who lives multitasking 24/7 isn't going to worry about the fact that something as inconsequential as the Mr. Greater Murray Open Whatever starts at ten in the morning on a Saturday. Looking good enough to win might be enough!

What does this all mean? We spend a lot of time talking about goals. Many of us understand our goals are linked to our behaviors. That alone is a million-dollar concept, and you should be sure to take some time reviewing your life through the idea of linking your behaviors to your goals. The great leap of understanding generational influence is to tie what you expect to be rewarded into your goal-setting process.

When I was young, standing on the Olympic podium with USA on my chest was my goal. Greg LeMond reportedly trained as a young man with a large dollar sign on his handlebars. Sure, winning the Tour de France was important, but more important to him was the money. Today, many cyclists use their GPS hookups to compare workouts and heart-rate monitor information with people all over the web.

There is nothing right or wrong about these approaches, but they're different. When discussing goals in this light...

Look at the rewards.
Look at your behavior.
Does your behavior match your rewards?

By the way, I'd like to know how one is rewarded for writing his name on a toilet seat.

I left him a little trophy anyway.

Thirty-Eight

Goal-setting for Motivation

Every time I write an article, I get a bunch of email from people who want me to design a training program for them. I'd be glad to do it, but the problem usually comes down to one thing. I hate to sound like a method-actor instructor, but what's your motivation? Why do you want to put a bunch of weight on a bar, or mix flax seeds in a blender with berries and protein, or sprint up a hill while dragging a sled, with a 150-pound backpack ripping a hole in your traps while lugging farmer bars?

Motivation is a funny thing. Coaches and trainers like to see motivated clients. Here's my idea of the perfect client:

Julie is attending her high school reunion in twelve weeks. At the reunion will be her former best friend who's now married to her ex-husband, who cheated on her with the former best friend. Phil will be there, too, an old boyfriend she never quite got over, who's now living well off the money he made when he sold his Cisco, Microsoft and Yahoo stocks.

Julie is twenty pounds heavier than her cheerleading weight and asks you to help her lose it before the big day. If you say, "Hmmm, first let's put you on a ten-week course of slowly building your ligaments and tendons up with some gentle movements to retrain the system," she'll be looking for a new trainer before you can further show your complete mastery of idiocy.

No, what she wants to hear is, "Right, eggs only for four weeks, two gallons of water each day. We'll hit the weightroom every morning and do sprint workouts at the track in the afternoons. I have some stuff banned by the FDA that might help, too."

Any form of hardcore, boot-campish death-march ideas will be fine. Stick moderation on the shelf for a while. Julie's motivation to look hotter than her ex-friend would be one thing, but add the ex-husband and a possible future mate into the mix and you have enough in the motivation pot to train blindly through exhaustion for the twelve weeks.

The worst client for most coaches and trainers is, well, most of us. We know how we want to look or how much we want to lift, but we're not sure how to get there and have no deadline spurring us on. Let's talk about goal-setting and how to figure out your motivations. Then let's explore how to put it all together and really make it work.

There are two major goal setting times each year. The obvious one is in January. Just try to find a gym with an open treadmill the first week of the year. The other time of the year is collectively known as Back to School time, even if we haven't been to school since the Beatles were in the *Top Forty*.

It's easy to set goals in school, especially high school. Each day there's a surge towards the gymnasiums, swimming pools, football fields, soccer fields and wrestling rooms as the athletes walk over to practice. Life, however, isn't like that. Your buddies in the cubicle next to you don't walk with you to the gym. Mom and Dad don't bring blankets to sit on while you get your upper-body workout finished, nor do you find a lot of cheerleaders tumbling when you rack the squat.

No, goal-setting is an adult pastime. Generally, I see the art of goal-setting breaking into three generations. The problem is simple: Most of us know what to do. Let me say this again: Nearly every reader knows what to do about losing fat or gaining muscle. It's like telling people they need to put on a seatbelt or stop smoking or floss daily. I mean, we know that, but sometimes, well, we just can't find the floss.

I've discovered three degrees of goal-setting that break down very easily into three terms.

Should
Could
Must

There's certainly a value to each level, but success in life and lifting only occurs during the *must* phase of goal-setting. Let's go through each one by one.

As we go through our first stages of life, we enter into a goal-setting phase I call the Should Phase.

You should mow the lawn.
You should get a job.
You should go to a nice college.

This suggests a better approach to what you're doing. Most of us who lift weights and watch what we eat live in the shadow of *should*. I went to a workshop and the speaker kept repeating, "Don't should on yourself." It was funny… the first time. But she did make a good point.

The *should* approach to goal-setting is where most of us live as adults:

I should lose a couple of pounds.
I should get to the gym a little more often.
I should try to keep an eye on my eating.

This approach is worthless. The person accepts the issue, then lets the problem slide past him as he reaches for the TV clicker and chips. Since you're reading this book, you are probably beyond *should*, but I bet you know a lot of people in your life who live in *should*.

The *could* phase is the beginning of the path to success. The concept behind *could* includes the belief and the knowledge one might possibly be successful in taking these steps. Generally, when people start using *could*, they seem to have a basic understanding of the path ahead of them. In fact, they may even know the destination.

You know, I could lose a couple of pounds.
I could do the low-carb thing.

You know, I could get to the gym a little more often
I could go right after work.

You know, I could keep an eye on my diet a little better.

Knowledge is power in the *could* stage. You know what to do, but just don't seem to find the power to do it.

And you know what? Not one thing I've written so far matters at all because to be truly great, you've got to make your goals *musts*. And that, my friends, is the key to success in sports and training.

The single best piece of diet advice I ever heard came from (don't laugh) peak-performance consultant Anthony Robbins. Robbins got his advice from one of his clients. It's called the Alpo Diet. Invite a dozen friends over to your house. Tell them by the end of the month you're going to lose ten pounds. Tell them if you don't, you'll eat the can of Alpo in front of them.

Well, as long as it has gravy.

For the next week, every time you feel the urge to take a piece of chocolate from the cubicle next to you, reread the contents of the Alpo can. If someone offers you something smothered in goo, open the Alpo can and take a deep sniff.

You see, this is the crux of goal-setting: Rarely do people improve because of the pleasure of the goal; rather it's pain that sets them toward a goal.

Robbins developed a simple solution to understanding this years ago. I use a four-square chart for my athletes. I ask them to fill in the four boxes; the easy part are the first two questions:

What pleasure will you get if you do get your goals?
What pain will you get if you don't get your goals?

The Goal	Pain	Pleasure
Do		
Don't		

You know, those are the obvious two, but it's these two questions that make the difference:

What pain will you get if you do get your goals?
(Be sure to re-read that!)

What pleasure will get if you don't get your goals?

I've worked with dozens of athletes with this simple chart and the remarkable thing about all of this work is few athletes have much to say about the pleasure of getting their goals.

"It would be nice to be an Olympian" certainly doesn't stir the imagination as much as "I'll have to eat a can of dog food if I fail."

Pain drives most goals! A woman might say, "I can't run a mile." If I tell her her child is roped to the railroad tracks a mile away and she had to get there in less than ten minutes, she might run that mile. The temporary issues of a rising heart rate and sweating do not compare to the fear of losing a child.

Does getting a goal cause pain? Oh, no question about that! Think of how many high school seniors will accept a college sports scholarship, and then sneak away after less than a week of practice. The new level of competition causes obvious problems, but even smaller goals have issues:

- Losing fat often means buying new clothes.

- Becoming Top Ten often leads to the question, "When will you be number one?"

- The diploma issue — Now I have a nice piece of paper, but no job and no idea of what to do.

You see, achieving a goal can cause pain. Can a person experience pleasure from not reaching a goal? Obviously, the pleasure we get from failure must be greater than the successful completion of a goal, otherwise (and I'm trying to be nice) there wouldn't be anyone available to appear on those daytime television shows with subjects like *People Who Date Their Cousins' Pets.*

Think of how many athletic careers have been ruined by love (sorry, guys, but I need to spend more time with Yolanda), cars, boats or whatever eats up all the athletes' time and resources. For the record, I can understand why someone would trade making love for making weight in wrestling, but we have to at least realize this is part of the issue with achieving goals. That stuff can certainly get in the way of accomplishment, so failing can be pleasurable in a sense. If you know this, you may be able to recognize and avoid it if you truly want to reach your goals.

Most of this, of course, has almost nothing to do with why Julie is going to be extremely successful in losing those twenty pounds. Julie is going to lose those twenty pounds or more because she's eating Alpo! The pain she feels when she thinks of the betrayal of her friend and husband will keep her forking down eggs long after the rest of us have pulled out the chips and TV remote. Pain motivates most people much better than pleasure. Sorry, but it's true.

How, then, do we make something a *must*?

A couple of ideas:

First, put it out there: Tell people what you want to do and enlist their help. Talk to people who've done what you're attempting. Let them know what you want to do.

Second, grab the Alpo or whatever will stimulate you to do or not do what you have to do or not do. What in your life would bring you enormous pain? Here's an idea: If you don't lose those ten pounds, your brother sends in your application, signed and sealed, to join the Marine Corps or French Foreign Legion. I guarantee those ten pounds will come off in boot camp.

Or how about this: Post your *before* photo on an internet forum. Tell everyone when you're going to post your *after*. Tell them if you don't, they should keep humping the shameful before shot until you come through with the after.

Next, and this is the odd one, start acting like you've already achieved the goal. Hit the beach like you lost those ten pounds or buy new clothes with the goal in mind. The brain is easy to fool; just go to Disneyland and look at what people wear. Start acting like you've accomplished something and, often before you know it, you've accomplished it.

When you succeed or fail, it comes back to the question that's plagued actors for a century: What's my motivation? Sniff some dog food and get back to the squat rack!

Thirty-Nine

The One-dumbbell Workout

According to recent studies — at least the ones cited in the mags my wife reads checkout line — the number of choices a person has in life is directly linked to the occurrence of depression. The more choices you have, the higher your chance of becoming depressed.

These days people have more choices than ever. That's good (I think), but it's also causing them to be confused and depressed. Think about it. Only this past century did most people get more than a very limited few options. Generally, if Dad farmed, the son farmed. For women, choice meant having a say in who her husband would be, and even that choice wasn't guaranteed.

The industrial revolution changed much of this rather quickly, and today, especially with the internet, there are more options than we can fathom. You may find this news to be, well, depressing, especially if you're a strength trainer. As a person involved in fitness, bodybuilding or sports, I can guarantee you've been exposed to this pandemic. In fact, I think one of the reasons most people fail to improve in strength training is this:

We have too many choices!

Fifty years ago, this wasn't an issue. If you were lucky enough to find a gym, it had weights. On the floor. Iron only. Usually rusty. Some advanced places like the University of Notre

Dame had low benches where you could lie down and pull over the bar to do a new fangled exercise called the bench press.

Oh, how times have changed! Today, you can venture into an airplane hanger that serves as a twenty-four-hour spa that'll cater to every whim of conditioning you might consider. You can climb mountains (by hand or bike), spin like you're in the Tour de France, or do some bizarre combination of yoga, weightlifting and martial arts... all at once.

If you decide to get in shape and build some muscle, the choices can be overwhelming. Not only do you have an infinite variety of machines, you even have a choice when it comes to barbells. You have regular bars, fat bars, EZ bars and those new padded bars some people actually use while wearing gloves! How much cushion do you need to build a hard body, anyway?

Add huge inflatable balls, pulley systems, balance boards, high reps, low reps, bodybuilding, powerlifting, kettlebell juggling... hey, I'm getting depressed just thinking about it.

The kicker is, you can make great progress without these options. I learned this the hard way a decade ago. I'd found the perfect gym. Squat racks as far as the eye could see, platforms all loaded with Olympic bars and bumper plates, a sprinting track, boxes for jumping, an area to stretch, and a clientele that included NBA players and Olympians from several countries. Each workout was an insight into the Olympics and the world of professional athletics.

Of course, it closed.

I was left having to train at home with a terrible bar I got at a garage sale, two thirty-five-pound plates and two twenty-five-pound plates... a total of 165 pounds. My options were just a wee bit limited. During the next six months, I made the best progress of my life. Why? I had no choice! I had to make do and work hard!

I'm not arguing we leave our gyms or move in as Tom Hanks' roommate in *Castaway* to train with coconuts and logs, although he did get pretty ripped. My point: An occasional round of simplicity, for as little as one workout or one week, can do wonders for our overall training.

Here are some ideas.

A few years ago I broke my wrist in a most convincing way, leaving it in several pieces that required two surgeries. I'm not one to stop training, but it became impossible for me to train in my normal fashion for almost a year.

Because I had few options, I purchased an adjustable dumbbell weighing eleven pounds, and popped two twenty-fives on each end. That sixty-one-pound dumbbell and I began a long and fruitful relationship.

The basic workout was… basic.

1. One-hand Clean and Press. Straddle the 'bell and grab it with one hand. Clean the bar to the shoulder and press it overhead. Clean the weight from the ground on each rep. Continue until you can't continue.

2. One-hand Clean and Press-Press-Press. This time, clean the weight one time to your shoulder and get in as many presses as you can.

By the time I finished these two lifts, my whole body was starting to feel a glow.

3. Waiter Walks. Lock the weight out overhead and walk as far as you can, like a waiter. Those funny muscles around your waist are called obliques. You may never have noticed them before.

4. Do a bunch of sets and reps with each exercise.

That was it. And it worked great!

If your wrist isn't actually broken, switch hands and do the whole workout again. If you choose to do both right and left hands in the same workout, start with your weaker hand.

One day I tried to bench my sixty-one-pound dumbbell with one hand. Why? I didn't have any other choice! Turns out, this is a great exercise.

The hard part of the lift is sticking your right leg out far enough to hold the body on the bench and finding a grip for the left hand. Otherwise, even a light dumbbell will drive you and your well-conditioned body right to the floor. The exercise, however, is worth trying; you'll discover a dumbbell that's one-quarter of your max is hell to lift if you only use one hand.

The next great idea came from a very cheap friend of mine who fitted his gym with garage-sale items. He had a mishmash of weights and dumbbells. You could get close when picking two dumbbells, like sixty-five and seventy-five pounds, but you could never find any that were the same weight. In hindsight, he was on to something.

Do this: Train with two dumbbells, *but of different weights.* When doing something like a dumbbell clean and press, you can squeeze out a lot more reps with the combination of different weights than you can usually do with one weight. Drop the 'bells on the ground, switch hands and go again. Mismatched-dumbbell bench presses can also give an intensity lesson to the best of lifters.

I'm not trying to tell anyone to quit the gym. The issue isn't the gym; it's the whole direction of the fitness industry. Everyone is trying to find a niche, and authors and personal trainers are doing their best to get a name. There's nothing wrong with that idea. The problem comes when an athlete gets so caught up in gadgets, rep cadence, foot placement and all the rest that he or she misses the big picture.

Certainly, part of the big picture is to *Go Hard, Go Heavy, and Go Home*, or whatever is on your T-shirt, but the other thing that's often missed is you need to give an exercise, a lift, a training program, a supplement, or a diet some time to work.

Back in the 1970s, I was an eyewitness to the greatest change in weightlifting history, the printing of Arnold's *The Education of a Bodybuilder*. College weightrooms literally filled up within weeks. It was hard to get near certain parts of the gym, especially the bench and the lat pulldown station. Most of the frat boys were on Arnold's six-day routine and not one single guy squatted (er, quarter-squatted) with more than 135, yet they were all supersetting every exercise. Guys would leap from preacher curl to triceps extensions, and back again with a fury that shocked people who hadn't yet seen *Pumping Iron.*

Rarely, if ever, did any of them improve. None, in fact, followed the advice of the book and marched up the level of intensity from whole-body calisthenics to three-day-a-week training to four-day-a-week training. No, instead they came in prepping for the Mr. Olympia, using the most advanced routine in the book!

They had too many choices. They didn't spend the time on the basics, the simple stuff, before they moved up. The moral of the story is easy to grasp: Start with the basics, give the basics time to work, then gradually move up to the fancy stuff, if you even need to.

Think about these four points:

1. Come up with a workout — weekly, biweekly, monthly, whatever — in which you get a little old school, toss out all the fancy stuff and just work hard. Work hard… simply.

2. Try some single dumbbell work or some mismatched dumbbell workouts.

3. Whenever you add a new exercise, something that involves inflatable balls or feet propped on benches, be sure to use old-fashioned exercises and good form, too.

4. Finally, give yourself some time before you move to the next great exercise, diet or supplement. Finish your last great program first.

You just might make the best progress of your life. And there's nothing depressing about that!

Forty

The Journey to Excellence

Recently one of the great mentors in my life died. He was Coach Ralph Maughan of Utah State, and he taught me one great lesson.

One day I was tossing the discus — throw after throw over 180 feet. Despite these being very good throws, Coach Maughan criticized me continually. Finally, I said something along the lines of, "Jeepers, Coach, these are good throws."

He took off his glasses, rubbed his eyes, and answered, "After seeing my athletes throw 230 feet from this ring, it's just hard to watch these kinds of efforts."

I reached down, pulled my ego out of my rear-end, and got back to work.

You see, once you have the vision of excellence, pretty good is hard to swallow. It's an odd topic, but I'd like to talk about this vision — this journey — toward excellence.

During the last century, a once-robust man was aging badly and dying fast. His son could've written him a short note.

> *Dear Dad,*
> *I guess you can't be too keen on aging, but, you know, let's hope for the best.*
> *Your son,*
> *Dylan*

Instead, the Welsh poet, Dylan Thomas, took pen in hand and wrote the greatest villanelle in history, a villanelle so good the poetry form has basically vanished. The last four lines, a call to arms for his father's heart and soul, are unforgettable:

And you, my father, there on the sad height,
Curse, bless, me now with your fierce tears, I pray.
Do not go gentle into that good night.
Rage, rage against the dying of the light.

This poem is recognizable as excellent by dullard high school sophomores and eulogists looking for a summary point for a funeral talk. You see, excellent is easily recognized by people who have no idea what is supposed to be excellent. Someone who's never seen an Olympic event can tell within seconds what is truly excellent in the sport. To quote sprint coach, Charlie Francis, "If it looks right, it flies right."

And that's my point: For those of us in this game of strength, health, fitness or just looking good, we often forget the standard of excellence. And it's easy to understand why we've forgotten excellence: We're fighting against forces that seem to want to dissuade any and all from any notion of the journey to the top.

We can't be part of this movement!

My brother, Gary, has a funny insight about education in America. We were both laughing about how our kids have thrown away their trophies. One of my dearest possessions is a cheap, tiny trophy that has *S.V. '67* imprinted on it. I earned that thing. I worked hard on my own time, asked for help, and battled through self-doubt to hit a ball in a little kids' softball league. I want to be buried with it. Gary said the same thing about his medals and trophies.

Why are our children tossing trophies away? Lindsay tossed her Most Valuable Player trophy. Before you sit amazed at my daughter's skill, understand this: Every kid in the league got that trophy!

Gary's boys had similar awards and the results were the same: The trophies ended up in the trash. Gary's insight? "They lowered the bar in the high jump to one foot. Anybody who jumps over gets a gold medal. The adults think it's good for their kid's self esteem, but the kids know it's BS!"

Here's my challenge: I want to redirect myself in my pursuit of excellence. The road to excellence is going to really hurt the self-esteem, like I discovered in Washington, DC, last year.

At a DC seminar, Dave Tate explained progress and programs in a manner that stunned the audience. He explained the four levels of programs:

Crappy
Sucks
Good
Great

Let me make two important points before you think about where you belong on this list. First, Dave asked the question: How many of you can bench 300? A lot of hands went up, including mine. Hell, I can snatch that!

"400?" Again, a lot of hands went up.

He then spoke of the large number of 800-pound benchers at his gym, then the 900-pound benchers, even the 1000-pound benchers.

"Any hands up?" I sat on mine . . crushed.

You see at forty-percent of the world record, my bench press is Crappy. I'd have to train long and hard to Suck. That's the first point: Where do you rate? Where do you really rate?

Dave's second point silenced the audience. You see, the road from suck to good is long and difficult! Each step up Dave's scale is laborious and not for the fainthearted. What are you willing to give up for excellence? Is it a goal worthy of even considering?

Let me quote Cervantes to help ease the pain here: "It is the road, not the inn."

In other words, even if you don't win Mr. Olympia and make action flicks, there's a lot of good in simply striving to achieve the best you can be. (Catchy slogan. I just invented it.)

Consider all of that before you begin your journey to excellence. It's a journey worth considering. Even if you choose to be sucky in an area of your life, at least go through the effort of admitting you are, in fact, choosing less than your best in some things.

I'm lousy at a lot of things, and I see little hope in getting better. My handwriting is horrific, my foreign language skills embarrassing, and my tact is lacking. I don't see me doing much work in those areas.

Two more considerations: One, what's considered excellent in your area of focus? For bodybuilders, in my opinion, look at Arnold in the early 1970s and Zane in the late 1970s. I don't like chemical gut or freaky face. I like the older look of bodybuilders during the 1960s and 1970s.

In performance sports, what are the top people doing? I used to spend a week each year with Mike Powell, the long jumper. It seems twenty-nine feet is a mark worthy of consideration.

And the high jump? The first height at the Track and Field Nationals — the opening mark — is seven feet! *Excellence is not easy.*

Two, take a few minutes to look at the pattern, the methods, and the plans of the best of the best. Generally, most of us will overlook the obvious elements that tie together the stories of most extraordinary people. Like what?

Here you go, an obvious one: time. The Greek weightlifters tell us it takes twelve years of training to prepare for their workouts. Most professional athletes will tell you they've been in the game for a decade, if not decades. If you've been training three months, the best of the best literally have fifty-two times more experience than you!

What do you do?

Learn from those who've been there before.

Here's a quick hint: Never accept a handball game from an old guy in a gym. Trust me. Gramps over there will be so kind and, you'll figure, "I'm in great shape." Gramps will make you run back and forth and back and forth while he stands like a statue in the middle tapping the ball slightly, ever so slightly back to you.

You'll lose, experience near heart failure, and Grandpa won't even be out of breath. Gramps not only beat me in handball, but got a towel for me to wipe off my face... a beautiful moment of kindness. A kindness that could kill.

You see, age is crafty. Old athletes figure out one thing from years of doing it wrong: Less is more.

You've heard it before. The Olympic lifting legend, Tommy Kono, has made a living on those words. *True excellence also reflects a silky smoothness about it. Less effort, more results.*

We've all heard the saying, now a cliché, that a journey of a hundred miles begins with a single step. The road to excellence shouldn't be rushed, but most of us do. The high school athlete who sees graduation right around the corner has a hard time hearing me tell him to go home when his practice is going horribly.

"But, I'm just having a bad day," he says.

"Right, so you're practicing to be crappy, or merely sucky today? Go home."

This is the great challenge of goal-setting. We set the wheels in motion after listening to Earl Nightingale or Anthony Robbins or Zig Ziglar, and chart master plans with numbered and bulleted points to be at certain stages at certain times, yet true excellence has that terrible skill of being effortless. Like the old guy at the handball court, there's beauty in simplicity.

And it's terribly confusing. I shake my head sometimes when I try to hold all these thoughts together.

- I want to get better than crappy, but to do this I need to do less.

- I want to stop sucking, but to do this I need to be more elegant in my performances that suck.

- I want to make the big jump, but I have to jump slowly to make the big jump.

- All the while, I must look pretty doing it.

Exactly! So, what can we do to get on the road to excellence and perhaps find that most elusive of goals?

First, know what the standards are for you. Make an honest evaluation today. Before and after pictures have been overdone, I agree, but it's still hard to argue with how great they are for honest assessment.

If your goals are athletic, look up the records in your sport, watch the championship DVDs, and read the articles reviewing the events. In other words, get a clue what you're facing.

Next (and this is the most difficult) map a flexible approach to your goals. If you decide to be the best powerlifter in the world and don't know how to squat, maybe that's something you can't be flexible about. Learn to squat!

However, everything else is negotiable. Champions have literally come to victory by opposite approaches. Outline your ideas, some broad strokes across a yellow tablet, and get an idea what you need to address.

Next, continually strive to look excellent while you attempt this challenge. When I first started Olympic lifting, there was always a bodybuilding contest after the lifting. My coach, Dick Notmeyer, used to tell me to watch how well the bodybuilding competitors dressed when they came to the competition. In street clothes, he'd tell me, you could figure out the winner because he looked the best. Perhaps something as simple as focusing on some perfect reps in the gym might be a start... or trading in your Members Only jacket.

Finally, excellence is rarely a stressed or rushed effort. It looks easy. Eliminate all the excess and strive for simplicity. If you can remember Wayne Gretzky playing hockey, he flat moved more efficiently than anyone else. You could say the same about Michael Jordan at his peak, too.

Eliminate the excess. Pare down what you do both in training and in movement. Generally, less is more.

It's funny. When I quit trying to throw so far with the discus, when I simplified the movement, it went a lot farther.

And Coach Maughan had a lot less to wipe his eyes about at practice.

Forty-One

The Philosophy of Physical Capital

My wife, Tiffini, has been working in banking since before we met in 1987. Today she's a bank examiner, and yes, she complains every time we watch *It's a Wonderful Life.*

Just as I roll my eyes when I watch a football movie starring geeky actors who couldn't play in a Powder Puff league, she also rolls her eyes dismissively over the errors of the evil bank examiners in the movie.

The upside of marrying an intelligent woman with financial expertise is that you marry an intelligent woman with financial expertise. And after we combine her career choice with the fact I can barely add two single-digit numbers, Tiff handles the money in our family.

Whenever I ask how much money I have, she says, "Honey, you have one hundred dollars."

That seems about right.

Anyway, it only makes sense that the key concept I hold in training would be stolen from the financial world. I insist on a concept I call physical capital. It's simply this: Physical capital is the sum of all your training, nutrition and recovery tools.

I call them recovery tools, but honestly, most of us sleep without giving a ton of consideration to the importance sleep holds in muscle-building and fat-burning. "Good night, dear, let's really drive out catabolic forces from our bodies for the next eight hours!"

I don't think there's anyone who would disagree with the concept of physical capital. In fact, I'm sure I don't go nearly far enough encompassing the concept. There are certainly emotional, financial, social and genetic factors that lend themselves to success for any and all of your goals. If you want to go to an Ivy League school and both Dad and Grandpa, graduates of said school, are also the largest donors to the school, there's a chance you might just get a break at admissions.

Physical capital is an account all of us can add to every day in some different way. I attend workshops, buy tons of books, experiment with supplements, and visit forums on the internet way too much to not be considered a geek.

Which leads me to an issue: When you write in forums covering lifting, you soon become an "expert." It's a rare day when I don't get at least one email asking for a program. For what? Well, it can be for fat loss or discus throwing or looking good nekkid or whatever, but nearly every day, some nice person asks me to design a foolproof three- to six-week program to take them from skinny-fat to Mr. Universe.

That would take nearly seven weeks, but for you, well, we can have this done in five!

The problem with program design via email is twofold: First, I don't believe in the correspondence-course approach to coaching.

Second, and more important, there are literally dozens of problems with a cookie-cutter (or an email cut-and-paste) training program. Before I can even begin helping my email writer, there are dozens of questions that have to be asked. And, after all those years sitting in philosophy and theology classes, I feel the need to ask the questions behind the questions.

It sounds so easy when I ask them:

1. What is your max front squat, deadlift, snatch and bench press?

2. Do you know *how to do* a front squat, deadlift, snatch and bench press?

3. What have you eaten for breakfast the last thirty mornings?

Question number two is the killer. You see, generally, before we can even begin ramping up a training program, athletes have to have a basic level of mastery in all the Olympic lifts and power lifts. Then, after a mastery of the lifts, my emailing friend needs to know his maximum effort on these lifts. And this simple question, "What's your max?" is the first problem to solve when I try to help an athlete. What is a max?

This is physical capital. You know how to perform the lifts, but can you do them at a level appropriate to your goals? So then, what is a max?

Recently, I was sitting with Mark Twight at dinner. If you don't know Mark, there's a chance you never climbed a mountain. If you have, yes, it was that Mark Twight. Mark is a genius in training athletes, most recently the cast of *300*. If you don't know about *300*, well, find out. I mean, really.

As usual, Mark and I were talking about getting to the next level in performance. Mark told me about a workout he has his athletes doing, a three-bar deadlift workout. Let's set this up exactly as you would need to do it.

Load three bars:
One with 95% of your best deadlift
The next with 90% of your best deadlift
The third with 85% of your best deadlift

Mark's athletes would then do a single with the first bar (ninety-five percent), then step over to the second and do a double (ninety percent), and finally step back and do a triple with the last bar (eighty-five percent). The idea of the workout would be to do up to three of these clusters.

Before you rush off to do this workout, please sit up and pay attention. I asked Mark an intelligent follow-up question, "Um, whoa, how uh… ?"

You see, I looked at this workout through one lens and Mark looked at it through another. With Mark's athletes — who are serious asskickers in the dojo, on the field and up the mountains — this workout was doable. As someone who lives in the weightroom, this workout might put me in the hospital! Why?

It's those words, best and max. I know everyone knows exactly what those mean, but I don't think so.

First, let's look at four highly scientific terms I use on a daily basis:

Sorta Max
Max
Max Max
Max Max Max

Not long ago, listening to Dave Tate speak, he basically said most programs he reads are, and I quote, "full of shit." It takes an elite powerlifter maybe fifty weeks to build up to something like a ninety-five-percent lift. Yet all of us read programs where athletes are asked to do ninety percent of this or that for eight sets of ten.

Folks, that ninety percent isn't ninety percent.

I agree with Dave completely. Most people have a *Sorta Max*. A Sorta Max is a concept I came up with a while ago when people were telling me what their maxs were in various lifts. Sorta Max is that heavy lift you do in the gym and call it a day. And, I must say this, hats off to you, you deserve it, here you go, good for you. That's great, nothing wrong with it. It's the heavy *today max*, if you will.

For many of us, we occasionally have a good day and nail a big lift, or in some cases, just have a great performance. That's where most people hail their *Max* numbers.

One time, I was asked to show a dip to a roomful of young women. The other instructor said, "Just do as many as you can." Now, usually, more than five dips for me is considered a marathon effort worthy of a good Gatorade dousing and tears of accomplishment. But, before a roomful of women, I knocked off a nice thirty-five reps. That's my max… and I ain't going to be doing that every day, thank you very much.

Max Max is the next step. That's the top end lift that maybe you spent the better part of a few months building up to with some kind of organized program. That's exactly what my best bench press reflects.

John Price and I decided at least three times both of us needed to bench press 405 — four big plates per side — and focused on the bench for two workouts a week. John's program, which I followed to its exacting principles, was this:

Monday: Bench Press

135 for 10
225 for 10
315 for 10
More weight — 335 or so for 10 or as many as possible

Thursday: Bench Press

135 for 10
225 for 10
315 for 10
365 for as many as possible

With this highly scientific approach, I usually benched 405 by the fourth week. The last time I did this, I bench pressed 405 in a polo shirt and a pair of khakis.

If I would have ever spent more than a month working on the bench, I'm sure I could have done more. But, for me, 405 is my Max Max. A few weeks of training focused on one lift and I made a good number.

In my opinion, the Max Max is the most underappreciated measure in sports and training. It's simply what you can do with some effort. If all your Max Max numbers are at a good level for your goals and interests, I can practically promise you have achieved a solid level in your chosen field. Maybe not the best, but you're good.

It should be obvious where *Max Max Max* is heading. This is a number that takes a lot of commitment and a lot of time to achieve. You'll probably need to do it in competition. All my top lifts are done in competition. Why? There's usually a story.

Why a 628 deadlift? Because after I pulled 606, a bunch of other guys missed, and then one or two went up and made a big show of missing something a bit heavier. I wanted to make sure there was no question: I took the next poundage (628) and made it. For days later, I felt lousy throughout my body and decided, "Hmm, that's enough for me."

Really, my best deadlift could have been more… and, honestly, less. But the circumstances led to the choice of weight as much as any intelligent training program on my part.

Max Max Max might be a lifetime achievement you planned for decades or, like me, you stumbled around long enough to do something max-worthy. And that's the issue.

Now, let's get back to Mark and me at dinner. You see, I heard Max Max Max, and Mark was talking about Sorta Max. Mark's athletes deadlift around 300. Therefore, the three bars would look like this… rounding the numbers to reflect easy plate selections:

One bar with 285
One bar with 265
One bar with 245

Total equipment:

Three bars
Twelve 45-pound plates
Two 25-pound plates
Six 10-pound plates
Two 5-pound plates

Maybe more than a home gym would have, but most gyms would have this many plates.

My workout idea, based on my Max Max Max:

One bar with 605
One bar with 575
One bar with 545

Total equipment:

Three bars
Thirty-two 45-pound plates
Two 35-pound plates
Two 25-pound plates
Two 10-pound plates
Two 5-pound plates

Hmmm, that's interesting. I don't need that many fives or tens, but thirty-two forty-fives? That would clear out many collegiate athletic team gyms!

Next, let's look at load. If Mark's athlete did his workout three times through (eighteen total reps), the tonnage would be 3,650 pounds. If I did the workout through once (six total reps), the tonnage would be 3,390 pounds… nearly the same load at one-third the volume!

I realize the numbers are boring, but most of us need to look at these numbers carefully. When you read an article and go back to Golden Spa 23/7, how do you determine how much weight you're going to lift? Do you simply just strut over to the Duo DynaBiceps Machine and pull the selector into "D," or do you pull out a calculator to decide whether to use the eighteen-pound dumbbell or the twenty-pounder?

Remember how easy the question was back in the beginning: What's your max front squat, deadlift, snatch and bench press?

Here's the question: Is your bodyweight front squat a Sorta Max, Max, Max Max, or Max Max Max? Doing a six-week front squat program designed to add ten percent (guaranteed!) to your max probably won't work if you're an elite lifter. Imagine the letter:

> *Dear Dan,*
> *After doing your miracle Bench Press Protocol, the BPP, I went from a 1000-pound bench to 1100 in just six weeks. I had never considered the importance of [fill in appropriate new miracle training idea or supplement here] until I tried your program.*
> *Signed,*
> *BiggGunz*

Let's be honest, to up your bench to 1100 might take (for some of our readers anyway) almost twelve weeks, double my imaginary program.

To understand the concept of physical capital, the first twin issues are:

1. Do you know how to do the exercises listed in standard training programs?

2. Do you at least have something beyond a Sorta Max for these exercises? Yes, it may take a few months of focus on each of the basic moves to progress to those carefully scientific terms Max and Max Max.

And before I move on, let's not forget the two other great issues I tend to beat to death in my lectures and presentations. First, and it's really so basic most people miss it, do you have the equipment to do the workouts I, you, or anyone else designs? If you decide to do Mark's deadlift workout, do you have thirty-two forty-five-pound plates? Do you have three Olympic bars?

Recently, I was given advice to begin doing horizontal rows, a form of pull-ups for the rhomboids, and it took me nearly a week to figure out a way to do these in my home gym. Great exercise, no facility!

Next, the other issue I tend to discover with many people far too late: Do you have the temperament to do certain kinds of training?

For example, I struggle with programs with percentages. I also struggle in programs that don't have a ton of variety built in. Yet I also thrive on short, brutal programs that demand total focus for a few weeks. Why? I have no idea, but it's worthless for me to help you design a training program if you:

1. Don't have the equipment to do the program

2. Don't know how to do the lifts demanded in the program

3. Don't have the capacity to train at the numbers required by the program

4. Don't have the mental skill-set to handle the program

Be careful about number four here. There are people who thrive on volume and no change. Another person might think those guys are mad. Sometimes, the problem with the cookie-cutter approach to training goes far beyond the issues of the body and really are cultural, social and mental challenges.

A buddy of mine recruited a fine young thrower from Germany who always did ten standing throws, then ten reps of this drill, ten reps of that drill, and ten reps of another. Always! His coach told him to do ten when he was a youth and, by all that is holy, ten is what you do!

That approach worked for this young man, but it would drive me crazy in one day. So, yes, physical capital certainly encompasses a lot of other areas of life, too.

I call this problem — the problem of trying to follow a program that fails to fit any of your equipment needs, exercise considerations, volume or intensity issues, or your personality — the Cinderella's Stepsister Syndrome. In other words, the shoe don't fit!

A few years ago, I spent far too much of my life trying to explain to a father that his daughter couldn't possibly follow a program I use called The Big Twenty-one. She wasn't strong enough to do the basic program. But, since my athletes did it, his daughter should be able to do it, too.

First, let's look at the program.

The athlete does three exercises (each and every day) for three workouts a week (Monday, Wednesday, Friday) for three weeks (week one, week two, week three) for a total of nine workouts. The three exercises are clean and press (clean the weight and press the weight for every rep), snatch and clean and jerk (clean the weight and jerk the weight for every rep).

It's so simple it confuses people. You do all three lifts, in that order, every workout. I've probably lost the bulk of my audience, but this is so important. The key to the workout is the rep-and-set scheme, and the built-in weight increases.

The most confusing part is this: Each workout, add five pounds to the opening weight. After three weeks, the opening weight will be forty-five pounds more.

Reps and Sets

Opening weight x 5
Add five pounds x 5
Add five pounds x 5
Add five pounds x 1
Add five pounds x 1
Add five pounds x 1
Add five pounds x 1
Add five pounds x 1
Add five pounds x 1

Total repetitions: 21

You see: The Big 21!

So, and this is all math-related now, if you want to finish with 225 on the last rep of the last workout, you start with 145 on day one. Let's look at those two bookend workouts:

Day One:

145 x 5
150 x 5
155 x 5
160 x 1
165 x 1
170 x 1
175 x 1
180 x 1
185 x 1

Day Nine:

185 x 5
190 x 5
195 x 5
200 x 1
205 x 1
210 x 1
215 x 1
220 x 1
225 x 1

For the psychos still reading:

Day two starts with 150 and ends with 190
Day three starts with 155 and ends with 195
Day four starts with 160 and ends with 200
Day five starts with 165 and ends with 205
Day six starts with 170 and ends with 210
Day seven starts with 175 and ends with 215
Day eight starts with 180 and ends with 220

Here's what you're still missing: That's for one lift! You still have to do two more each day! The Big Twenty-one is sixty-three reps of full body, explosive, big lifting. Just writing it down gives me wrist cramps.

What kind of physical capital does it take to do this workout? Let's look:

1. Equipment: One bar, a 310-pound set. It's easy and cheap for equipment.

2. Do you know how to do the lifts, the clean and press, the snatch and the clean and jerk? If you don't, please don't do The Big Twenty-one workout!

3. If you answer yes to both questions, can you do them with the weights suggested?

4. Finally, do you have the ability to stick to a program for nine workouts while hating the last three?

As a lark, I calculated the lightest a person could do this workout with a traditional Olympic bar set-up:

Day One:

45 x 5
50 x 5
55 x 5
60 x 1
65 x 1
70 x 1
75 x 1
80 x 1
85 x 1

Day Nine:

85 x 5
90 x 5
95 x 5
100 x 1
105 x 1
110 x 1
115 x 1
120 x 1
125 x1

The dad who wanted his daughter to do this workout couldn't figure out how to make it work when she can't snatch eighty-five; how will she snatch one-ten in a few weeks? You see, Mr. Cinderella's Stepsister, the shoe don't fit.

That's the whole point: *All too often, the shoe doesn't fit!*

Let's summarize with a few key principles that can help most of us adapt the programs we see online, in magazines or in email to fit our needs:

1. I strongly recommend at least a two-month focus on the major lifts. If we can just agree to get a Max Max squat, bench press and deadlift and work from there, we'll all be miles ahead. Yep, that will take about six months. If you can't deadlift double-bodyweight, you need to by the end of the six months.

2. You need to make an honest evaluation of your equipment. One of my workouts calls for four bars and several kettlebells. Now, if you don't have four bars, don't try it. There are several one-bar workouts and those will be fine if you only have one bar. If you don't have one bar… sorry, I forgot the question.

3. When you begin a program, if you don't know how to do a lift, move or exercise, spend a few workouts mastering it, and get yourself to a place where you're lifting weights that will actually make your body react. Hint: If they're foam and brightly colored, go heavier.

4. I'd strongly suggest you take some time to look at a bunch of different training programs to see which resonate with you. When I read the workout of the Iranian

Superheavy, something in my core says, "Yes, that sounds right." When I read about the 1,000 crunches a fitness model does before her hour of cardio, my brain looks for potato chips. Make sure the shoe fits.

Taking a few minutes aside every so often to account for your physical capital — your shortcomings and your assets — is like finding a vein of pure gold. Mine it.

Forty-Two

Improve Your Fitness Literacy

Growing up, my single source for lifting, strength, and fitness info, beyond a few books in the library, was *Strength and Health* magazine.

I was convinced, as were probably most readers of the York magazine, if I did eight to twelve exercises per day, three days a week, and drank my Hi-Proteen drinks, I'd be halfway to the Olympics or Mr. America in no time. Once I established myself, I could drive off to Pennsylvania and join the York Barbell Club to rub shoulders with the best and brightest while polishing off the be-all and end-all of energy supplements, wheat-germ-oil-based Energol.

Well, as it turned out, the protein gave me gas and the stories of York were all overblown. But, here's the deal:

- I believed in high-protein diets.

- I believed in heavy lifting, usually the Olympic lifts.

- I saw a path that had many goals: general fitness, the Olympics, a great body, a long life, an odd kind of fame, and success in any and all other pursuits.

Compare this to what the majority of gym members experience in a typical week. First, there are dozens of television commercials selling this and that for fitness, from little chairs that work the abs to hucksters selling a pill to eliminate the fat caused by stress. (The new infomercial on Ghetto Booty is offensive at so many levels I felt the need to cleanse after watching it.)

Always remember, unless I recommend it (insert Dan's smiling face), it can't be trusted.

I will never sell out... except for a lot more money than I've been offered. My integrity has a price.

Seriously, walk around a bookstore and browse these sections: health, fitness, cooking, sports, self-help. You'll find dozens, if not hundreds, of books that give you more information on strength, fat loss and conditioning than you could possibly retain.

For many of us, if we stacked all of our books, magazines and printouts from the internet, we could literally go from floor to ceiling several times. I have a bookshelf at work, three at home, and a storage closet of liquor boxes filled with books, magazines and articles. (The amazing thing about all of this is finding enough liquor boxes in Utah to hold my collection.)

You have an astounding amount of information at your fingertips, but the ability to discern what's right and what's crap is rarely considered. Sure, you may have typed "this sux" at the end of one my articles (and that hurt my feelings), but what tools do you use to determine whether or not an article, a workout or a diet is worthy of giving it a try?

In other words, what is your fitness literacy? How do you decide, literally? How do you cut through the crap? What's worthy of further reading and experimentation? As you go from one book telling you ninety-five percent of your diet should be carbs, to the next book that says five percent, how do you comprehend this?

I'd like to share how I go through the volumes of pages I read in a typical year, but first there's an important side note:

Reading all this stuff is great, but acting on it is greater. No one has said this better than the philosopher, Jerry Seinfeld:

"In a lot of ways, that's what a bookstore is. It's a 'smarter than you' store. And that's why people are intimidated. Because to walk into a bookstore, you have to admit there's something you don't know.

"And the worst part is you don't even know where it is. You go in the bookstore and ask people, "Where is this? Where is that?" Not only do I lack knowledge, I don't even know where to get it! So just to walk into a bookstore you're admitting to the world, 'I'm not so bright.' It's pretty impressive, really.

"But the pressure is on you now. This book is filled with funny ideas, but you have to provide the delivery. So when you read it, remember: timing, inflection, attitude. That's comedy. I've done my part. The performance is up to you." (Jerry Seinfield, *Sein Language*, page 3)

I speak for every strength coach when I say we've done our parts. The performance is up to you.

All those programs, workouts, diets and supplements you read about are all very good to excellent. The performance is up to you.

How should you read an article, book or forum discussion? First off, let's look at how you should read an article. Here's a quote from one of my articles, which you read earlier, assuming you didn't skip ahead:

"One of my favorite books has a title that caught my eye immediately when I saw it in the bookstore. It's *Great Books* by David Denby. Seriously, when you're looking around the bookstore for a new book to read and you see one called Great Books, how can you pass on it?"

That's what it said; now let's add how I read it:

"One of my favorite books (How often does this guy use I, my, and me?) has a title that caught my eye immediately when I saw it in the bookstore. (Bookstore? Is this guy so dumb he has to go to bookstores?) It's *Great Books* by David Denby. (What the hell is he talking about now? Why can't he just get to the point and tell us what he always talks about... whatever the hell that is) Seriously, when you're looking around the bookstore for a new book to read and you see one called *Great Books*, how can you pass on it? (I'm amazed he thinks this is funny)."

The problem with most readers — and there's actually research to back this up — is they aren't active readers; when I read an article, I literally talk with the author as I go through the points. When a writer states, "I don't know why I'm writing another article about X," I nearly always agree. Seriously, how many times does the same thing have to be hashed again?

But then, as I read the weightlifting forum posts about my article, *The One Lift a Day Program*, I'm stunned to continue to find people asking if two lifts a day are the same as one lift. I can't do the math, either.

If you only read opinions that agree with your opinion on everything, you'll just be a head-nodder. One of the best ways to expand your active reading skills is to read the opposite of what you tend to think.

With the fitness wave caused by the movie, *300*, it was funny to find some guys writing in forums they wished Mark Twight would've trained the Spartans like Arnold instead of training them like warriors. Aside to those people: Please go back to your pirated copy of *Hercules in New York* and leave the rest of us alone.

For my opposite reading, I go to pro-vegetarian websites, general fitness sites, and the HIT-Jedi websites.

There are places on the 'net where everybody kneels before the great training Oz and nods at their master's voice. But when you meet these people, they rarely look like they ever lifted a weight. As I remind people all the time: PVC pipe is great for learning the movement or practicing something specific; it is not a workout weight.

The next little technique I use to read strength-related materials is actually a tad arrogant, but true: I figure my needs are more important than the author's needs. In other words, I don't care what order the author wrote an article, I'm going to skim, pick and choose, skip, and jump and hop all over the article to discover whatever gems I can steal.

That's right, I steal ideas from other coaches. The amazing thing is I'm the only strength coach in the history of lifting to ever actually steal from others. As you can see, I steal and lie. It's not my fault; my parents were in the iron and steel business. My mother ironed and my father stole. Old joke.

I skim articles quickly. Part of the reason I have so many liquor boxes — besides the obvious reason — is I like to come back to articles to catch what I missed. It's funny how sometimes I'll come back a decade later and discover the answer to an issue that's plagued me for years. I'm not saying I'm a genius, but I usually find the right answer in thirty years or so.

Feeling free to skim relates to the next key point, one that's really important. How do you handle the vocabulary?

Seriously, when someone writes an exercise as "close-grip narrow-stance accelerating front pulls to the rack position," how do you go about performing the lift? I call this move the clean, and you might find that as difficult to understand, too.

When I start reading an article about neurons, I usually skip all the big words because I figure my nervous system has to be working okay since I'm still sitting in my chair. I go right to the bottom of these articles and look for the summary points.

If seven sets of four is the final answer to "Who wants to be the World's Strongest Human?" I want to be doing seven sets of four before anybody else finishes the article.

The vocabulary issue is beginning to stagger the fitness world. Just pick up any random issue of a fitness magazine. Here you find Y Squat, Wall Slide, Spiderman Lunge, Counter-Movement Jump, Warrior Lunge and Lateral Tube-walk. Once I see the picture and the description, I generally get it, but how much time will it take me to master these movements? By the next edition, there'll be a new breed of exercises I might try and spend another month mastering. I'm sure there's some value to that, but Y Squat? Why not?

One of the oddest bits of research recently pointed out an interesting phenomenon: As high school textbooks get bigger and bigger (because they have to cover more and more crap mandated by non-teachers), literacy goes down. In fact, it's believed one-quarter of today's students can't comprehend their textbooks.

Looking at freshman girls carrying over one-third of their bodyweight in backpacks, one wonders why the girls aren't in the best shape of their lives, and what an incredible waste of effort is going on if these students can't understand what the hell is on those pages.

Other countries are going to another model: slimmer, smaller texts that encourage the student to think and apply the information. That's probably good advice for all of us.

Finally, the best advice I can give is to use your own experience to resonate with the author.

Not long ago, I was reading *Play as if Your Life Depends on It: Functional Exercise and Living for Homo Sapiens* by Frank Forencich. On page 182, I found a short list of muscles. At first, I just skipped over it. It's embarrassing to think my thought process was something like, "Why pay attention to muscles when I'm in the strength training profession?"

I came back when I saw he was quoting something from Janda and I checked the list again. Forencich noted researchers found some muscles are tonic, or basically slow-twitch and prone to stiffening with age. Other muscles are phasic, fast-twitch and prone to weakening with age.

The author noted most masseuses and physical therapists had discovered the same thing in their practices. I sat in my chair and shortened the tonic muscles and instantly I had the look of an old man.

Well, I always have that look, but… more so.

The tonic muscles are hamstrings, pecs, upper traps, psoas, inner thigh, calf, biceps and forearm flexors. The phasic muscles are abs, butt, middle and lower traps, triceps, rhomboids and forearm extensors. It hit me: No wonder the Olympic lifts seem to keep me young. The simple clean and press might be the Fountain of Youth!

Then I pulled out one of my favorite workouts from the past. Ignore the lifts and just look how it ties into Forencich's point:

Day One: Monday

Power Clean and Press
1 power clean and 8 presses

Three sets of eight with a one-minute rest between sets. If there's a single key to the program, it's the one-minute rest period. By strictly monitoring the rest period, and of course keeping track of the weight, one can track progress.

Power Curls
3 sets of 8 with a one-minute rest between sets

Using a curl grip, slide the weight to just above the knees and curl-clean the bar. Let it come down under control. Again, get all eight reps in, don't change the weights, and monitor the rest period.

Finish with some kind of ab work.

Day Two: Wednesday

Power Clean and Front Squats
1 power clean and 8 front squats

Once again, three sets of eight with a one-minute rest. Stay tall in the front squats and keep your elbows high. We usually use this as more of a warm-up for the next exercise.

Overhead Squats
3 sets of 8 with a one-minute rest

Using the wide snatch-grip, lock the elbows with the weight overhead, and squat down. Athletes who do this exercise will not only develop flexibility, balance and leg strength, but also an incredibly strong lower back.

Again, finish with some kind of ab work.

Day Three: Friday

Whip Snatches
3 sets of 8 with a one-minute rest

With a wide snatch-grip, stand up and hold the bar at crotch level. Dip and snatch the bar overhead. Continue for eight reps. You'll be surprised how quickly this exercise can get into your blood. If you want big traps and explosion, this is the king.

Clean-grip Snatches
3 sets of 8 with a one-minute rest

With a clean-grip, stand up and dip the bar to your knees. Then explode up, driving the bar in one full movement overhead. It's like a clean and press, well… without the clean.

Ab work if you wish.

I call this the Transformation Program because I always literally feel transformed after finishing it. In other words, I feel good. Think about that for a moment: a training program that makes you feel good.

Reading Forencich's work tied into something my body already knew, but I couldn't wrap my brain around. Doing the Transformation Program and adding three simple stretches (the overhead reach, a biceps and shoulder stretch, and a hip flexor stretch) seems to resonate with me. I literally feel younger.

As I was reading one single paragraph of Forencich's book, I came away with an insight why some workouts appeal to me and others don't. I've passed my fiftieth birthday, and I need to rekindle those workouts that add life to my life, and walk away from plain brutal workouts.

What's the point of all of this?

- You have in books and on the internet more information than the bulk of history's great strength and conditioning coaches had access to during their entire careers. That's a problem. Why? Much of it contradicts the other.

- You need to learn to discern the material. It helps to read stuff you absolutely disagree with to develop this skill. Where's my Jane Fonda fitness book?

•   You're in charge of your reading. Learn to interact with your authors as you read them. Feel free to skip to around. At this time, I welcome all those who skipped to the end.

•   Listen to Seinfeld: "This book is filled with funny ideas, but you have to provide the delivery. So when you read it, remember: timing, inflection, attitude. That's comedy. I've done my part. The performance is up to you."

Hey, read all you want, but remember, the performance is up to you.

Afterword

This can not end. This work, like all works of the heart, will always remain unfinished.

As I reach back through these stories, I find myself sitting on that pink naugahyde bench at the Pacifica Barbell Club listening to Dick Notmeyer telling me, "Oh, you are just like this guy I once knew who struggled with this, too," as he told me a long story of how someone else with my problem overcame it with hard work. I see Ralph Maughan wiping his eyes from the wind and cold at the discus rings of Utah State University and telling me, one more time, to skip across the ring. I am walking with Jack Schroeder as we discuss my recent columns and whether or not I touched my audience, "People love stories, Dan."

I see my father standing out in the discus sector on a Sunday afternoon. I throw the discus, he marks it with his feet, then scoots back to recover the disc. He throws it back to me a few times and I remember being impatient to get another throw in. Today, it's my favorite memory of my dad. I sit here and remember my brother, Richard, and his wife, Diane, driving me to buy the book on track and field that opened my eyes to the faint possibilities I could be good in this sport. I can see my brother, Gary, just out of bounds on the sidelines of Westmoor High School cheering me to, "Just *hit* that guy!" Years later, we would compete together many times in track meets, but in my mind, I'm still fourteen.

I picture my wife, Tiffini, leaping over the platform at the Nationals to embrace me after I pulled out a lift few people thought I could make. And I remember my mom scolding me for getting two personal fouls in one football game.

Honestly, Mom, they had it coming.

Any and all lessons you may have learned in this book are the result of the teaching of others. My story would not be complete without the training programs of Dave Freeman and the insights of Bob Lualhati. The hours and hours I played street football with my brother, Phil, and our neighbors taught me to compete and run into cars, bounce off and keep playing. My brother, Ray, kept pushing the bar higher and higher for me throughout my life and career. I also learned how to pack children for long, boring track meets by watching my sister, Corinne, unpack bag after bag for my three nieces to survive the epic Saturdays of my youth.

When people first come to me for training advice, they want to discuss repetition schemes and set structure and the right way to open the hip joint. I pray they leave with an appreciation for detail, an understanding of the need for balance in life and sport and the importance of community. Anyone can write a training program that will ruin an athlete's day, but I want my students to build the blocks for a successful life. Honestly, I hope my lessons live long past my mortal body.

I never wanted to be a coach. I had dreams of a life in academics, which might explain those months of Intensive Turkish studies and my trip to the Middle East, lengthy visits to both coasts and detours to odd parts of our world that offered more opportunities for enrichment.

Yet, I kept getting drawn into coaching. There would be a young person who just *had* to learn the Olympic lifts and, I, of course, was reminded of another young guy who struggled with those lifts, too. I found myself repeating myself so often I came up with the corny axiom, *"Repetition is the mother of implementation,"* which drove many a young person crazy through the years. It was a lesson I couldn't skip.

And, time after time, I realized I was telling and retelling the same stories to my athletes about honors won and lost and championships that either slipped away or were won by the least of margins. Athletes love stories. And, many times I found myself merely walking with my athletes, because most of the time all we need is a companion on this journey. I am sure sometimes the athletes thought they wanted solitude, but I knew they needed someone to stand beside them.

I noticed at times my job was to show pictures, books and movies, and just open up possibilities to the athletes. There have been countless times I stood by and cheered others on and realized later sometimes the best thing we do is be present. Often, my joy might have been greater than my athletes because I could taste the thin line between success and failure. We must celebrate the joyful moments of life.

I never wanted to be a coach, but everybody calls me Coach. I remember shuddering when I heard *Coach* referring to me, yet now I embrace it. My attitude changed a few years ago when I met a man named Coach.

We met at a conference and he had taken voluminous notes from my talk. He came up afterwards and waited patiently while I answered the usual questions about all the things I didn't talk about during the lecture. Generally, if I don't talk about something, it is because I don't think it is important. He excused himself and asked for some clarification about a few small items.

I asked him his name and he said, "Coach."

"Fine," I said, "but what's your name?"

His answer changed my life. "When I was a young man, I was a terror. I did all the wrong things and I knew I was doing wrong. At the local community center, I started playing some ball. There was a man there who took no nonsense from me. He expected more. He demanded more. The man turned my life around. And, as soon as I could, I decided to dedicate my life to his memory. All I know of him is that we called him Coach. Please, all I ever want to be, and all I ever want to be known as is Coach. Call me Coach."

Call me *Coach*.

Suggested Reading

On Lifting

John McCallum, *Keys to Progress*
The Socrates of weightlifting. We are all just footnotes.

Pavel Tsatsouline, *Power to the People*
For those of you who didn't know the question, here is the answer.

Pavel Tsatsouline, *Enter the Kettlebell*
It might takes decades to discover the genius of
the Program Minimum.

Kenneth Jay, *Viking Warrior Conditioning*
This book changed my viewpoint on training.

Tommy Kono, *Weightlifting, Olympic Style*
Impossible to put down; it stands apart from all other
sports books: It's a life book.

Brett Jones and Gray Cook, *Kalos Sthenos — The Get-Up*
Rarely has a book turned me from hating something
to loving something.

Mark Twight, *Kiss or Kill*
No wonder I like Mark; this book is a line in the sand.

Dave Draper, *Brother Iron, Sister Steel*
It's not just about the barbell.

On Learning

T. H. White, *The Sword in the Stone*
Walk along with Wart as he learns the lessons of leadership
and life from the animals who tutor him.

Alexandre Dumas, *The Count of Monte Cristo*
From the depths of despair, a voice calls out to Edmund
and he discovers the world is full of wonders to explore.

On Learning, continued

Cormac McCarty, *The Road*
Love transcends doom.

Frank Herbert, *Dune*
There are risks on the road to destiny.

Sir Arthur Conan Doyle, *The Sign of the Four*
Sure, pick any of the adventures, but I love sitting next
to Watson in this one in utter bewilderment as the chase unfolds.

Douglas Adam, *The Hitchhiker's Guide to the Galaxy*
You know: Don't Panic.

On Life

Thomas Cahill, *How the Irish Saved Civilization*
We are forever indebted to those who copied a book.

Genesis, *Chapters One to Four*
It's all there. And, yes, we are our brother's keeper.

Dan Millman, *The Way of the Peaceful Warrior*
An extraordinary book about extraordinary moments. All of them.

Dylan Thomas, *Do Not Go Gentle Into That Good Night*
Rage on.

Be sure to also read the Collected Works of Calvin and Hobbes and
all seven of the Harry Potter books. Sometimes you are the hero and
sometimes you are the problem.

About the Author

Dan John has spent his life with one foot in the world of lifting and throwing and the other foot in academia. An All-American discus thrower, Dan has also competed at the highest levels in Olympic lifting, Highland Games and the Weight Pentathlon, an event in which he holds the American Record. His day job is the Head Strength Coach and Head Track and Field Coach at Juan Diego Catholic High School in Draper, Utah.

Dan is also a religious studies instructor for Columbia College of Missouri, both online and at the extension in Salt Lake City. As a Fulbright Scholar, he spent time in Egypt and Israel, and received advanced degrees in both history and religious education. He has been a columnist for the *Intermountain Catholic* and his articles have been published in the *Utah Historical Quarterly* and *Catechetical Update*. His passion for writing and lifting led to a series of articles in *Testosterone Magazine* (t-nation.com), which are the basis of this book. Dan has also been published in *Men's Health* as well as being highlighted in *Outside Magazine* and footnoted countless times in recent strength books.

At home, he is married to Tiffini, his wife of over twenty happy years, and his daughters, Kelly and Lindsay.

Index

409